Nehru

PROFILES IN **POWER**

General Editor: Keith Robbins

Nehru

Judith M. Brown

Longman

An imprint of **Pearson Education**

Harlow, England · London · New York · Reading, Massachusetts · San Francisco
Toronto · Don Mills, Ontario · Sydney · Tokyo · Singapore · Hong Kong · Seoul
Taipei · Cape Town · Madrid · Mexico City · Amsterdam · Munich · Paris · Milan

Pearson Education Limited
Edinburgh Gate
Harlow
Essex CM20 2JE
England

and Associated Companies around the world

Visit us on the World Wide Web at:
www.pearsoneduc.com

First published 1999

ISBN 0 582 43750 4

British Library Cataloguing-in-Publication Data
A catalogue record for this book can be obtained from the British Library

Library of Congress Cataloging-in-Publication Data
A catalog record for this book can be obtained from the Library of
Congress

10 9 8 7 6 5 4 3 2 1
04 03 02 01

Produced by Pearson Education Asia Pte Ltd.,
Printed in Singapore

CONTENTS

CONTENTS

LIST OF FIGURES

LIST OF MAPS

ACKNOWLEDGEMENTS

The last decade of the twentieth century has been a turbulent one in the lives of India's peoples. Many long-held public assumptions about Indian identity, about the proper role of the state, the nature of the economy and the role of religion in public life have been challenged, in a context of unprecedented political turmoil, and amidst evidence of a widening gap between the privileged and comfortable and those who live in abject poverty. The experience of the first fifty years of independent nationhood has raised anew many of the questions facing the founders of the new India in the years of the nationalist struggle for independence from British rule. It is thus fitting that Jawaharlal Nehru, India's prime minister from 1947 to 1964, should be the subject of a 'Profile in Power'. Moreover, India is no longer the distant land it once was for western travellers. Businessmen and tourists travel in unprecedented numbers to the subcontinent, while many people of Indian ethnic descent have made their homes in Britain, North America and elsewhere as a significant global diaspora. What has happened in India's recent past to make her what she now is, and to produce one of her most remarkable leaders, is consequently of proper concern to many people outside India. I am therefore most grateful to Keith Robbins, General Editor of this series, and to Andrew Maclennan of Longmans, for their invitation to attempt this essay in understanding Jawaharlal Nehru for an English-speaking audience who may know little about India. They have both been unfailingly supportive and patient, recognising the many pressures which conspire to deprive an academic of time to write. My thanks go, too, to Bill Jenkins,

Senior Higher Education Editor at Longmans, for help through the final stages of publication.

Any book written in mid-career rests on countless supportive relationships and debts of gratitude to colleagues, librarians and archivists. I must acknowledge particularly my gratitude to the Nehru Memorial Museum and Library in New Delhi, to its Director and staff, who made it possible to work on the papers of Motilal and Jawaharlal Nehru and many other prominent Indian politicians, as well as the records of the Indian National Congress. I am also indebted to Oxford University and my immediate colleagues in the fields of Commonwealth and South Asian history for providing not only a supportive scholarly environment but also the possibility of sabbatical leave; and to the Trustees of the University's Beit Fund which has enabled me to travel widely within the Commonwealth. Mrs Stephanie Jenkins in the Modern History Faculty has provided invaluable administrative and technical help in the preparation of the manuscript and in liberating time for scholarship. I would also wish to thank particularly Professor R. Frykenberg of the University of Madison, Wisconsin, for his constant and generous encouragement; and Professor Hew McLeod of Otago University who, while a Visiting Fellow at Balliol College, most graciously gave of his time and experience to read the manuscript. This book could not have been written without the continuing support and tolerance of my family, particularly my son James and my husband, Peter Diggle, who read the whole book as it was being written and ensured that I would not lose those readers who have a keen interest in but no professional knowledge of India.

Oxford,
May 1998

LIST OF ABBREVIATIONS

AICC	All-India Congress Committee
EIC	East India Company
IAS	Indian Administrative Service
ICS	Indian Civil Service
NATO	North Atlantic Treaty Organisation
RSS	Rashtriya Swayamsevak Sangh
SEATO	South-East Asia Treaty Organisation
UN	United Nations
UP	United Provinces (of Agra and Oudh)

IACOBO
FILIO DILECTISSIMO
HUNC LIBRUM DEDICAT
MATER AMANTISSIMA

INTRODUCTION

Jawaharlal Nehru (1889–1964) was one of the most notable and, arguably, one of the most influential Asian political figures of the mid-twentieth century. He ranks in stature and interest beside his great mentor, Mahatma Gandhi, and his Chinese contemporary, Mao Tse Tung. This study is, however, not another full-scale biography.[1] Like others in the 'Profiles in Power' series, it focuses on the individual who is its subject as a person of power. Of course there are dangers in writing history through the lens of individual lives; particularly of imputing far too great an impact on the course of events to individual talent, vision or indeed wickedness, at the expense of a more subtle understanding of the deeper forces moulding society, politics and the economic foundations of public life. Yet there are historical figures who at specific junctures in their country's history achieve a peculiar pre-eminence. Investigation of the reasons for their achievement of such a position, and the use they were able to make of it, is therefore a way to open windows into the past, and to probe the deeper processes of historical change. There is another reason why studies of powerful leaders are problematic. Most peoples have a tendency, perhaps even a need, to deal with their past in simple explanatory terms, often using individuals as symbols for particular episodes in their common experience which have been markedly traumatic or confusing. In the context of recent British history the older personification of the trials and triumphs of the Second World War in Winston Churchill is an example; as are later analyses focusing on 'Thatcher's Britain'. In the experience of India, Nehru's prime-ministership from 1947 to 1964 is increasingly interpreted after the passage of three intervening decades as the time of ill-chosen economic strategies, of disregard for the underprivileged, and of a misplaced attempt to achieve a secular Indian identity. Responsibility for the confusions and undoubted problems of the present is heaped on the convenient head of a dead leader, thereby absolving the living and Indian society of the burden. A profile of Nehru is thus timely, for particular as well as general historical reasons.

Why, then, is Nehru so important for someone seeking to understand the recent historical experience of Asia, and of India in particular? In the first phase of his public career, from about 1919 to 1947, Nehru was an outspoken and radical nationalist figure, notable in, and at times holding the presidency of, the Indian National Congress, the main anti-imperial movement on the subcontinent. He was prominent in Gandhi's campaigns of direct but non-violent resistance to British rule, and consequently for lengthy periods was a resident in imperial jails. He emerged from his final imprisonment in 1945 to become one of the most important Indians in the negotiations leading to the end of British rule in 1947. Thus his nationalist career opens up a host of questions about the nature of colonial nationalism and its leadership: questions of national identity in the face of geographical, linguistic and religious diversity, of the social origins and representative nature of nationalist orators and activists in societies marked by great differentials of wealth and resources, of viable tactics in relation to colonial rulers, and of the dynamics of imperial decisions to withdraw from empire. Nehru's personal experience and very real dilemmas of mind and action are particularly illuminating, because the Indian movement of resistance to imperial rule was one of the first and longest in duration in Asia or Africa. In a sense the Indian experience became a marker for subsequent nationalist movements and for imperial rulers under pressure, displaying the strengths and weaknesses of both imperialism in the twentieth century and the nationalist enterprise. As violence and partition of the subcontinent in the name of religion accompanied political independence, it was agonisingly clear that no one had emerged from the years of conflict and manoeuvre as a clear victor.

It was in this context of fear and fracture that Nehru embarked on the second great endeavour of his life, that of creating a new, secular and democratic India, engaged in self-sustaining economic and social change. His role was that of prime minister from independence until his death in 1964. His tenure of this high office, marked by great idealism, patched-up compromises and notable failures both in domestic policy and in foreign affairs (when China invaded India in 1962), displays many of the dilemmas inherent in the experience of nationalist leaders who attempt to transform themselves into democratic leaders of new nation states, and endeavour to do for their compatriots what they criticised imperial predecessors for failing to do. In this process they have to build on the ambiguous foundations laid by their own movements of protest and opposition, and the patterns of governance and control laid down by the colonial rulers. The enormity of this project demands emphasis. In India it consisted at the very least of creating a new national state structure with a new constitution, parliament, state legislatures, a vastly expanded civil service and a national rather than an imperial defence force; of enfranchising and educating in democratic practice a mass electorate numbering just over 150 million; of setting social and economic goals; of establishing a foreign service and constructing a stance in international relations. All this had to be done in a context of material scarcity, widespread illiteracy and confused public identities. The states of Africa and Asia which emerged out of the slow decline of European systems of world-wide imperial control in mid-century are now an integral part of the world community, with all their vast potential as well as their manifest problems, bound to each other and to older states by new economic and political ties and by the transformation of international communications and image-making. To understand this remarkable change in the nature of the world community a study of one of the most notable Asian national leaders is a good beginning.

Yet Nehru was not just a national orator and activist, and eventually a democratic prime minister. He was also highly intelligent, with a sensitive and lively mind which ranged over a wide spectrum of political, economic, social and moral issues. He was, furthermore, an accomplished author in English, recording the fruits of his lonely contemplations in jail.[2] To spend time with him, to listen to his personal agonisings, and to trace his quest for his country's roots and its appropriate future shape, is to have privileged access to the mind of an Asian intellectual living in a time of change and challenge. Through his mind a later generation can gain access to the intellectual and emotional experience of at least one generation of colonial subjects who wrestled with the nature and future of their indigenous traditions, who tried to make sense of their own history and the reasons for colonial rule, and who strove to envisage a new world where their peoples would achieve new national unities, bringing their strengths, insights and values into interaction with western influences and techniques, to create new equalities and opportunities at home and abroad. The generation before Nehru had agonised over many of these issues. Nehru had listened to and disagreed with his father, Motilal, and with Gandhi (his senior by thirty years), both of whom were in a sense colonial Victorian gentlemen.[3] The younger man came to intellectual maturity in the context of Edwardian Britain and its empire, witnessed the transformation of Europe's largest land empire by communism, and was part of the generation which had the task of attempting to turn visions of change in Asia and Africa into reality. Not all his contemporaries who graduated from being nationalists to taking the reins of political power shared the answers to these questions which he found through his undoubtedly privileged education, his subsequent reading and his phases of enforced contemplation. This study will show many of the conflicts he experienced with other Indians on such crucial issues as the nature of religion and of social structures and conventions, on questions of inequality, desirable strategies of economic change, and the role of violence in public affairs.

To approach Nehru by focusing on power is entirely appropriate. Throughout his career he was firmly convinced of its importance, for himself and for his country. At first he emphasised the priority of wresting power in India from the British – as the precondition of essential political, economic and social change. Unlike many other Congressmen he opposed any compromise on the issue of independence; for example by accepting 'dominion status'. He viewed with suspicion and misgiving the brief occasions when Congressmen took office in the legislatures set up by imperial rulers, fearing that even such a small taste of power would corrupt and divide those who collaborated with the British. After independence he was deeply perplexed by the nature of his own and of state power, recognising their centrality for what he saw as desirable change in India, yet aware of the ways in which those with influence and position could so easily become heirs to the practices and attitudes of their colonial predecessors, whose power had, in his view, been illegitimate because it had not been achieved through popular consent or tempered by democratic practices of review and responsibility.

In analysing Nehru's own position of power at various stages in his life there are three major themes which demand attention and will be interwoven through this 'profile'. The first is the inner world of the man himself: his personality, vision and interior drive. Why, when most people are uninterested in political careers, did this particular individual seek political position and influence, and at times ruthlessly eliminate those who would have circumscribed his freedom to manoeuvre and challenged his priorities? What were the goals he sought to achieve through the use of power? The second theme is the political system in which Nehru operated. This includes the patterns and institutions of politics, and the particular mechanisms of and pathways to power in India's political setting. This of course changed markedly in 1947, with the beginning of independent and democratic government in place of an imperial and more authoritarian regime. Such a change poses questions about the ability of individuals such as Nehru to operate in a changed political environment and to adapt to a new political system. Such adaptation is an exercise seldom required of political leaders in long-established political systems. Understanding how one person achieves, retains or loses power directs attention to such topics as political movements and organisations, the constitutions and conventions which lay down acceptable patterns of political behaviour, and the various layers of political institutions and public offices open to the aspiring. Thirdly there is the theme of constraints on the use of power and the ability of the individual to pursue and achieve his goals, even when he has apparently attained a position of preeminence in a political system. The constraints can be constitutional and institutional – designed to limit the authority attached to a particular office. Equally significant are the limits imposed, most markedly in democratic contexts, by the attitudes of colleagues and supporters. Even Gandhi, at the height of his influence in the nationalist movement, had only been able to do what his 'followers' permitted him to do; and at times he had abandoned work through and in Congress rather than be limited or manipulated in a way which would have compromised his ideals.[4] Nehru as prime minister was on several occasions tempted to do the same. As he was also to discover, there are often constraints on the use of apparent power stemming from the weakness or absence of appropriate instruments and material resources with which to implement policy. Perhaps even tougher (and more discouraging for the visionary who achieves power) are the constraints generated by social and economic conservatism and vested interest, which inhibits change in practice, even rendering reforming laws feeble in specific, local contexts, despite national reforming rhetoric and the apparent backing of democratic consent. Vision and reality are thus in constant dialectic in the lives of many leaders, not least in that of Nehru, as nationalist and then as national statesman.

. . .

NOTES AND REFERENCES

1. A number of substantial biographical studies of Nehru are available. Among the most useful are S. Gopal, *Jawaharlal Nehru*, 3 vols (London: Jonathan Cape, 1973–84); M.J. Akbar, *Nehru. The Making of India* (New York: Viking, 1988); B.R. Nanda, *The Nehrus. Motilal and Jawaharlal* (London: George Allen and Unwin, 1962).

2. Nehru's most accessible writings are *An Autobiography* (London: Bodley Head, 1936); *The Discovery of India* ([1946] rev. edn Bombay: Asia Publishing House, 1947). The collection of his regular letters to chief ministers of the states of India is also a remarkable political source: G. Parthasarathi (ed.), *Jawaharlal Nehru. Letters to Chief Ministers 1947–1964*, 5 vols (Delhi: Oxford University Press, 1985–89). (These are subsequently referred to as *LCM*.) The chief collection, still in print, of his writings and speeches, including his various jail diaries and a range of intimate private letters, is S. Gopal (ed.), *Selected Works of Jawaharlal Nehru* (1972– ; Ist series, New Delhi: Orient Longman; 2nd series, New Delhi: Jawaharlal Nehru Memorial Fund). (These are subsequently referred to as *SWJN* with series number in parentheses.)

3. An excellent introduction to the challenges faced by several generations of Hindu thinkers is B. Parekh, *Colonialism, Tradition and Reform. An Analysis of Gandhi's Political Discourse* (New Delhi, Newbury Park (Calif.) and London: Sage, 1989), particularly chs 1 and 2.

4. Judith M. Brown, *Gandhi. Prisoner of Hope* (New Haven and London: Yale University Press, 1989).

Chapter 1

A VOCATION TO POLITICS

. . .

THE WORLD OF INDIAN POLITICS IN THE LATE NINETEENTH CENTURY

Nehru was born in 1889, an Indian baby but a citizen of the British empire and a colonial subject of Queen Victoria. This was a time before imperial rulers suffered serious self-doubt about their role, a time when Britain seemed quite evidently the strongest world power. Yet British rule in India, the raj,[1] was a comparatively recent phenomenon in the time-scale of India's own history. Recorded civilisation on the subcontinent stretched back over 4000 years; and in the more recent past India had developed sophisticated state-systems in the form of empires and small regional states at least contemporary with the emerging states of early modern Europe. When English traders first ventured into Indian waters and settled in tiny numbers in small coastal 'factories' in the seventeenth and early eighteenth centuries they operated on Asian terms, as one of many international groups involved in the spice and textile trades. Only in the later eighteenth century did the men of the East India Company begin to exercise political control, by acquiring from Indians rights to gather land revenue. This revenue became the financial foundation of an increasingly powerful EIC government, backed by a large standing army, which controlled the whole subcontinent by the 1820s. The upheavals across north India in 1857 brought to an end Company raj, and India came directly under the control of the British Crown and parliament. (The great Indian territorial sway of the British sovereign was recorded in Latin on British domestic coinage until 1947.)

However, British politicians and parliamentarians were not in any simple sense land-hungry, despite the vast areas which came to be coloured pink on political maps of the world. Their preference was for less expensive means of furthering British interests globally, and they were deeply suspicious of direct governance in places where there was no large-scale white settlement. But when Nehru was born virtually all British opinion was agreed that the raj was an inescapable fact of British life, a special case for direct imperial control because it was uniquely vital to Britain's world-wide position. A century later the importance of India to Britain is less easy to comprehend. India was the home of the Indian army, a huge imperial reserve of fighting power numbering well over 100,000 Indian troops, paid for by Indian tax-payers. It was often deployed in many different parts of the empire for imperial purposes as well as defending India's own borders, particularly the north-western land frontier, the 'back gate' of imperial Russia. India was also highly significant for British trade and investment. Towards the end of the century nearly one-fifth of British overseas investment was in India. The subcontinent was the largest single market for British exports, mostly manufactured goods ranging from soap, books and textiles to railway locomotives and carriages. India exported raw materials such as cotton and jute, and of course tea, to Britain, Europe, North America and South-East Asia, not only supplying British domestic needs but also by exporting to other areas helping Britain to balance her trading books world-wide. India's public finance and the exchange rate of the rupee were managed in the imperial interest, thus supporting sterling as a strong international currency. Beyond this, in more personal terms, India also provided a small but significant area for the employment of expatriates, mostly from Britain's professional classes, in her administration, army, police, forestry and medical services, education, and in the Christian church, as chaplains and missionaries. Early in the twentieth century there were about 150,000 Europeans in India, of whom over one-third were women. Few of these were permanent settlers, because of the climate and the nature of their work: most returned to live out their old age in Britain in modest comfort.

Despite the centrality of the raj to Britain's world position, the British were essentially pragmatic imperialists, in India as

elsewhere, and were remarkably silent on the ideology under-
pinning their imperial enterprise.[2] Perhaps 'ideology' is itself
too strong a word, presupposing a coherent, articulated system
of ideas. More accurately most British people concerned with
India would have agreed on certain assumptions, often unvoiced,
about India, Indians and the nature of their own dominion. It
was assumed that the raj was virtually permanent. Even in 1912
Lord Hardinge, as viceroy, was writing that there was 'no question as to the permanence of British rule' and that the idea of
colonial self-government for India, as in the White Dominions,
'must be absolutely ruled out'. He dismissed the notion as
'ridiculous and absurd'.[3] Echoing through such protestations
was the assumption, too, that British rule was morally defens-
ible for a people who were Christian and democratic, despite
the apparent contradictions between what they found acceptable 'at home' and in India. British belief in the morality and
legitimacy of their raj rested on their vision of Indians and
'Indianness' as compared to their own assumed qualities of
character. Such a perception, which historians have labelled
'Orientalism', saw Indians as profoundly different in character
as well as historical experience. They were seen as weak and
effeminate, corrupt and unreliable, hopelessly divided among
themselves by religion and by the Hindu caste system, symptom
of a society in decay, waiting to be revivified by good government, economic advance and sound religion. Consequently
British rule was in British eyes a providential imposition, 'good'
for India's peoples. It would provide sound government and
just laws in place of chaos or despotic rule; and it would provide
an environment for the slow processes of educational advance
and social reform. It would also prevent Indians from exploiting or fighting each other. Thus armed with a good conscience,
generations of men (and the women who went as wives and
missionaries), often from the same small group of 'Anglo-
Indian' families, committed themselves to 'service' in India.

Yet it would be wrong to impute too much power and influence to the raj. Despite its panoply of civil and military power,
the British never had the financial or expatriate manpower
resources to run an efficiently authoritarian state. They could
threaten and punish: but they relied essentially on the cooperation or at least acquiescence of Indians in and with their
regime. Further, they had little real control over the deeper
forces in Indian society and economy. Yet the British presence,

their structures of rule, and their Orientalist assumptions about India and its peoples were the context in which Indians in the later nineteenth and early twentieth centuries lived, worked, prayed and played, and thought about life. The political and administrative structures of the raj, moreover, laid down the ground-rules for Indian political organisation and behaviour. They provided some of the foundations for the new nation state Nehru was to help create, but which Hardinge had found impossible to envisage when Nehru was a young man.

The enterprise of imperial governance

To understand the nature of imperial governance it is important to recognise the sheer size of the operation. The British had to attempt to understand and control a subcontinent infinitely greater and more diverse than their own islands. Nor did they have in the later nineteenth century any of the tools modern governments have at their disposal, such as swift communications, propaganda techniques or scientific methods of measuring social and economic forces. The area under the raj was 1,800,000 square miles, more than twenty times the area of Britain, and equivalent to continental Europe without Russia. Further, the subcontinent was even more varied than contemporary Europe. Within it there were major regions, such as Bengal, Madras or the northern plains, each distinguished by climate, crops, food, clothes, culture and language. There were also several distinctive religious traditions unequally represented across India. Hindus formed a majority of over two-thirds throughout the country, but a large Muslim minority was heavily represented in the north-west and in Bengal, owing its origins in part to the presence in earlier centuries of a Muslim empire over much of the subcontinent, following invasions of Muslims from the north-west. There were smaller groups of Sikhs, Parsis and Christians, and tribal groups who were often geographically isolated and barely touched by any of the world's organised religious traditions. The British perceived many of these distinctions between Indians, particularly those of religion and caste, as uniquely powerful and divisive in Indians' psyche and society, as central to 'being Indian', and therefore as evidence that Indians were incapable of modern national sentiment and organisation, let alone democratic practice. Later historians may discard such Orientalist justification of imperial rule. But the size and diversity of India has remained a critical issue for effective and acceptable governance on the subcontinent, as Nehru was to discover as he endeavoured to establish government on popular consent.

British imperial rulers, like the Indian rulers they replaced, were less interested in articulated consent. They saw Indians as subjects rather than participatory citizens and recognised that coercive power lay at the heart of their rule, buttressed by the operation of the rulers' prestige, a facet of government over which they took extraordinary care. By the later nineteenth century they had evolved a structure of government subject ultimately to parliament in London (see Figure 1). One-third of India stayed in the control of the remaining Indian princes, subordinate allies left in place as a reward for loyalty during the turmoil of 1857. In the remaining two-thirds, 'British India', the lines of civil and police power flowed down from the viceroy or sovereign's representative, through the provinces into which India was divided, some being equal in area to Britain itself. The raj's main local representative was the district officer, who was magistrate, collector of revenue, the man with clout who could get things done and whose path it was unwise to cross. He often controlled an area as large as an English county. This autocratic style of government was buttressed, and somewhat tempered, by the creation and gradual expansion of consultative councils for the viceroy and provincial governors, whose members were part nominated and part elected, to represent what the British saw as significant 'interests' in Indian public life, such as large landholders, universities or in certain areas business associations. Simultaneously Indian cooperation had been sought in the running of local government – in town councils and district boards, as an exercise in political education and in cheaper administration. The whole edifice was designed for essentially static, conservative governance, its goals being tax collection and social and political stability. The role of government was assumed to be limited (as in contemporary Britain, of course) and there was very litle human investment in such areas as education, health and social welfare. Only about 4 per cent of government expenditure went into such areas, less than in the princely states, and much less than in Britain itself.

What roles were there for Indians in this regime, what routes to power in India's public life? In the formal business of imperial

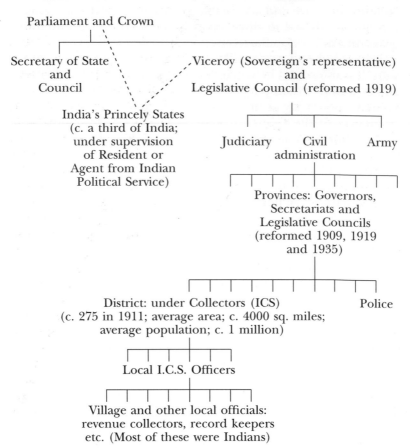

GREAT BRITAIN   INDIA

Parliament and Crown

Secretary of State and Council

Viceroy (Sovereign's representative) and Legislative Council (reformed 1919)

India's Princely States (c. a third of India; under supervision of Resident or Agent from Indian Political Service)

Judiciary   Civil   Army
administration

Provinces: Governors, Secretariats and Legislative Councils (reformed 1909, 1919 and 1935)

District: under Collectors (ICS)   Police
(c. 275 in 1911; average area; c. 4000 sq. miles; average population; c. 1 million)

Local I.C.S. Officers

Village and other local officials: revenue collectors, record keepers etc. (Most of these were Indians)

Figure 1 The structure of imperial government in India

security and civil administration Indians outside princely territory had a severely limited role except in very subordinate positions. The army's officer corps and senior police ranks were expatriate preserves. Despite a royal pledge in 1858 of equality among imperial subjects, in practice even the few Indians qualified by western education to attempt entry into the prestigious Indian Civil Service (ICS) found it difficult because of practical barriers such as the young age required of candidates for the entrance examination, and the fact that for many years it could only be taken in London. By 1909 only about sixty out of 1142 ICS officers were Indian. By contrast the lower ranks of the army, police and civil government were filled entirely by Indians. More informally, Indians of substantial social standing, 'native gentlemen' such as landholders, business men and some of the western educated who had risen to new status and wealth through the professions of law, medicine and education, were co-opted into the enterprise of imperial government through the consultative councils and local self-government institutions, and through the *durbari* system of open access (particularly for notable people) to the representatives of empire. At the base of the raj district officers, for example, kept their own local *durbar* lists, and ranked their trusted locals in strict precedence for public gatherings: their names were also recorded in the handing-over notes when officers left the district. At the highest levels invitations to viceregal and royal *durbars* and indeed the imperial honours system displayed the value of a range of notable Indians to their rulers and the routes through which they could achieve a certain standing in the eyes of the raj and of their countrymen.

Although the official British in India were prepared to welcome certain types of high-born or gentlemanly Indian into their structures and formal functions, and had a high regard for those they categorised as 'martial races', the raj as seen and experienced by most Indians was clearly and sometimes crudely racial. Lord Curzon as viceroy at the turn of the century forcefully condemned this aspect of the British presence despite his contempt for educated Indians. British attitudes of racial superiority and separation had become increasingly strident during the nineteenth century, particularly after the 1857 mutiny. They were never enshrined in legislation, but British social conventions made their assumptions abundantly clear, in ways which were deeply offensive, particularly to western-educated Indians.[4] They tended to live apart from Indians in urban areas, their large homes in elegant gardens safely built on broad well-maintained roads away from 'black town'. In the districts the bungalow, with its size and structure, its grounds and servants' quarters, marked out the European home. Here British people created a conservative version of upper-middle-class life 'at home', which was itself profoundly stratified, where every family knew its place in relation to others in the imperial hierarchy. Its conventions, manners and morals were strictly policed by the *memsahib*, or European wife, to maintain a clear distinction between the domestic lives of rulers and their subjects, and of course to prevent any sexual intimacy between the two races. Europeans also took their recreation apart from their subjects, in their clubs, and in the 'hill stations' such as Simla where they attempted to reconstruct versions of an English rural idyll in a cooler climate. Informal and easy social relations between Indians and the British were hazardous and fraught with potential for misunderstanding, even where they were sought. It was hardly surprising that British officials felt most at ease in the role of paternal patron, in the company of those they saw as simple rural folk and the heart of 'real' India.

Social and economic change

Another element in the European image of India was a supposed conservatism which locked people into social relations dictated by tradition and prevented social mobility or economic innovation. Historical research has recently shown how wrong it is to characterise Indian society and economy as 'unchanging'; and also how the British themselves helped to construct and solidify 'tradition' in their attempts to enquire into and describe the society over which they now ruled. Yet it was true that India had not experienced the radical upheavals in the economy and in social organisation produced in parts of the western world by the processes of large-scale industrialisation and later by the growth of the professions. The nature of Indian society and its economic foundations thus had profound implications for the nature of politics on the subcontinent, and in particular framed the world of Indians who in new ways began to speak for 'India' and to organise a new style of 'national' politics.

In the 1890s India's population was in the region of 300 millions. The numbers were severely restrained by the lack of modern medicine and awareness of public hygiene among the vast majority, which in the later twentieth century were dramatically to reduce infant and maternal mortality, and to control such killer diseases as smallpox, cholera, plague and malaria. Poverty, leading to malnutrition, often made women, the old and very young particularly vulnerable: and wide-scale famine was still a real threat to life in some areas. Life expectancy at birth was under twenty-five years. Yet in the last quarter of the century forces were working to change the life experience of all Indians in ways unimaginable to their parents. For their own purposes of security and government the British began to draw India together into a new geographical and political unity with a web of reinforcing ties – particularly by their common administrative institutions and by new means of communications. The latter included metalled roads, railways and the telegraph and postal services, all of which linked areas once separate or isolated. People, goods, news and ideas began to flow more freely across the subcontinent. Moreover, in English, the new language of government and higher education, educated Indians had a common means of communication which came to be more widespread even than Hindustani, the trans Indian language which had evolved under the earlier Mughal empire.

When Nehru was born most Indians were still country people, living in the many thousands of villages scattered across the land. In the decade 1892–1901 between 9 and 10 per cent of the population lived in towns and cities. But rural society was not uniform, as strong differences had developed from area to area as a result of local ecology, social formations and different economic and political experiences. In some provinces such as the UP (United Provinces of Agra and Oudh) in the north there were large landholders for peculiar historical reasons – the post-1857 British policy of conciliating the local landlords whose attitudes had been crucial in determining local loyalties or disaffection in the region. Here men whose power was now reinforced by imperial support controlled great estates and thousands of unprotected tenants. The more common rural pattern of power was seen in many areas where there were locally dominant castes of substantial peasant farmers, who held land individually or in family groups. Whatever the regional pattern, land was the key to local wealth and to power over the lives and labour of men and women; it also lay at the heart of much local political activity.

In the countryside many were still engaged in subsistence agriculture, working small plots they owned or rented. In some areas, new crops, road and particularly rail transport had encouraged commercial agriculture, and farmers produced food and raw materials such as cotton for a wider domestic and overseas market. By the end of the century, however, there had been no agricultural revolution to shift rural patterns of power and dominance overall, or to benefit those at the base of society who had only their labour to sell. Yet India's rural folk were now more tightly locked into world-wide patterns of trade under the aegis of imperial rule, and were consequently vulnerable not just to domestic disasters such as a failed monsoon, but also to the shifts in those broader patterns of demand. This was to become painfully clear in the subsequent decades marked by world wars and slump, and was the context for Nehru's political apprenticeship.

Although a small percentage of Indians were townsmen, towns and cities had for many centuries played a central role in Indian society, economy and politics. Long-standing urban centres still in existence included those which were administrative in origin and nature, like Delhi itself, the capital of the Mughal empire; trading marts on well-worn trade routes across the land; or centres of culture and religion such as the famous Hindu holy city of Benares. In the nineteenth century some older towns decayed, their rationale undermined by the presence of new rulers. Some flourished and were joined by new urban centres as a result of the British raj, its new communications networks and the beginnings of modern industrial activity. Industrial development was small and geographically limited in the nineteenth century. Only about 500,000 Indians worked in factories in 1900. But Calcutta and Bombay, for example, began a dramatic process of expansion in size and range of occupations on the back of modern cotton and jute industry, as on a lesser scale did numerous provincial towns such as Kanpur in UP. Industrial workers migrated from nearby areas to take advantage of new jobs; and increasing numbers of them raised their families in new urban environments, creating new generations of men and women who had never lived in the countryside, despite the British tendency to see urban workers as peasants at heart. Much modern industry and business was in British hands at least until after the First World War. The 'unofficial' British community particularly in Calcutta included businessmen whose wealth made them objects of envy but also of snobbish scorn in official imperial society. 'Box-wallah', in origin a historical description of a man of trade, was by the end of the century a term of social deprecation! Increasingly Indian family and kin groups with traditions in trade, business and banking across the subcontinent began to use their skills, connections and credit in more modern enterprises, to co-operate with expatriate business and eventually to challenge its dominance. The Marwaris of Calcutta were a prime example. Having migrated as a small caste of traders from western India, their notable diversification into modern business and industry came early in the twentieth century. One of their most successful men, G.D. Birla, became a significant supporter and financier of Gandhi.

More significant than these industrial developments for the urban India in which Nehru was brought up was the increasing availability of western-style education in English. Education in vernacular languages was itself a comparative luxury; and literacy rates were low. By 1911 only just over 11 per cent of Indian men in British (as opposed to princely) India were literate, as were 1.1 per cent of women. The highest levels of literacy were in those areas where there was greatest urbanisation – Madras, Bombay and Bengal.[5] Education in English was less widely available and English-medium schools and colleges were found only in larger towns. Any education, at school or college level, was only for those who could pay for it. Although the EIC had encouraged English education early in the nineteenth century, by the end of the century the raj still only spent tiny sums on any form of education, and increasingly channelled its contributions through 'grants-in-aid' to recognised institutions to create a broader educational base. Yet western education flourished and was largely self-financing because so many Indian parents saw it as the route to advancement for their sons in the environment of British imperial rule. In 1857 the first three universities were founded – in Madras, Bombay and Calcutta. By the 1890s there were around 100 arts colleges educating 12,000 pupils: by 1900 there were nearly 30,000 Indian graduates in all, roughly one to every 10,000 of the population. Access to such education was highly restricted – by geography and by finance. Consequently the vast majority of students were males from high-status, urban and Hindu families who had long traditions of professional employment and despised manual labour. Women, lower-caste groups of Hindus and many Muslims (for reasons of geography and social status) were effectively excluded from participation in this significant force for change.

Although the English-speaking, western-educated Indians were a tiny percentage of the population their significance for the political future of India became out of all proportion to their numbers. These were the men exposed to a wide range of new scientific, social and political ideas, who had the skills necessary for modern professions, and who had the common

17

language with which to communicate across the subcontinent. Not surprisingly it was in urban areas that a vibrant Indian press developed, using both English and a range of vernacular languages. These educated men became lawyers, doctors, teachers, lecturers and journalists. Many became in time deeply frustrated professionally and personally by British racial exclusivity, by constraints imposed by the raj – whether in journalism, for example, or on access to the prestigious ICS – and by the growing experience of unemployment.[6]

Indian society was clearly changing by the 1890s. There were new routes to influence in public life, particularly for those who made it to the top of the modern professions, or for those in business who adapted to new modes of production and international markets. Yet the rural nature of most of India made it understandable that ICS men still clung to their dream of an idealised 'village India', and of peasants as 'real Indians', particularly when compared to urban, educated men whom they castigated as unrepresentative upstarts. It also indicates why in any development of really large-scale politics the countryside would be the key, as would those with powerful rural roots and connections.

The world of self-understanding

While the British tried to maintain their image of an unchanging India it was inevitable that sensitive Indians, particularly those receiving western education or in close contact with their rulers, would experience deep inner questioning – responding to the apparent challenges to their customs, beliefs and identities presented by their enforced and closer contact with the world and culture of the industrialised west. The very fact of colonial rule by an insignificant number of foreigners had from its outset produced deep introspection. As the century progressed, more Indians were drawn into closer consideration of Europe by education, literature, news and travel. Britain's own ideals of national identity and freedom, and of individual liberty, and her increasingly democratic government, western scientific discourse, manners and social relations, and the Christianity preached by missionaries, all demanded of Indians reflection and choice. Many were highly articulate about their inner questioning and the resolutions they achieved.[7] The repercussions in the world of Indian self-understanding were visible, too, in a wide range of new movements and activities.

For example, the later nineteenth century was a time of considerable religious upheaval and redefinition in India. India's major religious traditions all found responses to the issues raised by contact with the west and in particular to the criticisms of Christian missionaries who, though distinct from the imperial rulers, came to India and elsewhere in Asia and Africa as the British empire expanded. Their criticisms of Indian traditions were not only theological, but strident in hostility to social customs apparently sanctioned by religion. Indian responses ranged from text-based defences and definitions of religion to match British assumptions that holy texts were the basis of all genuine religion, to movements of purification, modernisation and revivalism.[8] In nearly all traditions there was an enhanced sense of who belonged and who was an outsider, as the boundaries of religious identity became more clearly drawn – by these internal movements and also by the external force of British attempts (as in their decennial census) to count the adherents to what they assumed to be coherent religious 'communities'. Linked to religious self-questioning were the beginnings of a social reform movement, particularly among Hindus exposed to western education who were developing a more western professional and domestic life-style.[9] Among the reformers' earliest concerns were issues relating to the treatment of women – early marriage, the ban on widow remarriage, the rare custom of *sati*,[10] the practice of *purdah* or seclusion (among some Hindus as well as Muslims), and the lack of female education. The battle against social conservatism was tough and some of the most articulate reformers were subject within their own families to intolerable pressures to conform. Patriarchal societies are not notable for their willingness to change the place of women within them; particularly as in India when gender was at the heart of imperial perceptions and criticisms of Indians and their society. Caste and the practice of untouchability were also on the reformers' agenda; and the latter became a divisive issue in the nationalist movement only decades later.

Self-questioning extended to matters of political theory and action. Increasingly from mid century, educated men began to ask what it meant in political terms to be an Indian subjected to imperial rule, and what British dominion told them about their own past, their weaknesses, divisions and possible unities.

They began to interpret India and Indianness in terms of a modern national identity, focused in the legitimacy of the nation state, an interpretation deeply embedded in the content of western liberal education but at utter variance with the Orientalist image of India held by the British. In earlier centuries notions of Indianness had certainly existed but had been predominantly cultural, and senses of political identity had seldom developed beyond the linguistic region. This political vision of being Indian was new and remarkable; but the subcontinent's multiple diversities – of ethnicity, language, religion and social status – were to make the new ideal of a nation and national belonging deeply problematic. In India, as in Europe and elsewhere, the idea of the modern nation and movements of nationalism were minority commitments and enterprises at the outset, and had solid foundations in sectional interests and grievances. In the Indian case a wide range of grievances among the western educated, not least about access to opportunities in and under the raj, united those who came together in new voluntary and secular associations across the country to consider their problems and press for change. This culminated in the emergence of new types of political association, and ultimately of the first and major pan-Indian political organisation which was to last until independence and beyond, the Indian National Congress, first held in 1885.[11] Despite its profound significance for the future of Indian politics, Congress was until the impact of the First World War a very limited political enterprise. It only met annually in Christmas week, and had at this stage no permanent organisation, secure funding or even coherent policy. It was essentially a mouthpiece for articulating discontents, and reflected only the interests of a tiny segment of the population. Attendance lists show how men in the modern professions dominated its meetings, as did high-caste Hindus from Madras, Bombay and Bengal. Based on essentially local groups of western-educated men it also suffered from internal cleavages and split seriously during the 1900s on personal and ideological lines. Another serious limitation on its 'representative' or 'national' character was its failure to attract Muslims. In part this was because Muslims tended to have less access to modern education than high-caste Hindus, not because of their religion as such. It also reflected the concern among some Muslims that in an India as envisaged by Congress (with a greater role in government for Indians) the main beneficiaries would be high-caste Hindus precisely because of their educational achievements. A group of northern Indian Muslims consequently led a new political initiative in 1906 by forging a Muslim League and using it as a vehicle to press for special consideration by government of the Muslims' position in a changing India, particularly in the form of separate electorates and reserved seats in the legislatures to be created by impending constitutional reform.[12] Like Congress, the League was tiny, made up of the highly educated, and unrepresentative of the vast mass of India's Muslims, who were in any case a diverse set of regional groups rather than a single 'community' with common problems and interests.

None the less, the emergence of both political bodies was immensely significant in the long run – for Indian politics and for those who aspired to political power in India. They were both means for a modern style of political organisation and articulation – using English as a common language for men from different regions, but at a deeper level using the political language and assumptions of the British in their demands and formulations of 'India', 'nation' and 'community'. They were the beginnings of a new institutional environment for political leadership and activity; though at this stage their lack of funds meant that there was no possibility of a paid profession of politics. Further, they were both laying foundations for new types of political authority and status in relation to their compatriots and their rulers, as they claimed to 'represent', to speak for all or sections of the Indian people. Older patterns of local political power and activity, centred on control of resources such as land, credit and commodities, persisted alongside these new developments, and increasingly found articulation through these new forms of political organisation, in turn being influenced by their assumptions and patterns of behaviour. So a new political style took deep root on the subcontinent, which those interested in power and the processes of decision-making, be they Indian or British, could ill afford to ignore.

.   .   .

The young Nehru was thus born into a world marked both by conservatism and movements for change in society, where the economy was being changed by new patterns of employment and wealth creation, despite its apparent traditionalism. It was a world which many of the British imperial rulers would have liked to have 'mothballed' according to their static vision of it as different and uniquely in need of their presence. By contrast, a highly significant minority of their Indian subjects were coming to see themselves and their present position in very different ways, and were organising to pursue a vision of change and reconstruction.

.   .   .

THE YOUNG JAWAHARLAL, 1889–1923

A world of privilege

Jawaharlal was born into a family in many ways typical of those marked by these new forces of change. The Nehrus were Hindu, high-caste, with a tradition of government service and professional work, located in a city with schools, a university and a high court. Where the family was untypical was in its great wealth. Jawaharlal's father, Motilal, was one of the most successful, and richest, civil lawyers of his generation. Such was his own success in the context of the British raj that he was determined that his only son must be prepared to take advantage of even greater opportunities in a changing India: power and influence in some walk of life must be his goal.

The Nehrus were Brahmins, the highest caste group in Hindu society. Originally from Kashmir, in the early nineteenth century they took service with the British in Delhi (in the law and police) and began the tradition of English literacy for their men-folk. The family left Delhi during the upheavals of 1857. Motilal was born in 1861 and eventually moved with his older brother, a lawyer, to Allahabad, provincial capital of what was to become the United Provinces. There he attended Muir College, a new higher-education institution named after the province's lieutenant-governor, and to become the nucleus of the University of Allahabad in 1887. In Allahabad Motilal ultimately made his home and legal practice. In professional terms his eminence was recognised when, despite being Indian-trained rather than called to the English bar, he was admitted as an advocate in the Allahabad high court in 1896, and in 1909 given permission to appear in Britain before the judicial committee of the privy council. Financially his success was plain for all to see. His changing life-style mirrored on the grand

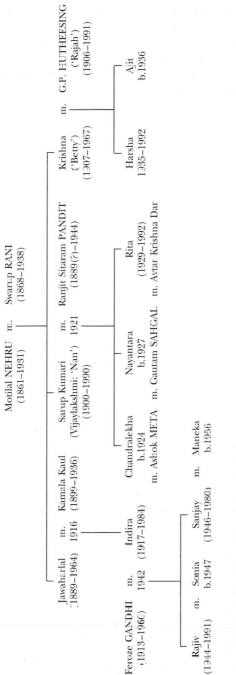

Motilal NEHRU m. Swarup RANI
(1861–1931) (1868–1938)

Jawaharlal m. Kamala Kaul   Sarup Kumari   m. Ranjit Sitaram PANDIT   Krishna   m. G.P. HUTHEESING
(1889–1964) 1916 (1899–1936) (Vijaylakshmi: 'Nan') 1921 (1889(?)–1944) ('Betty') ('Rajah')
                              (1900–1990)   (1907–1967)   (1906–1991)

Feroze GANDHI m. Indira (1917–1984)   Chandralekha   Nayantara   Rita   Harsha   Ajit
(1913–1960)   1942   b.1924   b.1927   (1929–1992)   1935–1992 b.1936
                                       m. Ashok META m. Gautam SAHGAL m. Avtar Krishna Dar

Rajiv m. Sonia   Sanjay   m. Maneka
(1944–1991) b.1947   (1946–1980)   b.1956

Figure 2 Jawaharlal Nehru's close family

scale patterns of mobility and adaptation visible among many English-educated families. Before his son was born he had moved from the 'Indian' part of town to the spacious civil lines where Europeans lived, and in 1900 he bought 1 Church Road, a large but dilapidated house which he transformed into a luxurious home for his extended family. Jawaharlal's boyhood was thus spent in a world of remarkable privilege and comfort. Theirs was the first house in Allahabad to have electricity, piped water and a swimming pool. There were two kitchens (for western and 'Hindu' food) and a retinue of servants. The men-folk wore western clothes, adopted western table-manners, and enjoyed the western luxuries of good wines and cigars. The children had bicycles and rode horses from their father's stable. Some of Motilal's clothes were tailored in London; and in 1904 he brought the first car to Allahabad. Money also meant education. Motilal bought the best not only for his son, but for his two younger daughters. It was to take the son to England in his teens.

By that time the cultural ambience of the Nehru home had marked the son for life in deeper ways than the comforts money could buy. It was an ambience of urbane cosmopolitanism and tolerance, and of concern for public affairs. The Indian world of Allahabad was itself mixed, reflecting layers of social change as the Mughal empire had declined and the British had established their raj. There were migrant professional Hindu families from different parts of India, like the Nehrus themselves, local Hindus, many of whom were taking up the commercial, professional and educational opportunities Allahabad offered as a provincial capital city, and local Muslim families of considerable social standing and with traditions of learning. The common culture of the city's educated owed much to Hindu and Muslim traditions, as did their colloquial language, Hindustani. Motilal himself had studied Persian and Arabic before changing to English-medium education at the age of 12. Despite clear awareness that Hindus and Muslims had distinct beliefs and religious practices, relations between them were usually cordial. This distinctive cultural background distanced father and son from comprehension of and sympathy with Hindu 'revivalism' and the 'communalism' which was to mar social relations and eventually to influence politics profoundly and violently in the twentieth century. Although Jawaharlal learned much about Hindu tradition from his mother and aunt, and participated in the great public Hindu festivals like other children, the men in the household were casual about religious practice, and the young boy imitated them and had no serious religious commitment, apart from a brief flirtation with Theosophy. He also imbibed a deep commitment to social reform. In the family group no *purdah* was observed, and the girls received education and learned English like their brother. Motilal publicly spoke of social reform as the parent of political reform and attacked the treatment of women and the caste system in particular – an attitude his son strongly supported.[13] Motilal himself had resolutely refused to undergo ritual purification on his return from a visit to Europe in 1899. He ignored the excommunication imposed on him by caste members; and he did not hesitate to send his son to England.

Motilal's expanding horizons made him a gracious (and welcome) host to both Indians and Europeans. The ease of his relations with English barristers and officials was unusual for the time: it made his son's passage to England less culturally strange than for many of his contemporaries, and gave him the capacity throughout his life to make relationships across barriers of race and nation. It did not, however, prevent Jawaharlal from recognising the racialism endemic among the British. Adult male talk in the house 'often . . . related to the overbearing character and insulting manners of the English people, as well as Eurasians, towards Indians, and how it was the duty of every Indian to stand up to this and not to tolerate it'.[14] Motilal none the less remained studiously loyal and moderate in his politics. As he became an increasingly notable public figure and was drawn into public political debate he made it plain that he believed in the good intentions of the British towards India and the efficacy of constitutional politics to gain redress of real grievances from the raj. It was precisely men like Motilal whom the imperial rulers wished to associate with their government through measures of reform at various levels of decision-making from the later nineteenth century. After the constitutional reforms of 1909, which enlarged the provincial legislatures, freed them from an official majority and provided for the election of non-official members, Motilal stood and was elected to the expanded provincial legislature. Moreover, his ambition for his son was entry into the ICS, the ultimate symbol of acceptance into the imperial structure as well as a route to public power. As the epitome of the 'native gentleman' the British wished to incorporate into their imperial endeavour Motilal was invited in 1911 to Delhi for the *durbar* held by George V. With his wife and two daughters he went with the entourage of the UP lieutenant-governor. His son, then in London, ordered his father's full court dress – somewhat ironically since a decade later they would both again be guests of the raj, but this time in jail.

Motilal had been educated entirely in India: he was determined otherwise for his son. After providing predominantly private tuition at home, he took his son at the age of 15 to England and secured his entry to Harrow, one of the most notable English public schools, where Jawaharlal studied from 1905 to 1907. 'Joe' Nehru, as he was known, more than held his own, socially and academically. His letters home are full of schoolboy preoccupations, though he later admitted: 'I remember how miserable I was weeks after you left me at Harrow both times. I do not think I have ever felt so lonely as I did then.'[15] This was almost the only sign he gave of the dimensions of the upheaval in his life in the transition from Allahabad to Harrow. When he left he realised how attached he had become to the school. He then went to Trinity College, Cambridge, and read Natural Sciences, from 1907 to 1910. These were in his words 'three quiet years ... moving slowly on like the sluggish Cam'.[16] The earlier loneliness persisted, though not as acutely, and he had many casual acquaintances and engaged in the usual undergraduate practice of semi-highbrow talk, often late into the night, which made him and his fellow students feel very sophisticated. He admitted his knowledge was superficial and theoretical, on matters ranging from sex to philosophy. Life was pleasant, intellectually and materially. The latter was hardly surprising – as his father gave him an allowance of £400 a year, which was a princely sum for an undergraduate and nearly half a professor's salary! Later he admitted he was unaware and insular at Cambridge.[17] More seriously, from Motilal Nehru's point of view, he was clearly not destined for singular academic success; and this put an end to the paternal ambition for an ICS career for his son. Having coasted through his academic work, Jawaharlal achieved a lower second-class honours degree. But even this gave him a serious understanding of the importance of science in the modern world, which was unusual among Indians of his generation, who tended to study arts subjects and law. Jawaharlal next went to London for two years to study law, enrolling at the Inner Temple, a legal career being the obvious course if the ICS was not a viable option. His London days were a striking contrast to the painful experiences of the unsophisticated Gandhi in London a few years earlier, dogged by shyness, poverty and cultural confusions.

Jawaharlal thrived as a fashionable man about town, travelled in the British Isles and on the continent, and succeeded in spending very considerable sums of money which perturbed even Motilal, who was regularly asked for further funds. In 1911 Jawaharlal spent £800 and was quite blunt to Motilal about his extravagance; in mid-1912 his expenditure caused a serious disagreement between them, and the son again had to ask for more money, admitting that he was at his wits' end over his debts.[18]

Although Nehru's English education had not fulfilled his father's hopes, it had given him a superb command of the English language, visible in his letters, speeches and later books. It also gave him a cosmopolitan ease and vision, far greater than he could have gained in Allahabad – qualities which later marked him out in Congress politics and fitted him for negotiations with the British in the final years of the raj, and for an international leadership role. Whether it fitted him for the realities of Indian politics is debatable. As his Indian critics were deriding within a few years, he was too decent to be a politician: he was a gentleman, and worse, an English gentleman.[19] His English experience was that of assured ease, of the wealthy in the Edwardian years before the First World War shattered their world. Yet the England he inhabited was also an environment of serious political and social concern and debate, at least in political and academic circles. The Webbs, Richard Tawney and George Bernard Shaw were active; a Liberal government was expanding the state's role in providing social welfare. But though Nehru was eager to see Shaw when he lectured in Cambridge, he seemed more interested in the man than the message. There was little evidence at this stage that Nehru was giving serious thought to social and economic issues or to the role of government. Nor did he show any signs of a vocation to politics. He was happy to go along with Motilal's idea of an ICS career until his father dropped it; and only gradually and in an academic way did his politics begin to diverge from his father's moderation and belief in British good faith. The most that can be said is that he kept up with Indian politics through the newspapers and his father's letters. It was assumed that he would, like Motilal, take on a public role on his return to India, as would befit an articulate English-trained lawyer.

Back home in Allahabad, Jawaharlal was once more enveloped in the life and expectations of his extended family. Foremost among these expectations was his marriage, a topic on which he had corresponded with his parents while in England. He had agreed, somewhat reluctantly, to an arranged marriage within the Kashmiri community; for Motilal, despite his modernity, this was far too significant an issue for the family as a whole, as well as for his son, to be left to free choice. Jawaharlal wished for the decision to be delayed until he could see his intended bride, but Motilal in fact made the choice while his son was still in London. She was Kamala Kaul, daughter of a Delhi-based Kashmiri businessman, ten years younger than Jawaharlal and educated quietly at home in Urdu and Hindi (the two literary languages of northern India as opposed to the colloquial Hindustani). Motilal immediately saw to it that his heir's proposed wife should be groomed and educated by the European governesses who had taught his own daughters. Kamala was thus unwittingly prepared for a tragically brief married life which was to be marked not only by her own ill-health but by political prominence, domestic disturbance, separations from her husband and foreign travel. They were married in February 1916, amid sumptuous celebrations which lasted for days. Their daughter, Indira, was born the following year. Jawaharlal, the young family man, now settled to life as a lawyer in Allahabad, with all the openings his father and his colleagues could provide. But he found no real fulfilment in his profession, and disliked the parochial atmosphere of the local Allahabad bar. Nor did there seem to be any opening for worthwhile political activity, though he attended Congress sessions. Looking back in jail in 1922 he described the pettiness of the life to which he had returned, despite its comfort and security.

Ever since my return from England I have done little reading and I shudder to think what I was gradually becoming before politics . . . snatched me away from the doom that befalls many of us. Freedom in many of its aspects is denied us but the freedom and the glory of thought is ours and none can deprive us of it. But the life

I led and that so many of us lead, the atmosphere of the law courts, the uninspiring conversation of bar libraries, the continuous contact with the sordid side of human nature – all this and the absence of any organised intellectual life gradually kill this power of free thought. We dare not follow up the consequences of our thought . . . And so we live out our lives with little said or little done that beautifies existence for us or for others, or that will be remembered by any one after we are dead and gone.[20]

A new vision and vocation

Jawaharlal unexpectedly found a sense of purpose and a vocation to politics in this situation of discontented ease. In May 1922, at his trial for participating in a new political movement of non-cooperation, he spoke eloquently of true loyalty to the Indian motherland, rather than to the British raj:

in almost every jail in India will be found loyalists who have put their cause and their faith and their country above everything else and have been true to them despite all consequences. To them has come the great call; they have seen the vision of freedom and they will not rest or turn away till they have achieved their heart's desire.

He counted himself among a privileged band, glad to go to jail, as to a place of pilgrimage, and marvelled at his good fortune.[21] The change in his sense of purpose and self-esteem was the result of the world war and its influence on India, and of the emergence of M.K. Gandhi as a compelling new leader in Indian politics, the man who, apart from his father, was to have the most personal influence on his life, as he later acknowledged.[22]

The First World War had a major impact on India, though the subcontinent itself was never threatened as it was in 1939–45. Fulfilling its expected role in Britain's imperial enterprise, India sent well over a million men overseas to help fight the war, and raised over £146 millions to help pay for the conflict. Everyone in India, from the highest official to the poorest agricultural labourer, felt the effects – in higher taxes, shortages of essentials and spiralling inflation. More important than the physical impact were the political repercussions, both on Indian opinion and on British thinking about the nature and purpose of their rule.

Almost within a year of the war's outbreak the essentially moderate Congress was asking for an advance towards self-government and an acceptance that this was Britain's goal for India. The role of Indian troops in an imperial war and the western allies' own apparent advocacy of 'national self-determination' boosted the Indian claim. Moreover that claim was made with a unanimity never seen before in Indian politics. By 1916 long-standing splits between 'moderate' and 'extremist' factions were healed; and Congress joined forces with the Muslim League on this common political platform, following the conclusion of the 'Lucknow pact', in the drafting of which Motilal had played a significant part. In return for articulate Muslim support, vital to put real political pressure on the raj for constitutional advance, Congress accepted that Muslims had a distinctive political status in India which should be recognised through the provision of separate electorates and reserved seats in any reformed legislatures. The whole style of modern politics also began to change significantly, as two home rule leagues were founded to spread the idea of home rule and generate wider public pressure for it than the decorous demands of Congress's Christmas gatherings. Motilal became president of the Allahabad branch, and Jawaharlal one of its secretaries. It was indeed a sign of political transformation if such a one as Motilal now felt moved to join the more populist demand for home rule.

The British, with their backs increasingly to the wall, acknowledged political reality. Pragmatic as always, they embarked on a search for a strategy which would satisfy as wide a range of significant political opinion as possible, while safeguarding the essentials of British control and thus of the role India must be made to play in Britain's international network of political and economic power. The result was a declaration in 1917 that Britain's goal for India was the increasing association of Indians in administration and the gradual development of self-governing institutions, 'with a view to the progressive realisation of responsible government in India as an integral part of the British Empire'. Although a cautious compromise, this was a development inconceivable before the outbreak of war; and it led the way to a restructuring of government and decision-making which would offer certain types of Indians far greater scope for participation – and real power – in the politics and governance of their own country. At the same time as the more rapid Indianisation of the officer corps of the army and the ICS, the legislatures in the provinces and in Delhi were to be enlarged and freed from an official majority. Although little was to change otherwise in the Delhi government, in the provinces real changes in authority and responsibility occurred as some topics were to be transferred to the control of Indian ministers responsible to the legislature, and through it to the enlarged electorate – admittedly of only about one-tenth of the male population. Reserved topics would still be dealt with by the governor and his executive; and predictably these topics included such areas vital to imperial control as land revenue, administration, policing, justice, prisons and control of the press. True to their vision of India, the British allocated more seats to rural than to urban areas and provided special seats for important 'interests', including representatives of religious 'communities', who also had separate electorates. In the case of Muslims, the Lucknow pact of 1916 served as a guide to allocations of seats.

Although British intentions were extremely limited, what soon became clear was that new and highly significant power was available to politicians in the provinces; and that the pathways to that power were through the mechanisms of elections which in turn demanded that those who aspired for place and power in the new structures would have to find ways of forging new contacts with a far wider spectrum of society. There were, of course, drawbacks – the limited franchise, the nature of the transferred topics, the poor financial resources available to responsible ministers, and the reserve powers of the viceroy and governors. But it was an opportunity for incorporation into the raj's structures of power undreamed of by Motilal's generation. At first it seemed that virtually all Indian politicians would accept the reforms of 1919 and take to the politics of elections and work through the legislatures. But in 1920 this strategy was wrecked by the forces which enabled the emergence of Gandhi as a powerful force in India and in Congress politics.

M.K. Gandhi (later known as 'Mahatma' or Great Soul) was a virtually unknown figure in India before 1917–18. He came from western India, and from a far less privileged and more traditional Hindu family than the Nehrus, and had struggled as a student against personal diffidence, poor English, poverty and cultural strangeness to qualify in London as a lawyer. This did not guarantee him professional success in India; and he went to South Africa in 1893 on a short contract to ease his financial predicament. He stayed until 1914, making a legal career and a political reputation as a champion of Indian rights. On his final return to India two aspects of his life and experience marked him out from most westernised Indians and indeed made them think him a curious and unworldly figure. The most obvious was his rejection of what he called modern civilisation, on the grounds that it lured men and women away from the search for fundamental truth by its false standards of gain. He abandoned the trappings of a westernised life style in favour of celibacy and simplicity of food and dress, and lived in an *ashram* or religious community. He advocated for India *swaraj* or self-rule – in terms not of political freedom from the raj but of moral and social transformation. For him true work for *swaraj* was radical transformation of India's society and polity from the bottom up, rather than clamouring for concessions from the British. The second feature of his work which was peculiarly his own was the evolution in South Africa of a strategy of non-violent resistance to wrong of any kind, including acts of constituted authorities: he called it *satyagraha*, truth force. He had taught himself to lead movements of resistance to racially discriminatory law, preferring to suffer the legal penalty, including jail, rather than accept and thereby become implicated in the wrong-doing. No wonder Nehru commented that when he first met Gandhi in 1916 'he seemed very distant and different and unpolitical to many of us young men'.[23]

Gandhi himself did not contemplate a political career in India, and concentrated on establishing his *ashram* and on a range of local issues which seemed amenable to the strategy of *satyagraha*. However, several all-India issues changed his vision of his own proper role and threw him by 1920 into direct political and moral conflict with the raj. One of these was legislation (the 'Rowlatt Acts') designed to control terrorism, and in effect to retain for the raj specific coercive powers once war-time defence regulations lapsed. When the government ignored Indian political opinion and pushed the measures through the Delhi legislature, Gandhi advocated peaceful protests on an all-India scale. In the ensuing disturbances, caused partly by war-time conditions rather than Gandhi's own campaign, there occurred the infamous shooting of an unarmed crowd in the Jallianwalla Bagh, an enclosed space in Amritsar, Punjab, which left several hundred dead and many more injured. Gandhi called off his campaign, confessing to a 'Himalayan miscalculation'. But he was central to a Congress committee of enquiry into the incident, of which Motilal Nehru was also a member. By early 1920 when both the Congress and the British Hunter committees had completed their enquiries, Gandhi and Congressmen became convinced that (despite considerable British criticism of the event) British rule was fundamentally racist and that the Hunter report and subsequent government despatches were little more that whitewash. In July 1920 Motilal wrote to Jawaharlal of the need to 'raise a veritable hell for the rascals', just weeks after Gandhi had advised Indians to 'refuse to submit to this official violence' and to withdraw cooperation from the raj.[24] A further issue which combined to throw Gandhi into conflict with the raj was the treatment of the Turkish sultan, the Khalifah of world-wide Muslims, by the victorious western allies. Many Indian Muslims, though owing him no political allegiance, became deeply concerned that his territorial power would be so curbed in the post-war settlement that he would not be able to perform his religious function of protecting Muslim holy places. Gandhi supported the growing 'Khilafat' movement because, as a religious man, he felt that fellow-Indians should support Indian Muslims on a religious issue vital to them; and he hoped that this would cement the unity between Hindus and Muslims which he saw as crucial for genuine *swaraj*. He also hoped to demonstrate the efficacy of *satyagraha*, where the politics of moderation and petitioning had manifestly failed, but also as an alternative to the violence he abhorred as immoral and destructive.

By mid-summer of 1920 the Khilafat movement merged with concern about the Punjab shooting to form a single movement in favour of non-cooperation; and by the end of the year Congress had accepted this as its policy and abandoned the idea of working the reforms. Not without considerable misgivings, certainly without any total or permanent conversion to Gandhian priorities and political style, Congressmen launched into a populist programme of opposition to the raj, which included resignation of titles and honours, boycott of government schools and the law courts, refusal to participate in elections and legislatures, boycott of foreign cloth, and a commitment to social renewal. Gandhi had become the central figure in this new political movement, increasingly known and revered across India as no other political leader had been, and presenting a fundamental challenge to the ideology and style of Congress and its adherents since its inception. The impact on the Nehru family was dramatic. In 1919 Jawaharlal had wished to join Gandhi's campaign against the Rowlatt Acts, but this had distressed his father deeply. To the older man, jail was 'most repulsive' (he had tried sleeping on the floor to see what his son might have to endure). Nor was he convinced of the political efficacy of the suggested strategy. Both men recognised, as Jawaharlal later noted, 'that big issues were at stake involving a complete upsetting of our lives'. Motilal asked Gandhi to visit them, and after the two older men had had long talks alone, Gandhi advised Jawaharlal not to cause a rift with his father. It was evident that even now he had a powerful influence over the young man, who later wrote in a private letter, 'I shall never forget the advice that Bapu gave me . . . when the conflict in my mind was almost too great for me to bear. His healing words lessened my difficulties and I had some peace.'[25] But by the end of the next year both father and son recognised the force of Gandhi's new politics in the particular circumstances when British policies on the Punjab and Khilafat issues seemed to negate the 1919 reforms and their apparent promise of a new British vision for India and genuine cooperation between rulers and ruled. Consequently Motilal ceased his legal practice, the luxury of the great Allahabad home was pared down, the trappings of westernisation abandoned, while the men-folk discarded western dress in favour of *khadi*, Indian homespun. Father and son threw themselves into the non-cooperation movement, and within a year both of them were in jail.

Jawaharlal had no doubt that the emergence of Gandhi into Indian politics, and into the Nehrus' privileged world, was the great turning-point of his life, the time when he became fired with a new vision of Indian freedom and convinced of his own political vocation in pursuit of that goal. He remembered the exhilaration which had seized him at the time, an intoxication and excitement, and a powerful sense of freedom from fear. Gandhi recognised that the raj depended on Indian acquiescence and cooperation, and his 'non-cooperation' strategy was designed not just to withdraw active support from the British but to cut the psychological roots of colonial control of Indians. Liberating Indian hearts and minds and overturning the accepted politico-moral order was his goal – hence his attack on such key or symbolic aspects of British prestige and influence as honours, the courts and government-approved education. He succeeded in full measure for Jawaharlal, who now lost his 'old feeling of oppression and frustration' and found 'the happiness of a person crusading for a cause'. The movement wholly absorbed him; he gave up his old friends and pleasures, and even 'almost forgot' his wife and small daughter. (Looking back he marvelled at Kamala's patience and tolerance.[26]) The power of the movement and of Gandhi's inspiring personality swept Nehru and his colleagues along, and there was with the euphoria a remarkable vagueness in their minds about their goals and techniques. Although Gandhi's presence was so dominant, Nehru never became, even at this juncture, a 'Gandhian'. He was concerned about Gandhi's stress on religion, and the religious flavour of the Khilafat movement, though the idea of bringing morality and spiritual awareness into politics appealed to him. Nor was he convinced of the absolute priority of non-violence, or of its guaranteed efficacy in practical politics. Indeed, when he heard in jail that Gandhi had suspended non-cooperation in the spring of 1922 after outbreaks of violence he was deeply perturbed – in Gandhi's own words 'terribly cut up' – and feared that any non-violent movement could in future be undermined if their opponents chose to provoke violence.[27]

Gandhi's non-cooperation movement did not just mark the beginning of Jawaharlal's political vocation. It also took him for the first time into the countryside of his own UP, and made him aware of peasant India. One of the great strengths of non-cooperation was its ability to adapt to particular localities, to mesh with existing movements and to provide articulation for specific local grievances. In many parts of India it was nourished by this process of political symbiosis. In parts of UP well before Congress adopted non-cooperation there existed a peasant movement of protest against landlord strategies of exacting old dues to make their estates pay in post war economic conditions. Congressmen and Gandhi himself were deeply anxious not to stir up class conflict in the province, for fear of precipitating violence and alienating some of their own allies. None the less Nehru for the first time spent hot and dusty days in the villages, listening to those at the very base of rural society, and seeing what he had never grasped before, the poverty and harassment suffered by them. He was horrified at what he saw, and perhaps even more at the ignorance of educated, urban Indians of conditions in the countryside. He never lost the new sense of responsibility this experience produced in him or his 'sorrow at the degradation and overwhelming poverty of India', and all his subsequent politics were marked by this 'new picture of India . . . naked, starving, crushed and utterly miserable'.[28] There was a further benefit of this exposure. Earlier Nehru had been diffident, even frightened, about public speaking, partly because he doubted his command of Hindustani in such situations compared with elegant English. Now he lost that shyness, adopting a person-to-person style, and gained valuable practice in speaking before large rural audiences, whose response in turn boosted his confidence.

When Nehru spoke at his trial in 1922 for participating in the boycott of foreign cloth, he noted wryly how far he had travelled politically since his return from England. Then 'perhaps more an Englishman than an Indian', now he was a rebel against the raj, committed to preaching and practising disaffection against the evil he believed British rule represented.[29] He settled philosophically into prison, taking advantage of the enforced rest to think, to spin (the hallmark of Gandhi's associates), and to read – mostly novels and history, at the rate of about two books a week. He kept in good health and spirits, though he missed the ordinary things of life such as the voices of women and children and the barking of dogs, and found the lack of privacy a trial. But he was convinced that his life had been transformed, that he had a vision to follow, and in Gandhi a mentor who would help him strike a new and moral path to political freedom.

Outside the walls of Lucknow jail, however, non-cooperation lay in disarray. Gandhi was himself in jail and many Congressmen were anxiously looking for a return to the politics of the reformed legislatures, convinced that *satyagraha* had failed them. Thus it was profoundly unclear whether Nehru's commitment to Gandhi would be a route to political power or merely the door to work for moral renewal and social reconstruction in the changed world which would greet them on their release.

NOTES AND REFERENCES

1. 'Raj' is Hindi for 'rule': it is often used to denote Britain's imperial regime in India.
2. Because of this ideological reticence, the historian has to tease out the beliefs underlying a wide range of imperial policies, decisions and wider administrative and social activities. See T.R. Metcalf, *Ideologies of the Raj* (Cambridge: Cambridge University Press, 1994).
3. Lord Hardinge to Lord Crewe, 4 July 1912, Lord Hardinge to Lord Sanderson, 25 July 1912, Hardinge Mss. (University Library, Cambridge).
4. Fiction often provides the best insight into such matters – particularly, for example, the Indian novels of E.M. Forster and Paul Scott.
5. The highest figure for male literacy in 1911 was in Bengal (14 per cent). By comparison there were only 6.1 per cent literate men in UP and 6.5 per cent in Punjab, both of which were predominantly agricultural provinces.
6. Classic works on the nature and significance of western education are B.T. McCully, *English Education and the Origins of Indian Nationalism* (Columbia, SC: Columbia University Press, 1940); A. Seal, *The Emergence of Indian Nationalism. Competition and Collaboration in the Later Nineteenth Century* (Cambridge: Cambridge University Press, 1968).
7. See T. Raychaudhuri, *Europe Reconsidered. Perceptions of the West in Nineteenth-Century Bengal* (Delhi: Oxford University Press, 1988); B. Parekh, *Colonialism, Tradition and Reform. An Analysis of Gandhi's Political Discourse* (New Delhi, Newbury Park (Calif.) and London, 1989). An accessible example in English translation is M.K. Gandhi, *Hind Swaraj* (*Indian Home Rule*) in *The Collected Works of Mahatma Gandhi* 90 vols (Delhi: Government of India, 1958–84), vol. 10, pp. 6–68. (These volumes are subsequently referred to as *CWMG*.) *Hind Swaraj* is also available in A.J. Parel, *M.K. Gandhi. Hind Swaraj and Other Writings* (Cambridge: Cambridge University Press, 1997).
8. See K.W. Jones, *Socio-Religious Reform Movements in British India* (Cambridge: Cambridge University Press, 1989) for a survey; a case study is his *Arya Dharm. Hindu Consciousness in 19th-Century Punjab* (Berkeley and Los Angeles: University of California Press, 1976).
9. An excellent case study is M. Borthwick, *The Changing Role of Women in Bengal 1849–1905* (Princeton: Princeton University Press, 1984). See also C.H. Heimsath, *Indian Nationalism and Hindu Social Reform* (Princeton: Princeton University Press, 1964).

10. *Sati* is the 'voluntary' self-immolation of a Hindu widow on her husband's funeral pyre.
11. J.R. McLane, *Indian Nationalism and the Early Congress* (Princeton: Princeton University Press, 1977); Judith M. Brown, *Modern India. The Origins of an Asian Democracy*, 2nd edn (Oxford: Oxford University Press, 1994), pp. 167–93.
12. F.C.R. Robinson, *Separatism among Indian Muslims. The Politics of the United Provinces' Muslims 1860–1923* (Cambridge: Cambridge University Press, 1974).
13. J. Nehru to M. Nehru, 29 April 1909, *SWJN(1)*, vol. 1, p. 66. For Motilal's speech in April 1909, see B.R. Nanda *The Nehrus. Motilal and Jawaharlal* (London: George Allen & Unwin, 1962), pp. 106–8.
14. J. Nehru, *An Autobiography* (London: Bodley Head, 1936), p. 6.
15. J. Nehru to M. Nehru, 29 October 1908, *SWJN(1)*, vol. 1, pp. 58–9.
16. Nehru, *Autobiography*, p. 19.
17. J. Nehru to Indira Nehru, 30 January 1938, 11 March 1938, *SWJN(2)*, vol. 3, pp. 448, 458.
18. J. Nehru to M. Nehru, 2 June 1911, 29 December 1911, 21 June 1912, *SWJN(1)*, vol. 1, pp. 88, 93, 97–100.
19. Recalled by John Gunther, the American writer, and cited in B.R. Nanda, *Jawaharlal Nehru. Rebel and Statesman* (Delhi: Oxford University Press, 1995), p. 262.
20. J. Nehru to M. Nehru, 1 September 1922, *SWJN(1)*, vol. 1, pp. 333–4.
21. Ibid., pp. 256–7.
22. Note for John Gunther, enclosed in J. Nehru to J. Gunther, 16 March 1938, *SWJN(1)*, vol. 8, p. 869. On war-time politics in India and the emergence of Gandhi, see Brown, *Modern India*, pp. 194–231; Judith M. Brown, *Gandhi's Rise to Power. Indian Politics 1915–1922* (Cambridge: Cambridge University Press, 1972).
23. Nehru, *Autobiography*, p. 35.
24. M. Nehru to J. Nehru, 27 July 1920. Nehru Papers, Nehru Memorial Museum and Library, New Delhi (NMML); Gandhi in *Young India*, 9 June 1920, *CWMG*, vol. 17, p. 483.
25. J. Nehru to M. Desai, August 1923, J. Nehru Papers, NNML. ('Bapu', diminutive of 'Father', was an affectionate name for Gandhi used by his close circle.) See also account in Nehru, *Autobiography*, pp. 41–2.
26. Ibid., pp. 69–70, 77.
27. Ibid., pp. 82–6; Gandhi to J. Nehru, 19 February 1922, *CWMG*, vol. 22, pp. 435–7.
28. Nehru, *Autobiography*, p. 52.
29. *SWJN(1)*, vol. 1, pp. 252–7; Jail Diary, May 1922–January 1923, ibid., pp. 258–308.

Chapter 2

APPRENTICE TO POWER: GANDHI'S HEIR, 1923–*c*. 1945

Early in 1923 Jawaharlal Nehru was released from jail and his time of enforced rest and reflection. This chapter focuses on his life from then until 1945, when he was given his final release from an imperial prison and was clearly destined soon to take up high office in an independent India. These two decades, from his early thirties to his early fifties, were a time of personal and political maturation. In them he left behind all normal family life, travelled widely in India and Europe, and became central to the politics of the Indian National Congress and the nationalist movement as Gandhi's closest younger colleague.

Nehru was primarily engaged in the project of wresting power from the imperial rulers. In this engagement he learnt about the operations of state power and the practice of government from below, and was often on the receiving end of its arrogance and violence. It was an experience which was to influence his own priorities and style when he assumed the highest elected government office. He was also an apprentice to power in another sense, learning in these years about the organisation of India's political life and the interlocking of the different parts and levels of its political system, learning by trial and error about party organisation and management, the techniques of making a mass appeal and those of electoral politics, and wrestling to conceptualise and spread a national vision and ideal of his country's future. Yet he was not at this stage powerful in his own right. He had no established power base in a region or in an ideological or socio-economic group. His unique, and indeed peculiar, position, at least in Congress, was due to his relationship with Gandhi and to his status by the late 1930s as

Gandhi's recognised 'heir'. There was ironically nothing con-
crete or material to inherit: what he gained by association with
Gandhi was legitimacy in an all-India role. This position, which
at times he felt to be most uncomfortable, raises questions
about the nature of 'leadership' in India and in Congress which
became even more acute after independence. This chapter
explores themes relating to power in the context of imperial
India: particularly the inner world of this man and his attitude
to his own role and influence, and the outer world of politics
and governance, with its opportunities for and constraints on
the exercise of power by an aspirant Indian leader.

. . .

THE INNER WORLD

The euphoria Nehru had experienced in 1919–22 under
Gandhi's novel leadership turned on his release into a permanent commitment to a political career, to a passionate if more
measured concern about the exercise of state power and to a
personal aspiration to wield power. No other profession had
appealed to him, and he was fortunate that the family wealth
and tradition of public service gave him an unusual degree
of choice and the material resources to embark on a political
career. Increasingly in these decades the normal bonds of family life and physical stability collapsed around him, in a sense
freeing him to become a public figure, rather as Gandhi had
deliberately chosen that freedom for public service by a vow of
celibacy and the rejection of family life. The political activities
of the whole family and the subsequent experiences of police
raids and prison sentences took their toll on the family base in
Allahabad and their life together. His sisters married, though
he kept on close terms with them. Then death removed those
relatives who had been closest and most significant for him. His
father died in 1931, his mother in 1938, and most tragically his
wife died in 1936 of tuberculosis, in a Swiss sanatorium, after a
long period of ill-health. His growing daughter led a nomadic
life with relatives and in various educational establishments in
India and Europe, deeply influenced by her early experiences
of loss and instability. They were in close touch by correspondence and in person when possible, and their relationship was
an unusually close one for an Indian father and daughter. In
her letters she sometimes signed herself 'Indu-boy', and they

were open in their expressions to each other of great affection. He poured out his thoughts to her in a stream of letters which were a measure of his personal isolation and his commitment to giving her a broad and stimulating education, perhaps in acknowledged contrast to the more traditional upbringing of her mother.[1]

Nehru's emotional isolation and loneliness drove him into a frenetic life of public activity in association with Gandhi. He consciously led a simple and disciplined life, maintaining his physical health and stamina by exercise, good sleep and simple food, a regimen he recommended to his daughter.[2] But he recognised in himself the personal loneliness which lay behind the public man, and his failure in the sorts of close personal relationships which sustain a rewarding domestic and private life. He wrote publicly in his *Autobiography* of spiritual loneliness, of feeling like an exile in his own country, and privately of 'the shell in which I live, encompassed and cut off, and from which I seek escape in activity'.[3] Gandhi had recognised this as early as 1924 when he told Motilal that he thought his son was 'one of the loneliest young men of my acquaintance in India'.[4] Nehru's relationship with Gandhi was enabling and supportive, and the more vital for the younger man after his father's death. But it was also fraught with tension. When they disagreed on vital issues such as Gandhi's religious commitment and language, his technique of fasting to influence public events, and his political strategy, or when they temporarily drifted apart, this increased Jawaharlal's loneliness. He called a chapter of his *Autobiography* 'Desolation', in which he relived his doubts about Gandhi's actions while he himself remained in jail in the early 1930s. A decade later his prison diary voiced equally poignant distress at Gandhi's actions.[5]

Nehru was intensely self-aware. He saw himself as a traveller, a discoverer, even as a pilgrim, and as one who could never rest. This questing lay behind much of his literary output, including his *Autobiography* and *The Discovery of India* which was written in jail during the Second World War. He was aware that in contrast to many of his associates in the nationalist movement he was a modern intellectual, one who read widely in western literature and for whom thought could be a burden and even a bar to decisive action. As he wrote deprecatingly, 'The vagrant mind, finding no haven, still wanders about restlessly, bringing discomfort to its possessor as well as to others.

There is some envy for those virgin minds which have not been soiled or violated by thought's assault, and on which doubt has cast no shadow nor written a line. How easy is life for them. . . .'[6] Unlike his mentor he found 'no haven' in religious belief. Even in the exaltation of his early association with Gandhi he had been troubled by the religious dimension and flavour to Gandhi's politics, and in the 1920s he moved even more firmly away from any religious stance. He believed religion of any sort was the negation of reason and rational behaviour, could all too easily become a means of exploitation and a cloak for vested interest, and in setting its sights on otherworldly values had little conception of basic human and social values and social justice. As he wrote to Gandhi in 1933, he very unwillingly agreed to participate in the religious ceremony associated with a forth-coming family wedding, but, 'I am becoming more and more hostile to the religious idea. Exceptions apart . . . it seems to me the negation of real spirituality and only a begetter of confusion and sentimentality.'[7] The opposite of a religious attitude was what he called a 'scientific' attitude, one based on clear reasoning; and with this stance he aligned himself. It was only later in life that his hostility to religion seemed to mellow into an appreciation of a non-sectarian spirituality.

In 1937, partly as a joke, he wrote an anonymous article for the Calcutta periodical, *The Modern Review*, about himself and the man behind the actor for the mass audience who was receiving such public adulation.

> Jawaharlal has learnt well to act without the paint and powder of the actor. With his seeming carelessness and insouciance, he performs on the public stage with consummate artistry. Whither is this going to lead him and the country? What is he aiming at with all his apparent want of aim? What lies behind that mask of his, what desires, what will to power, what insatiate longings?

He did not answer these questions, but warned his readers how such a driven personality, and one with such a talent for public appeal, could be unsafe for democracy. 'A little twist and Jawaharlal might turn a dictator sweeping aside the paraphernalia of a slow-moving democracy.' This was an acknowledgement of his fascination with power, and of the capacity he had for holding a public stage, and, as he commented in a personal letter discussing the article, an admission of a self-centred stance which worked against close personal relationships and masked an inner poverty.[8]

Although Nehru did not reveal in this article the political conviction and vision which drove him on during these hard years as a nationalist opponent of government, it is clear that behind the public persona there was both belief and passion. Gandhi certainly saw this, and would not have worked with and on a man without depth, honesty and sincerity. In the 1920s the Indian National Congress was still a very diverse and loosely knit body, although it was the main vehicle for the articulation of nationalist sentiment and for the organisation of pan-Indian movements of protest against or cooperation with British rule. Many of its members were still mainly local politicians who at times used the all-India body for local ends. Those who were concerned with India's long-term future were nationalist in the sense of wanting to inherit the raj, but few thought beyond this to any radical reconstruction of India's polity or society. Most indeed came from socio-economic groups which had a vested interest in opposing major social change – professionals, businessmen, landowners. Even as Congress expanded its social base in conjunction with the extension of the franchise to the legislatures in these decades, its social complexion remained conservative. The group of committed Gandhians who followed the Mahatma in his vision of a radical transformation of India by non-violent means were tiny in numbers, and some preferred to remain outside Congress and work through the range of constructive agencies Gandhi founded to begin the processes of social and economic change.

By contrast with most active politicians of the time Jawaharlal Nehru was deeply thoughtful, widely read and increasingly well travelled. He had already visited Europe during his years of education in England, but now he returned as a mature political adult eager to make international contacts, although his absences from India were primarily driven by his wife's failing health and his search for a better climate and good treatment for her. In 1927 he participated in the International Congress against Colonial Oppression and Imperialism in Brussels and met not only established European left-wingers but delegates from Asia, Africa and Latin America. In the same year he visited Russia and saw the bewildering challenge to established social values and experiments with planned economic change, at a juncture of high idealism before the imposition of draconian state control under Stalin. The depth of his reading in western history and political philosophy combined with his international experience gave him an intellectual coherence and power possibly unsurpassed among his compatriots. He visualised India and its problems in a historical and international sweep of events and influences as few of his compatriots were able to do. An eminent Indian lawyer and politician, former member of the Government of India and friend of Motilal commented on this despite his own hostility to what Jawaharlal stood for.

> He is honest, desperately honest, but he lives in a world of his own, he hates the British and the present system equally and my fear is that even if you could bring about a settlement between him and the British he would continue to be at war with the present social system. It is sad to think that such a fine intellect and such a fine character should have nothing but jail for its immediate prospect.[9]

Nehru's early nationalism had been relatively simple in its conceptualisation. He opposed foreign rule and hated the arrogance of its representatives. As he matured he placed this almost instinctive reaction to the raj in the context of a considered understanding of the processes of history which relied heavily on Marxism. By the early 1940s when he wrote *The Discovery of India* he had developed a vision of the nature of India's past which had paved the way for imperial rule. He believed that India's once great and creative society and culture had fallen into decay long before the arrival of British traders. Unlike some Hindus he did not blame Muslim influence on and rule over India for this, but placed the ebbing of India's creative spirit even earlier. The reasons for this were obscure. But what was clear was that by the nineteenth century or even earlier, Europe had far outstripped India in technical expertise, which was the outer sign of a great inner vitality.

> Behind this technical progress was the spirit of science and a bubbling life and spirit which displayed itself in many activities and in adventurous voyages of discovery. New techniques gave military strength to the countries of western Europe and it was easy for them to spread out and dominate the East. That is the story not only of India, but of almost the whole of Asia.[10]

He saw British imperialism in India in a broader economic context as well – that of the development of capitalism and Britain's search for and exploitation of the resources, labour and markets of India. By the early 1930s, after the great collapse of western financial systems and the world-wide impact of the subsequent depression, he began to voice the opinion that capitalism had had its day.

> Capitalism has been of the greatest service to the world and individual capitalists are but tiny wheels in the big machine. The question now is whether the capitalist system has not outlived its day and must now give place to a better and a saner ordering of human affairs, which is more in keeping with the progress of science and human knowledge.[11]

That comment was part of an extended musing published in October 1933, soon after Nehru's release from yet another period in jail, and was entitled *Whither India?* Increasingly he spoke and wrote of what had to be done now for his country. Part of the appeal of Gandhi was his vision of an India reborn and revitalised from the innermost psyche of her people, a vision Nehru shared as the way of stopping the cultural decay he discerned in his attempt to 'discover India'. Nehru perceived the dimensions of this enterprise, and the need for change on many fronts. First and foremost was the need to achieve political freedom. He wrote in 1933, 'I am quite sure that the only alternative to a continuation of our present struggle is some measure of cooperation with imperialism . . . Personally I am not prepared . . . for any such compromise, whatever happens. It is better for the cause, I am convinced, that we should carry on the fight and even be crushed . . . than that we should compromise with imperialism.'[12] He acted on this principle, placing himself in opposition to Gandhi and other Congress leaders at several crucial junctures, when many Congressmen were prepared to settle for concessions and compromise – in 1931, for example, when Gandhi negotiated a 'pact' with the viceroy by which civil disobedience could be honourably called off in anticipation of concessions and constitutional reform, or in 1937 when Congress decided to take up provincial office after its success in elections. In 1943 he lamented in prison Gandhi's lack of defiance towards the government, and even at that low ebb of morale opposed any sort of compromise with the British.

But for Nehru, as for Gandhi, political freedom was not enough. He noted in *Whither India?* that they had 'got into an extraordinary habit of thinking of freedom in terms of paper constitutions'. This was to miss the essential point that India's struggle for political freedom was linked to the struggle for radical social and economic change, for the ending of hunger and want, just as its mirror image, political imperialism, was inseparable from economic and social exploitation. India's goal therefore had to be the ending of internal exploitation, of class privileges and vested interest. An Indian government replacing British rule which maintained existing vested interests 'would not even be the shadow of freedom'. As he expounded,

> The real question before us ... is one of fundamental change of regime, politically, economically, socially. Only thus can we put India on the road to progress and stop the progressive deterioration of our country. .... Whither India? Surely to the great human goal of social and economic equality, to the ending of all exploitation of nation by nation and class by class, to national freedom within the framework of an international cooperative socialist world federation.[13]

Nehru was equally sure that religion played into the hands of vested interest, and in the Indian context showed this unsavoury face in the increasing prevalence of 'communalism' in Indian society and politics – that privileging of religious identity above other identities in the political arena, which in turn bred violence and threatened the very existence of an inclusive and national body politic. He criticised communalism as a contrivance of reaction; and argued that communal issues were bogus ones compared with the real issues before the country – freedom, poverty and unemployment. In his presidential speech to Congress in April 1936 he castigated communal leaders as political reactionaries, and communal issues as a diversion from the central issue of imperial rule. For him India's future must be that of a socialist and secular state, and the nation was to be defined in secular and inclusive terms. As he faced the imminent future of a free India in 1945 he told the press he felt communalism to be a medieval outlook, inconsistent with democracy or modern perceptions of politics and economics.[14]

But how was this vision of a transformed India to be attained? Nehru had before him a variety of answers to this question. The western European political philosophy in which he had been nurtured spoke of the power and legitimacy of democracy. Contemporary Marxist example emphasised the ruthless mode of violence masterminded by the state. Gandhi preached non-violence, even in the face of a Hitler, and argued that the ends never justified the means and that wrong means would lead inevitably to evil ends. Nehru wrestled openly in his published works with the issues of coercion and peaceful change. Throughout his life he remained a committed democrat, and was insistent that people and events could be changed by rational argument. But he recognised the enormity of the changes he envisaged for India and the likelihood that those with vested interests might well not listen to reason or to the arguments of democratic politics. Although he did not agree with Gandhi that ends and means were indistinguishable and insisted on the primacy of the goal, he nevertheless cared deeply about means. In situations of conflict, and particularly in the circumstances of India's nationalist struggle, he saw non-violent methods of pressure as the most moral and civilised, and that was central to his alliance with Gandhi. But he insisted that he did not accept non-violence as an absolute ideal and creed. He was prepared to accept that in the last resort some more coercive form of pressure might prove necessary. 'Compulsion will often be necessary, in addition to conversion, and the best we can do is to limit this compulsion and use it in such a manner that its evil is lessened.'[15] This was the voice of a mature politician who had learned to ask the hard questions in his apprenticeship to power and had before him goals to achieve, for which access to the power of the state was vital. The private and public agonising about India's goals, priorities and means were the other side of the man who portrayed himself as a glamorous demagogue who could endanger democracy.

. . .

THE WORLD OF GOVERNANCE AND POLITICS

Nehru's practical apprenticeship to the exercise of power took place in the context of imperial India, which offered to Indians opportunities for a political role but also severe constraints on the manner and scope of their political activity. Ironically it was as he strove to overthrow the imperial regime and became practised in the politics of opposition that he acquired much of the experience and skill which enabled him eventually to take up the reins of government when the British left India. The external context of this practical learning was the changing political world of the inter-war decades, when a range of forces were creating a context very different from the one in which, before the First World War, his father had gained professional and political influence. It was a turbulent and controversial world in which there were new opportunities for Indian leadership and power, yet still severe limitations on such influence imposed both by the British as they struggled to control India for imperial ends and by India's own socio-economic and political structures and organisations.[16]

The most striking formal change in the political system stemmed from British strategies to retain control over what they saw as crucial interests of the raj, and through it of the empire as a whole. The constitutional reforms of 1919 worked after a fashion throughout the 1920s, and attracted considerable Indian political participation. A core of Gandhians, however, refused ever to participate in them or in electoral politics; while those Congressmen and others who did choose to avail themselves of this type of institutional power were discontented with the regulations which hedged them around and with the paucity of financial resources made available through them. When it became clear that they were not a prelude to more genuine self-government, despite the 1917 declaration of the British goal for India, Congress embarked on another movement of civil disobedience under Gandhi's leadership. This forced the British to see that in any further attempt to resolve the constitutional future of India Congress was a significant force to be reckoned with, and that no reforms would be solidly based unless they attracted some measure of Congress support. The result of prolonged negotiation and parliamentary discussion was the 1935 Government of India Act, which made provincial governments autonomous and gave Indians elected to reformed provincial legislatures control over all branches of government, subject to the governor's emergency powers. The act envisaged a fundamental reform of the central government in Delhi, once a federation had been formed of British India and the Indian princely states. The central part of the plan never came into operation as the princes were still engaged in discussions on the outbreak of the Second World War. But the provincial part of the package became reality after elections in 1936 in which over 30 million Indians were now entitled to vote. For the first time elected Indian politicians came to control their own affairs at that highly significant level in the political structure.

The British had thus revised their understanding of who was entitled to 'speak for' the Indian population, and had recognised the legitimacy of elected politicians even when these were so often the educated urban men they had once despised as unrepresentative of some imagined 'real India'. They had withdrawn from their earlier style of paternal control based on the district officer and his alliance with local notables, and had opened up new pathways to power for politicians who could win votes and form alliances in the country and in the legislatures. Ironically the very means they had chosen to buttress their raj had in turn helped to generate wider political aspiration and broader-based politics, which in turn could only be channelled and to an extent controlled by further constitutional concession. It had become evident that new forms of consultation and devolution of power were the only way forward for the representatives of a raj who still saw British control over India in some form as essential to Britain and to India, and as likely to last for several generations. But they were prepared to use their coercive powers when Indians failed to cooperate with their strategies, as thousands found at the price of liberty and of police violence when they participated in civil disobedience movements in 1920–22, 1930–34 and particularly during the Second World War.

British initiatives were not the only source of change in the world of India's governance and politics. This was also a time of considerable socio-economic change and upheaval which again offered opportunities to Indians who aspired to leadership to claim to speak for and organise disadvantaged groups and those who felt they had no voice in the emerging political structures and institutions. The impact of war and of worldwide economic depression on prices and credit, for example, created severe dislocation in the countryside, setting patron against client and landlord against tenant, and generating rural discontent which the British could not control by their old methods of paternalism. Those rural people with a stake in land and the new resource of a vote increasingly looked to their local member of the provincial legislature to voice their problems and protect their interests. The landless sometimes found educated leaders who would voice their interests, but more often generated leadership from among their own ranks and reacted to pressure in turbulent ways which frightened both imperial rulers and educated politicians. In towns and cities population growth became even more evident than in the countryside as industrial production increased and as people migrated to urban environments in search of work. Between the wars the urban population grew significantly – from around 30 millions to nearly 50 millions. Pressure on employment, housing and basic civic amenities became urgent problems, and officials in common with the more comfortable Indian middle classes became concerned at the prospect of an emergent urban underclass, undisciplined in manners and morals. They responded with a variety of devices for control and reform, ranging from town planning to primary education to the organisation and recognition of moderate trade unions. From the government's point of view, most disquieting was the apparent alignment of parts of Indian labour with international communism: on this it stamped with the full ferocity of the law.

In contrast with western Europe the urban population was still small and the vast majority (just under 90 per cent) of Indians still lived in the countryside. But in both urban and rural settings these decades were marked by unrest and at times violence born of religious revivalism and the activation of religious identities in politics. Movements of renewal among most of India's religious groups were an element in this, as were movements for social self-improvement among the lowest castes in Hindu society. But minority groups, particularly Muslims, also began to fear a future in which sheer numbers of voters were beginning to count, despite the imperial provision for special minority representation in the legislatures. Politicians were not lacking who found it useful to trade on religious identity and minority fear. One result in these years was the growth of specifically communal political groups, amongst minorities and within the Hindu majority. Another was an upsurge in riot and murder in the name of community and religion.

In response to these new issues and opportunities modern style political organisation in Indian politics became more significant as a resource and platform for individuals who aspired to public position and influence. It was also a strategy for con-

trolling those forces which disturbed and threatened the educated, who had increasingly learned to deal with their imperial
rulers in the language and style which the British had shown
that they accepted as legitimate and increasingly encouraged
for their own purposes. Although the British lamented in pat-
ronising style the lack of 'proper' political parties in India to
use the constitutional structures as parties used the structures
of local and national government in Britain, Indians were ex-
perimenting with a range of political organisations and devices
to enable them to exploit the opportunities of inter-war politics. Foremost among them, and most significant for Nehru's
career, was the Indian National Congress. Many of its provincial leaders recognised its potential importance as an electoral
mechanism and as a mode of making coherent blocs of allies
in provincial legislatures; while Gandhi and his closest allies
saw that only a disciplined body of workers could make non-
violent strategies work as practical politics. In these two decades Congress struggled against the pulls of factionalism and
regional diversity to turn itself into a proper political organisation with a clear goal and programme, with secure finances, and
with control over membership which would make it properly
representative of the whole of British India. It was an uphill
struggle, and Gandhi's attempted reforms of 1921 appeared to
have borne little fruit when he and Jawaharlal came at the end
of the decade to review the party organisation in anticipation
of a renewed civil disobedience movement. Membership had
slumped, and in many areas provincial organisation let alone
lower-level party structures did not exist. Further, its finances
were in a parlous state, unable to sustain full-time party work or
a nation-wide campaign. It was not until the later 1930s, when
the 1935 reforms had raised the stakes of electoral success, that
the Congress became a better-organised and successful party,
as aspiring and existing political activists flocked into its ranks
and submitted, however reluctantly, to party discipline in recognition of what it could do for them in the new political
environment. The growing significance of political organisation
and of Congress in particular in turn opened new pathways for
political careers and new bases for political activity for Jawaharlal's
generation of activists.

However, it was not until after independence that Congress
became primarily a machine for winning elections and sustaining a party of government. At this stage it was still also a broad

movement of nationalist opposition, and many of its problems stemmed from this dual function. From 1920 to 1945 it had to be prepared to change from one *modus operandi* to the other, using the official institutions of consultation and decision-making when these seemed profitable, but abandoning them for confrontation when constitutional activity appeared to be leading to a dead end. Decisions to switch from one mode to another were always hotly and even bitterly debated, as Congressmen had to consider their clients and followers and the British themselves, and calculate the balance of advantage in the short and longer term between cooperation with and opposition to the imperial regime. It was the presence of Gandhi which enabled Congress for so long to perform this dual role and thus to build up a unique place for itself in the world of Indian politics, in the eyes of the rulers and of the Indian people. It had become the recognised voice and vehicle for nationalist politics at least for Hindus, and in 1937, after the elections, it formed the government in seven of the eleven provinces of British India. Not only was it now nation-wide in geographical spread; it drew its support from a broader and deeper social span than before, gathering among its supporters a range of substantial rural men as well as those with business interests, in contrast to the educated and professional elite who had gathered in Christmas sessions with Motilal Nehru and his kind before the First World War. Its most significant failure now lay in its inability to persuade Muslim voters to support it. They had tended to vote, not for the Muslim League, but for a series of provincial parties and local groups who offered to safeguard Muslim minority interests through the new electoral mechanisms and legislatures.

Jawaharlal's personal political trajectory was inextricable from these changes, and indeed enabled by them. He was by temperament and philosophy a doer, an activist and campaigner, and most assured and fulfilled in such roles. He was at his happiest when participating in Gandhi's great civil disobedience movements, being in the forefront of each and then suffering imprisonment. Prison was a harsh school, even though leading Congressmen were normally dealt with under emergency ordinances rather than the ordinary criminal law. Nehru, Gandhi and their colleagues were given reasonable facilities, apart from the normal jail population, and were allowed some books, letters and family visitors; and in one jail term Nehru even had a small plot of garden to cultivate. But months and years of confinement were deeply frustrating to those whose political life-blood was action. Nehru was like Gandhi in his reaction to jail. Both were physically self-disciplined and able to cope with the stark simplicity of prison life. Both had the inner intellectual and spiritual resources to deal with the experience without becoming demoralised or embittered, even though Nehru at least suffered phases of near despair, as his prison diaries make poignantly clear. Both put jail to positive use and Nehru used the enforced leisure for extensive reading and also for his own writing, producing two major works in prison.

In the inter-war years Nehru participated and took up a leadership role in a wide range of protests linked to the cause of nationalism. These included the peasant movements in his own United Provinces in 1921 and 1931 against local landlords, and the dramatic expressions of hostility to the parliamentary commission of 1928 under Sir John Simon which toured India to investigate the working of the constitution but was opposed by a wide range of Indians because it included no Indian representatives. Nehru was also widely in demand as a speaker at a range of radical and sectional group gatherings. He never ran for election to the legislatures when Congress as a body permitted or encouraged its members to cooperate with the reformed institutions of government. Indeed, although he was deeply concerned that Indians should gain political power, he was suspicious of taking responsibility within government at this stage, without real power. In April 1936 in the Congress subjects committee he argued that Congress should postpone the issue of whether they would take office if they were successful in the elections, for office acceptance would encourage 'reformism'. In his presidential speech to Congress the following day he argued, 'It is always dangerous to assume responsibility without power, even in democratic countries; it will be far worse with this undemocratic constitution, hedged with safeguards and reserved powers and mortgaged funds, where we have to follow the rules and regulations of our opponents' making.'[17] His forebodings were fulfilled and two years later he was expressing great distress to Gandhi about Congressmen's lapse, as he saw it, into 'Tammany Hall' politics. Congressmen seemed to be adapting to the old order and to be at risk of losing their popular repute. 'We are sinking to the level of ordinary politicians who have no principles to stand by and whose work is governed by a day to day opportunism.'[18] His one experience of formal government at this stage was a spell in local administration as chairman of the Allahabad Municipal Board (1923–25), which he took very seriously and began (to his surprise) to find both interesting and enjoyable, though he had feared it might be a deflection from the struggle for freedom.

Despite his unease at constitutional politics and their effects on Congressmen, Nehru recognised that his political base had to be in Congress. His one abortive attempt at political organisation on the fringe of Congress in 1929 was a lamentable failure, and thereafter, even when his radicalism put him at odds with many other Congressmen he insisted that he could not part company with Congress itself. As he wrote in 1933,

> I have long felt that the Congress is far the most effective radical organization in the country and it is easier to work great changes in the mass mentality through it rather than through any other means. So long as I feel that, I shall gladly and most willingly work with this great organization, which has done so much for the country, even though it may not go far enough from my point of view.

Or again, slightly later, in his *Autobiography*, he wrote of the 'wonderful awakening of the masses' by Congress under Gandhi's leadership, despite its 'vague *bourgeois* ideology', insisting that desertion of Congress 'seemed to me thus to cut oneself adrift from the vital urge of the nation, to blunt the most powerful weapon we had, and perhaps to waste energy in ineffective adventurism'.[19] He was deeply involved in Congress organisation and policy-making, at times holding office as general secretary or as president, as in 1929–30 and for two years from 1936. The fact that there was a new leader in the making was plain. In 1920–22 Jawaharlal had been little known in India at large, while in local political and professional circles in the United Provinces he was known as Motilal's anglicised son. By the later 1930s he was a tireless and popular election campaigner for Congress. In 1943 the southern Indian politician Rajagopalachariar told the viceroy's private secretary bluntly of Jawaharlal's future importance, even though he was then in jail.

> Of the [Congress] Working Committee he said . . . that the only person who mattered at all was Jawaharlal Nehru. There was no hope whatever of getting him into position as a future leader except with Gandhi's help and guidance; and only Gandhi could

keep his excessive vanity in order. Such work as was to be done in the future must be done with Nehru.[20]

Nehru's political base in Congress was due to his relationship with Gandhi. As a party which was also at times a popular movement it represented many regional groupings and accommodated many viewpoints. It was, however, fundamentally conservative in its socio-economic base and in its vision of India's future, despite its radical technique of non-violence and Gandhi's idiosyncratic rhetoric of social and moral transformation. Although Gandhi declined to hold formal office in Congress as the years passed, he remained a towering influence behind it and in the country at large, and there emerged a group, often referred to as 'the old guard', who managed Congress with a firm regard for his advice. Nehru's relationship with this group was uneasy, but he had no other base within the party and his standing and influence depended largely on his relationship with Gandhi. To the ageing Mahatma Gandhi, Nehru was a deep emotional solace, but also a vital asset in his hopes for a new India. He saw Jawaharlal as intelligent and talented, fundamentally honest, and filled with passion and vision for the transformation of India. He was not only well travelled and well connected internationally; he represented a rising generation of younger men who were coming to maturity between the wars, had more radical hopes and had to be welded into the nationalist movement. To Jawaharlal, Gandhi was an inspiring and much-loved mentor, despite his peculiarities and apparent faults. He was also the key to Congress's ability to appeal to a mass audience, and the initiator of strategies which, unlike the politics of compromise and 'reformism', seemed likely to bring about India's freedom, which was in turn essential for the changes Nehru felt were crucial for his country.

It was Gandhi who manoeuvred the election of Nehru to the Congress presidency in 1929. He had earlier agreed with Motilal that the time had come to let a representative of the younger end of Congress take up the reins of power, and that no one was better fitted for the 'crown' than Jawaharlal. Jawaharlal insisted that he represented no one but himself and that he did not wish to be shackled by office.[21] As he later remembered, 'I have seldom felt quite so annoyed and humiliated as I did at that election. It was not that I was not sensible of the honour. . . . But I did not come to it by the main entrance or even a side entrance; I appeared suddenly by a trap-door and bewildered the audience into acceptance.'[22] Gandhi's wishes similarly precipitated Jawaharlal into the presidency in 1936, for the crucial period of the election under the new constitution and its aftermath. It was Gandhi who managed the tensions among Congress leaders, ensuring that the radical tendencies of the younger Nehru did not endanger Congress unity, yet also working to keep Nehru on board the Congress ship and retain his talents for the Congress enterprise. This was clear in 1929 and 1931 when Nehru was deeply out of sympathy with the possibility of compromise with the government instead of civil disobedience. Or again, in April 1936 when Nehru as Congress president alienated the Congress Working Committee with plans for action on various socio-economic issues, matters reached breaking-point and Nehru offered his resignation in view of the ideological conflict. Gandhi was called in to advise, and, according to the somewhat laconic minute of the meeting 'his advice was that the Committee should pull together. This advice was accepted and the Committee proceeded with its business.'[23] In July the same year Nehru still felt embattled and frustrated in his relationship with the Working Committee; again it was Gandhi who urged him not to precipitate a crisis but to be more tolerant and to keep a sense of humour.[24] The younger man was not easy to work with. For all his charm he did not suffer gladly those whom he perceived as fools or reactionaries, and he was notable for his flashes of blazing anger and rash behaviour. It was the Mahatma who could control him, and who had no hesitation in rebuking him when he felt he had overstepped the mark.

Although Gandhi's protective patronage and good management secured Nehru's place at the heart of Congress, it did not give him access to power. Rather, it gave him a significant position and then severely constrained what he could do with it. He was unable to change the conservative stance of most Congressmen, and of the core of those who gathered round Gandhi, even on issues he considered vital. This was a reality he recognised and resented, but swallowed for the sake of unity. Others were delighted at this restraint of an uncomfortable radical. One of Gandhi's most prominent business supporters, G.D. Birla, commented to a colleague with obvious satisfaction that despite Nehru's radical and forthright presidential speech in Congress in April 1936 he for one was 'perfectly satisfied with what has taken place. Mahatmaji kept his promise and without his uttering a word, he saw that *no new commitments were made.* Jawaharlalji's speech in a way was thrown into the waste paper basket because all the resolutions that were passed were against the spirit of his speech.' He noted that Nehru recognised his own limitations and behaved perfectly properly, not attempting to abuse his position in the face of opposition. He also commented that the forthcoming elections would be controlled by Vallabhbhai Patel, Gandhi's henchman from Gujarat, and that there was every likelihood of Congressmen ultimately accepting provincial office – despite, of course, the impassioned opposition to this stance of Nehru.[25]

Although Nehru was unable to alter the composition or complexion of Congress, within its ambit he acquired a range of political skills and experience which were an essential preparation for the taking and use of power when the raj ended. Ironically for a future prime minister, Nehru during these years gained little actual experience of legislative work or administration by comparison with some of his Congress colleagues. Many of those Congressmen whose power bases were specifically local and provincial did participate in the reformed legislatures and in provincial government after 1936, and went on to become chief ministers in their former provinces. Nehru's only taste of this aspect of governance was his brief spell in the Allahabad municipality, which led him to consider town finance and a wide range of local issues, from the quality of local employees, municipal improvements, roads, water supply, infant mortality and education to the treatment of prostitutes. However, by the 1930s it was clear that he was setting his sights on big issues of future government. He was Congress's most wide-ranging thinker, who saw India's own problems in the context of world events and trends, and Gandhi relied on him to speak for Congress when foreign issues demanded a response. As early as 1935 he wrote to the younger man, 'But I have great faith in you in these matters. You have undoubtedly a much greater grasp of the situation than any one of us has, certainly than I can ever hope to have.'[26] The price of this world vision was deep anguish when Nehru found himself caught during the early years of the Second World War between his loathing of fascism and his desire to gain his country's freedom.

Nearer home, in the late 1930s, he turned his attention to planning for India's future, a task to which he was stimulated by the example of planning in Soviet Russia. In his own mind internal economic strength was linked with external standing, for without economic self-sufficiency India would remain within the grasp of wider economic imperialism. He took up the chair of a new National Planning Committee which brought together Congressmen in government, representatives from several major princely states, and a range of professionals with skills to offer their country – businessmen, economists, industrialists and the like. Gandhi could see no point in all this. But to his daughter Nehru explained how this very new type of work enthused and stimulated him. He discovered in middle age that he had not lost the knack of learning.[27] As a diverse group the committee found it difficult to agree on any basic social policy or prin- ciples except that of ensuring an adequate standard of living for India's masses. This alone took them into plans for improved nutrition, housing, clothing, the need for increases in agricul- tural and industrial production, and an attack on illiteracy and unemployment. It was clear that such a broad strategy would need considerable state regulation and control. To Nehru it seemed that such control would not lead to the concentration of power he saw in Russia, but rather to an enlargement of freedom if pursued within the context of a democratic state. Prison in 1940 put an end to this activity; but it had begun an educational and intellectual process to which he returned with enormous enthusiasm once power was within his grasp.

Between the wars Nehru's main experience lay in the realm of large-scale politics, and diverse aspects of its organisation and management. This was central to his creation as an all- India rather than a local figure, and as a potential leader of what was to be the world's largest democracy. Despite his un- easy position in Congress during these years he learned a great deal about the nature of the party, its social origins and its organisational structures from his position as a United Prov- inces Congressman in close touch with a powerful provincial leadership, and from his periods of office. Under Gandhi's guidance he had investigated the state of party organisation in the late 1920s and found it lacking. All this showed him how vital Congress was to Indian politics – as a mechanism to link together the different elements in the political system from the locality through the province to the all-India level. If it worked efficiently it could function as an agitational or electioneering organisation depending on the strategy of the moment; as a means to tie local interests into an all-India movement, and in reverse to explain all-India policies to local people; to recruit workers for the national cause and socialise new groups and generations into the ways of democratic politics; and ultimately to select election candidates and discipline those who succeeded once they took their seats in the provincial and central legislatures in order to sustain a democratic government.

However, beneath the organisational features of Congress lay even deeper issues of the type of 'nation' Congress really represented. Despite its expanding base after the First World War, Nehru was painfully aware of its socio-economic limitations, and the likeness it still bore to the elite institution of his father's day. Those at the very base of Indian society, in town and country, had no role in it, except as temporary allies (who were often feared by the leadership and carefully controlled) when local issues precipitated them into Gandhian campaigns of non-cooperation. Moreover, ordinary Muslims as well as the majority of articulate Muslim politicians were outside its ranks, in spite of its claim to speak for the whole of India.

In 1936–37 Nehru was involved in two campaigns to enlarge the Congress base in terms of class and community. The 'mass contacts' issue, however, fizzled out in the wake of Congress's remarkable electoral success, and it rested content on its laurels rather than address seriously the thorny issue of the representation of the truly poor and underprivileged in Congress. Similarly the later Muslim 'mass contacts' campaign petered out, never vigorously enough pursued at local level by provincial Congress leaderships, hindered by opposition within Congress from those who felt on class and communal grounds that it was undesirable and destructive of the Congress which represented their interests. The conservative and limited class-base of Congress, the presence within it of those with sympathies for and connections with Hindu communalism, and its failure to attract more than a small number of Muslim members came back to haunt Nehru with a vengeance, as the British prepared to dismantle their raj, and as he in turn struggled to construct an Indian nation. Despite the rhetoric of an inclusive nationalism, Congress still represented distinctive and comparatively privileged Indians, and was predominantly Hindu. The 'nation' remained a deeply disputed concept and identity. The disputes increased after independence, to Nehru's distress, further constraining his ability to pursue his vision of a transformed India.

Whatever the limitations of Congress at this stage, working within and for it did prepare Nehru for many of the tasks of a genuinely popular and national leader, for a role which had never before been required or indeed even possible in quite this way before the emergence of a more genuinely democratic political system. The shy man who had stumbled into the world of rural India in 1920–21 had found by the 1930s that he had immense skills as a mass campaigner and speaker. He campaigned tirelessly during the elections of 1936 and found that he revelled in the work and in the response he elicited from quite ordinary people he had never met personally. He reckoned he spent 130 days touring the country, covering 26,000 miles, by air, boat, rail, car, lorry, horse-drawn vehicles, on varieties of animals (horses, elephants, camels) as well as on foot. As Congress president, rather than as a candidate, he chose to speak in broad national terms about India and its future, and how the end of foreign rule would enable them to deal with the real problems of ordinary people – poverty, debt, hunger. For him personally this was a revelation of his own capacity for popular leadership, as well as an opportunity to spread his message of radical change and reconstruction. In so doing he built on his experience since 1921 of some of the real problems faced by rural people, gathered during his leadership of peasant movements associated with Gandhian noncooperation.

Despite his deep concern at the failure of Congress to attract Muslim voters, his personal failure of vision at this stage was to underestimate the power of what he dismissed as communalism. He insisted that Congress was for all Indians, and that its programme addressed the problems of all Indians, regardless of creed. As a result he became locked in public controversy with M.A. Jinnah, leader of the Muslim League, and denounced his insistence that Muslims formed a third distinctive group in India (over against government and Congress) as 'medieval and out of date'. He argued that communalism bore 'no relation whatever to modern conditions and modern problems, which are essentially economic and political. Religion is both a personal matter and a bond of faith, but to stress religion in matters political and economic is obscurantism and leads to the avoidance of real issues.'[28] He proceeded to denounce the League as representing only a few upper-middle-class Muslims and said that he himself knew more about the conditions of ordinary Muslims than did Jinnah and his League. In the privacy of his prison diary in 1942–43 he was even more bitter about Jinnah, as an unpleasant opportunist, as pompous, abusive and destructive, and as one who had lowered the tone of public life by spreading bitterness and hatred.[29] This failure to understand the real fear of minority groups as well as the manipulations of politicians underlying 'communalism' ultimately undermined Congress even more as a truly embracing body with a vision of an inclusive nation, and paved the way for the Muslim League's creation of a broader support base as well as a powerful bargaining position during the war, when the Congress leadership were in jail.

. . .

The inter-war years had done much to transform and educate Nehru. Once war ended and he was released he was poised to take advantage of new pathways to power opened by the British, who now conceded the impossibility of maintaining India within the empire. He was now a notable national figure, experienced in many of the skills of politics, nurtured and blessed by Gandhi who was himself by the war's end frail and old, and whose skills in managing mass campaigns of opposition were now less important to Congressmen who saw the imminence of real power. Despite the ambiguities of Nehru's position in Congress, Indians and British realised in the final months of the raj that he was vital as a spokesman for Indian aspirations and as a crucial representative of Congress. But he was aware that he was ageing. He confessed to becoming less achievement-orientated. In jail he had wondered about his future but indicated that the hope to lead his country and to embark on radical change was still there.

What of the big things and brave ventures which have filled my mind these many years? Shall I be capable of them when the time comes? Or will the time itself come for me to play an effective part in moulding events? To some extent, I suppose, I have made a difference to events in India in the past. But I hunger for constructive work on a vast scale. The time for that will surely come to India – but to me?[30]

. . .

NOTES AND REFERENCES

1. There is a useful collection of letters between Jawaharlal and Indira for this period: S. Gandhi (ed.), *Freedom's Daughter. Letters between Indira Gandhi and Jawaharlal Nehru 1922–39* (London: Hodder and Stoughton, 1989).
2. J. Nehru to Indira Nehru, 15 March 1938, *SWJN(2)*, vol. 3, pp. 460–1.
3. J. Nehru, *An Autobiography* (London: Bodley Head, 1936), p. 598; J. Nehru to Padmaja Naidu, 2 March 1938, *SWJN(1)*, vol. 13, p. 695.
4. Gandhi to M. Nehru, 2 September 1924, *CWMG*, vol. 25, p. 65.
5. Nehru, *Autobiography*, ch. LXI; Nehru's jail diaries, 1942–45, are in *SWJN(1)*, vol. 13. See Judith M. Brown, 'Nehru's Relations with Gandhi', in M. Israel (ed.), *Nehru and the Twentieth Century* (Toronto: University of Toronto Press, 1991).
6. J. Nehru, *The Discovery of India* ([1946] rev. edn Bombay: Asia Publishing House, 1947), p. 491.
7. J. Nehru to Gandhi, 25 July 1933, *SWJN(1)*, vol. 5, p. 491.
8. 'Rashtrapati', *The Modern Review*, November 1937, *SWJN(1)*, vol. 8, pp. 520–3; J. Nehru to Padmaja Naidu, 20 October 1937, ibid., pp. 523–5.
9. T.B. Sapru to M.R. Jayakar, 22 March 1934, National Archives of India, Jayakar Papers, Correspondence File No. 408.
10. Nehru, *Discovery of India*, p. 41; see also B. Parekh, 'Jawaharlal Nehru and the Crisis of Modernisation', in U. Baxi and B. Parekh (eds), *Crisis and Change in Contemporary India* (New Delhi, Newbury Park (Calif.) and London: Sage, 1995).
11. 1933 *Whither India?*, *SWJN(1)*, vol. 6, p. 8.
12. 27 November 1933, ibid., p. 28.
13. 1933 *Whither India?*, ibid., pp. 1–16.
14. Presidential speech, 12 April 1936, *SWJN(1)*, vol. 7, p. 190; press interview, 14 July 1945, *SWJN(1)*, vol. 14, p. 41.
15. Nehru, *Autobiography*, pp. 73, 552. Chapter LXIII, which concludes thus, is an extended debate on 'conversion or compulsion'.
16. Details of Indian political developments between the wars can be found in Judith M. Brown, *Modern India. The Origins of an Asian Democracy*, 2nd edn (Oxford: Oxford University Press, 1994); B.R. Tomlinson, *The Indian National Congress and the Raj 1929–1942* (Basingstoke: Macmillan, 1976); R.J. Moore, *The Crisis of Indian Unity 1917–1940* (Oxford: Clarendon Press, 1974).
17. Speech at Subjects Committee, 11 April 1936, presidential speech, 12 April 1936, *SWJN(1)*, vol. 7, pp. 168, 186.
18. J. Nehru to Gandhi, 28 April 1938, ibid., p. 388.

19. 27 November 1933, *SWJN(1)*, vol. 6, p. 30; Nehru, *Autobiography*, p. 365.
20. Linlithgow to L. Amery, 24 February 1943, *India. The Transfer of Power 1942–47* (London: HMSO, 1971), vol. III, p. 723. Henceforth *TP*.
21. M. Nehru to Gandhi, 11 July 1928, NMML, Motilal Nehru Papers. File No. G–1; Gandhi to M. Nehru, 15 July 1928, *CWMG*, vol. 37, p. 64; J. Nehru to Gandhi, 13 July 1929, *SWJN(1)*, vol. 7, p. 156.
22. Nehru, *Autobiography*, p. 194.
23. Handwritten minute of CWC proceedings at Wardha, April 1936, NMML, AICC Papers, File No. G–31 (1936).
24. J. Nehru to Gandhi, 5 July 1936, Gandhi to J. Nehru, 8 and 15 July 1936, NMML, J. Nehru Papers.
25. G.D. Birla to P. Thakurdas, 20 April 1936, NMML, P. Thakurdas Papers, File No. 177.
26. Gandhi to J. Nehru, 17 October 1935, NMML, J. Nehru Papers.
27. J. Nehru to I. Nehru, 22 December 1938, *SWJN(2)*, vol. 3, p. 473; Nehru, *Discovery of India*, pp. 400–9.
28. Press statement, 10 January 1937, *SWJN(1)*, vol. 8, p. 120.
29. 31 May, 21 September 1943, *SWJN(1)*, vol. 13, pp. 154–5, 244.
30. 13 November 1942, ibid., p. 28.

Chapter 3

THE TRANSFER OF POWER: 'TRYST WITH DESTINY'

Locked in an imperial prison, Nehru had wondered during the war whether the time would ever come for him to embark on the radical reconstruction of India he had so long envisaged. Within five years, on 14 August 1947, he stood in India's parliament, the Lok Sabha, and made his famous speech marking the nation's independence, when he spoke of the arrival of the moment when they could keep their 'tryst with destiny'. Deeply moved by this rare historical moment, the ending of an era, he pledged himself to the service of India and to humanity.[1] The next day he became free India's first prime minister.

This chapter addresses two key aspects of the 'transfer of power', as British decolonisation in India came to be known. First, there was the handing over of state power from the colonial rulers to their nationalist successors, and the making of a nation state with new structures of authority, new policies and new connections between it and the governed, the 'nation' whom it claimed to represent. Nehru's personal life was intermeshed with this process, and his own pathway to power, in high government office, depended on it. So, secondly, there is the issue of the new leadership, and how opponents of the raj transformed themselves into administrators and decision-makers, taking on unprecedented responsibilities while they were subjected to pressures and constraints very different from those they had experienced as nationalist politicians. Nehru had longed for power, for himself and for his country, though he denied that he was a career politician. He told a student audience in Calcutta in 1945,

I may confess what has been my one moving urge in politics. I am not a politician as you perhaps know. Politics irritates me . . . But the Indian politics of today at any rate . . . has still an idealistic element which appeals to me. Therefore I have entered politics in spite of the fact that I am not a politician in the professional or the literal sense of the word. Politics in India, fundamentally considered, is not getting elected to the council. It is a question . . . of the freedom of India, and . . . of ending poverty by rapid economic advancement. It is a politics of revolutionary changes.[2]

Between 1945 and 1950 Nehru faced reality. There were no precedents to guide him and his colleagues, as India was the first Asian or African part of the British empire to attain freedom, and they had need of remarkable resources to deal with the demands on them within India and in a fast-changing external world.

. . .

THE CONSTITUTIONAL TRANSFER OF POWER

Nehru had been jailed in August 1942 for his implication in the Congress resolution to embark on a campaign to force the British to 'quit India' during the war. Earlier that year the British had, in fact, conceded that *after the war* they would be prepared to grant political freedom, in the course of the abortive mission of Sir Stafford Cripps to secure Indian political cooperation in the war-time government of the country. So, when Nehru was released from jail in 1945 he found that his political role as opponent of an obdurate imperial ruler was gone. By this time the British were anxious to leave India, and to transfer power to Indian leaders, but with honour and safeguards for British interests, and if possible to leave behind a peaceful and united country. Gandhi's campaigns of noncooperation had never made British rule impossible, but by 1946 it was clear to the viceroy, Lord Wavell, that the raj could not endure, and must be brought to a dignified end as rapidly as possible to prevent the descent of the subcontinent into chaotic ungovernability. He urged the cabinet in London to recognise the danger of the situation and accept his 'breakdown plan'. To his journal he confessed on the last night of the year that 'the administration has declined, and the machine in the Centre is hardly working at all now . . . while the British are still legally and morally responsible for what happens in India, we have lost nearly all power to control events; we are simply running on the momentum of our previous prestige'.[3]

The reasons for this erosion of imperial power and commitment to rule India were complex. Between the wars British economic interests in India itself had declined significantly, as had the significance of India for Britain's world-wide economic relations. The subcontinent was less important for expatriate careers as a result of the progressive Indianisation of the services. Further, Britain was less able to use the Indian army throughout the empire at India's expense, once Indian politicians had come to influence Delhi's financial policy from the 1920s. With the constitutional reforms of 1919 and 1935 India had become increasingly difficult and 'political' to rule, while the raj's older allies, including the princes and substantial landholders, were themselves losing authority as a result of economic and political change and were less able to sustain their imperial masters. By 1946 even the capacity of the paid services to sustain the raj was in doubt, most obviously in the case of the police, but even of the ICS, which was now exhausted and undermanned as a result of the war, and whose Indian members (over half the total) naturally shared much of the national aspiration of India's political leaders whose background they shared. (Jawaharlal himself could so easily have been a senior ICS officer by now, had his work at Cambridge been more distinguished!) Britain itself was suffering from the aftermath of war and had neither the money nor the manpower necessary to re-establish a viable raj. Even if there had been a will to do so, the pressure of her American allies would have been a powerful argument to the contrary.

The problem for the Congress leadership was no longer the raj, but the nature of Muslim politics in India. Muslims' self-perceptions and political demands at this stage are one of the most controversial aspects of the history (and historiography) of the subcontinent. They were a diverse community with distinctive regional interests stemming from local factors such as their local numerical strength and socio-economic position, and until the late 1930s this was reflected in the failure of Jinnah and the Muslim League to speak for them or command their loyalty. Although many Muslims felt they were a distinct community which needed a specially guaranteed status in any devolution of power from imperial to Indian hands, there was little notion of Muslims forming a separate 'nation' in the modern sense of the word. Even when the Muslim League in 1940 demanded autonomous and sovereign zones in north-western and eastern India, where Muslims were a majority, in any plan for independence from British rule, the details were vague, and nowhere was the word 'Pakistan' used, though it came into common parlance to denote the Muslim demand.

However, by the time Congress leaders emerged from jail they found themselves confronting a League which had a very different standing among Indian Muslims, and a formidable leader who could not be dismissed as Nehru had done before the war. The war had given the League the opportunity to estab-lish itself in provincial government, and to garner growing popular support as well as the adherence of substantial local Muslim leaders of different kinds. In addition, Cripps's nego-tiations of 1942 had made it plain that the British would not permit any section of India's peoples to be coerced into joining a single successor state. Once it was clear from 1945 that the British were indeed going, Jinnah was able to bargain hard with his new-found strength and status as a 'Muslim spokesman'.[4] Meanwhile beneath the reasonably polite world of political negotiation popular attitudes were hardening, among Muslims, Hindus and Sikhs, all of whom began to look to the future with degrees of fear depending on how they saw their position once the British left. 'Communal' violence between the wars had been sporadic and small-scale, but now it became a terrifying and widespread reality in some areas where the balance of population was sensitive. One of the worst-affected areas was Calcutta and Bengal in late 1946 when possibly over 10,000 people were butchered, Hindus and Muslims, and many thou-sands more were injured and made homeless. This was the time when the governor said that parts of Calcutta were as bad as anything he had seen on the Somme; while Gandhi went on a personal pilgrimage through the most violent country areas to quieten fears and tension. The all-India politicians, whether Muslim or Hindu, could not control these local outbreaks, and they increased the bitterness of the atmosphere in which polit-ical solutions were negotiated.

In this highly charged and much changed situation Nehru became a significant element in a composite Congress leader-ship which contained many of the 'old guard'. Although Gandhi was still an important figure, he increasingly withdrew from an active and central role in Congress decision-making. His skills as the architect of popular movements of non-cooperation were not needed at this juncture by his colleagues. He, himself, was becoming more aware of and much saddened by the gulf in sympathy and priority opening up between him and his associates, who now had their eyes set on state power. He felt he was being true to his personal vision and vocation by trying to stop violence, and by working for his *ashram* community and through his long-standing constructive programme. Congress now needed men who could argue and negotiate, and Nehru was a lawyer, had superb command of English and was at home in the world of the departing rulers. He came to play an increasingly key role in 1945–47 in Congress's internal discussions, as a drafter of its key documents, and as its major spokesman, particularly from July 1946 when he became its president. Wavell was pleasantly surprised to find how much more practical he seemed compared to their previous encounter during the Cripps mission. The more he saw of him, the more he liked him. He thought him sincere and personally courageous, but lacking in 'balance' and tending towards the fanatical and doctrinaire, rather than being able to see differing viewpoints. With the last viceroy, Lord Mountbatten, Nehru's relations were far better. The Mountbattens deliberately threw open their doors to Indian politicians, consciously abandoning much of the stuffy protocol which had marked imperial rule and underlined the difference between ruler and subject. Nehru responded to their friendship and hospitality, forming a relationship with them both which lasted throughout their lives. Nehru developed a particularly intimate bond with Lady Mountbatten, which to an extent compensated for the absence of a normal family life and close emotional bonds which had marked his life and personality. Not only did this easy relationship with the viceroy enable negotiation: it also contributed to the remarkable spirit of cordiality between British and Indians which marked the end of the raj.

In jail Nehru had learned of the growing support for the idea of 'Pakistan' and for Jinnah. He admitted to his diary that he thought the whole idea of Pakistan was mad and destructive. Tellingly, he noted as early as the end of 1943, 'Instinctively I think that it is better to have Pakistan or almost anything if only to keep Jinnah away and not allow his muddled and arrogant head from interfering continually in India's progress.'[5]

On his release he reiterated publicly that he felt partition of the country was the wrong solution to its communal problem for it would only weaken India and make her a prey for stronger nations, and would neither solve the communal problem nor be in the interests of Muslims. However, he also agreed that no one could be forced to remain within India at independence and that Congress had accepted this as far back as 1942.[6] Even Gandhi, who had spent so much of his life working for harmony between all India's peoples and communities, had realised at least by 1940 that some sort of partition might become necessary.

However, all attempts at a negotiated compromise to achieve a unified subcontinent at the end of British rule came to nothing.[7] The conference called by Wavell at Simla in June 1945 to begin a new era of cooperation between Indian politicians and the government and lead to a more representative government to pave the way for a final solution collapsed. The stumbling block was Jinnah's insistence that only the Muslim League could nominate Muslim members. This stance was of course anathema to Congress leaders who had always claimed that Congress was representative of all Indians, and would have meant betraying their Muslim colleagues, including A.K. Azad, who was at that time Congress president. In 1946 the plans of a Cabinet Mission to India, offering a loose three-tiered federation which would have given Muslim areas a degree of autonomy, also petered out on the communal issue – with Congress insisting that no non-Muslim area could be forced into a group where Muslims would be in a majority, and the League fearing that Congress would use its majority in any constituent assembly to steamroller safeguards for Muslims. The other aspect of the plan, the formation of an interim government, stalled because Jinnah insisted that only the League could nominate Muslim members. However, Wavell went ahead with the reconstitution of his government without the League's agreement and on 2 September its members were sworn in, with Nehru as vice-president. A month later Jinnah nominated five more members.

The operations of central government began to grind to a halt as the two parts of the interim government found it impossible to work together, and this, with the deterioration of order throughout the country, forced the government in London to take drastic action. Attlee's government sacked Wavell in February 1947 and replaced him with Lord Mountbatten, indicating that Britain envisaged an end to the raj by June 1948. Mount-batten arrived in March and soon saw the seriousness of the situation and realised that it would be impossible to retrieve the Cabinet Mission plan. He worked rapidly towards independence accompanied by partition of the country, including partition of Punjab and Bengal, the provinces where numbers of Muslims and Hindus were evenly balanced, which Jinnah had hoped for in their entirety. Ultimately he produced on 3 June a plan which all parties accepted – though reluctantly. With enormous energy he drove his staff and the politicians in the heat of summer to achieve the necessary partition of government assets and personnel and the required voting for the disputed areas. On 14 August, at midnight, power was transferred to two successor states, both of which remained for the immediate future as Dominions within the Commonwealth.

It is hardly surprising that great controversy surrounds the complex bargaining of these final months of British rule, partly because British participants, Congressmen and the founders of the new Pakistan all wished to throw the blame for partition on another party, and because 'history' became part of the national self-imagining of both India and Pakistan. There are many question marks about the whole bitter process, and much criticism has been directed at Nehru from several angles. Some have argued that his outspoken comments about 'groups' within the Cabinet Mission plan wrecked the delicately balanced project. Others (including his former colleague, Azad, in a posthumously released portion of an autobiography) were to lament that he agreed to partition. However, it must be remembered that Congress had a composite leadership, and that even after Nehru became Congress president, it was the Working Committee, including the formidable figure of Vallabhbhai Patel, the Gujarati leader, and Rajendra Prasad from Bihar, which made the key decisions. By early in 1947 this core group was clearly accepting that some form of partition was inevitable, including that of Bengal and Punjab, and the Working Committee formally accepted the necessity in March 1947. However, it is likely that most of them had recognised even earlier not only that it would be impossible to compel Muslims to become Indian citizens if they did not wish to be, but that also the price of accommodating them was too high. Jinnah's own hopes for 'Pakistan' are disputed by historians, and there is considerable evidence that he was using the idea of Pakistan and his bargaining position to attempt to achieve an autonomous Muslim bloc in a loose federation on the subcontinent rather than a totally separate nation state. But even this was potentially too destructive of India as the Congress leadership envisaged it. All of them, even those without Nehru's socialist convictions, wanted a strong and centralised state which had the authority, legitimacy and power to reconstruct the country. To have accommodated Muslims in a loose federal structure would have destroyed the very architecture of the state with which they hoped to work change. So the 'tryst with destiny' was, as Nehru acknowledged, incomplete; but it still held out the prospect of the creation of a new India which had been his goal for over two decades.

· · ·

UNFINISHED BUSINESS: FORGING THE NATION

The partition of the subcontinent into two nation states did not resolve fundamental issues of national identity, either in India or in Pakistan. Many of these troubled Nehru's premiership long after independence, focusing on the subcontinent's religious, ethnic, linguistic and regional diversity, as also on the gross social inequalities which persisted. But in the immediate aftermath of independence and partition Nehru's government was all but overwhelmed by several urgent pieces of unfinished business which posed potentially destructive challenges to the new nation and its state.

The first of these was the upheaval and violence which engulfed parts of northern India in the summer of 1947. Communal violence had already marked Bengal and Punjab before partition. Now it spread and escalated out of control, as groups took their revenge for earlier killings, and particularly as they attacked the streams of refugees who tried to cross to the 'safe' side of the new international border. Trains were stopped and passengers butchered, with no quarter being given for age or gender. Women were abducted and subjected to forced sexual relations with men of feared and hated communities. A whole generation of Hindus from Pakistan and Muslims from India began new lives deeply traumatised by loss of property and close kin, and by experiences of shocking human brutality. No one knows the scale of this human disaster. Estimates of fatalities reach as high as one million: and probably over 14.5

million people became refugees, crossing the border in equal numbers each way. But India's Muslims had been scattered throughout the country, and those living far away from the border often had neither the capacity nor the wish to migrate. Nearly 30 millions remained, forming around 11 per cent of the Indian population, making independent India one of the world's countries with the largest number of Muslim citizens.

Nehru threw himself into the work to restore order and a measure of peace and security to people of all communities. Some of his Congress colleagues were less than sympathetic to the plight of Indian Muslims, and Nehru turned to Gandhi and Mountbatten for moral reassurance and help as he tried to abide by secular principles of national identity. An emergency committee of the cabinet was set up under Mountbatten to coordinate action to deal with the vast range of problems which stemmed from this massive displacement of people. Nehru worked tirelessly and in practical ways at issues of relief and rehabilitation, including medical care, housing and the long-running problem of abducted women, whose families refused to accept them back even when they could be found. He was distressed because so many elements in the administration did not share his commitment to resolving the miseries of ordinary people. He had been surprised and horrified at the extent of the violence, and poured out to Mountbatten his surprise, shame and horror at what his compatriots had done, yet his determination to rise to the challenge despite his sense of helplessness. To his old colleague in Congress, Rajendra Prasad, he wrote,

> I must confess to you that recent happenings in the Punjab and in Delhi have shaken me very greatly. That would be a small matter; but what is a much more serious matter is that they are shaking my faith in my own people. I could not conceive of the gross brutality and sadistic cruelty that people have indulged in . . . I am fairly thick-skinned, but I find this kind of thing more than I can bear.

He admitted that he had no wish to lead a people who seemed so demented.[8]

A significant part of his leadership role at this juncture was his determined discourse on the need for India to retain her identity as a secular and composite state which incorporated and nurtured citizens of many different communities. He paid particular attention to the plight of India's remaining Muslims and their fears and sensitivities, insisting that India must do everything to assure them that they and their culture were welcome in and integral to India. He was carrying on, in a new context and to a different audience of Indian Hindus, his insistence that Hindus and Muslims were not two 'nations', which had before independence been aimed primarily at Jinnah and the League.[9] Meantime he insisted in public and in private that he wished India and Pakistan to build a relationship of cooperation and good neighbourliness, despite his dislike of the ideology on which Pakistan had been built.[10]

Interwoven with the problems which partition itself generated was the problem of enduring strands of Hindu communalism in India itself. This perturbed Nehru greatly, and he saw it as a profound internal challenge to the integrity of the new India as he envisaged it. It was visible at different levels of public life, ranging from local-level hostility to Muslims to a more considered privileging of Hindu culture and history as the foundation of Indian identity. A small number of Hindus belonged to overtly 'communal' organisations such as the Hindu Mahasabha or the militant RSS, whose definition of Indian nationality rested on a sense of Hindu ethnic and cultural belonging. But there had always been considerable overlap in personnel and sympathy between such overt Hindu nationalists and some important as well as lower-level Congressmen who placed great value on Hindu tradition, in contrast to Nehru's secularism or Gandhi's individual piety combined with great religious tolerance. Among the Hindu nationalists was Vallabhbhai Patel, who made no secret of this difference between him and Nehru.[11] It was a contributory factor in the increasingly strained relations between the two men which nearly ended in total breakdown of cooperation early in 1948.

However, the most dramatic challenge of Hindu communalism to India's identity and stability came late in January 1948, when a single gunman, a young Hindu, shot the aged Mahatma at close range as he walked to address one of his regular prayer meetings in the grounds of Birla House, New Delhi. He died immediately. Nehru was broken-hearted, and his sense of loss was enduring. He had lost a personal, moral and political friend and guide, and would later remember how he still felt the urge in difficult situations to run to Gandhi and ask his advice. But he saw the potential implications of this death for the whole nation, and the possibility of devastating violence between India's component communities. With an enormous effort of personal control and composure he led the nation in dignified mourning, broadcasting within hours of the death to tell Indians of 'the light [which] has gone from our lives' and to urge them to root out the poison of communal hatred in the strong but non-violent way Gandhi had preached. He used every possible occasion to invoke Gandhi's image and exhort Indians to follow his example and teaching on non-violence. He preached the message that India was to be a nation where all communities were welcome, and whose strength and identity lay in its composite and secular nature.[12] Almost immediately all communal organisations were banned, both Hindu and Muslim, for several years. But even in spite of this tough measure and his own constant discourse, Nehru recognised that there was a groundswell of sympathy in the country with a more overtly Hindu definition of the Indian nation, and that some of his Congress and cabinet colleagues shared this view. Even when the immediate crisis of partition and Gandhi's assassination was passed he feared for the future. In 1949 he wrote, 'I have viewed with dismay and sorrow the narrow and communal outlook that has progressively grown in this country and which shows itself in a variety of ways. I shall cease to be Prime Minister the moment I realise that this outlook has come to stay and that I cannot do my duty as I conceive it.'[13]

A further piece of business, unfinished at independence, seemed likely to threaten India's identity, both secular and democratic – the remaining princely states, covering one-third of undivided India. The British had hoped that they could be welded into a federal India after productive constitutional discussions in 1930–31. But when war broke out in 1939 negotiations for princely cooperation were still in process, and the issue of their future was shelved. When war ended, it rapidly became clear that the British could do nothing for their former allies, given their own weakened state and the difficulties they were encountering in extracting themselves from their Indian empire. But in practice the problem was allowed to drift; and Mountbatten admitted on 11 July in a personal and top-secret report to the London government that he had 'not been able to grip this States problem before'.[14]

Nehru had long been hostile to those he called 'feudal chiefs', whom he saw as undemocratic and an aspect of the vested interests he wished to uproot in the drive for greater equality within the nation. In 1933 he had argued that 'the whole Indian state system must go root and branch'. He had also been prominent in Congress's rapprochement just before the war with democratic campaigns within the states. In 1945 he returned to the argument, insisting that the princely order, as it existed, would have to go, and that the princes could no longer rely on the British. However, his tone had mellowed somewhat and he spoke of a 'friendly' approach to the princes, inviting them 'to join hands in the great tasks ahead'.[15] In the last hectic months of the raj Nehru was not the main Congress member of government to deal with the states. That task fell to Vallabhbhai Patel with the home portfolio, who, with an able civil servant, V.P. Menon, and the full backing of the viceroy, 'persuaded' the princes that on the lapse of British paramountcy over the states they would have to throw in their lot with either India or Pakistan. The mechanism for the immediate transfer of power would be standstill agreements covering urgent issues of mutual concern – defence, foreign affairs and communications – and their positions would be finally resolved after independence. Almost all the rulers agreed to this device. Those who opted to remain in India found that they were eventually forced by popular pressure and the new Delhi government to become part of a fully democratic nation state. Although the princes 'lost' their states and ruling positions, they were given substantial personal concessions which sustained their own and their families' positions, and some remained important in the new nation's public life. India meanwhile had secured geographical and political unity within her new borders, and acquired land and people in such quantity as to outweigh the loss to Pakistan by partition.

Although Patel and Menon dealt with the details of this potentially disruptive episode in the forging of the new nation, the future of two major states caused ongoing problems with which Nehru as prime minister had to deal. They mattered greatly to him because they challenged his vision of a noncommunal and secular India, and in both instances he showed he was prepared to use armed force when he thought the integrity of the nation was at stake, however temperamentally averse he was to the use of violence. In southern India, Hyderabad, one of the largest princely states, had not acceded to the Indian Union at independence, and as the months afterwards dragged on it appeared to Delhi that the Nizam was buying arms abroad and expanding his army, and taking legal advice, with a view to claiming independence or to joining Pakistan. This unfinished piece of princely business became entangled with other issues crucial to the new nation, as the Nizam was a Muslim and the majority of his subjects were Hindus. Among the Hindu peasantry there developed a movement originating in rural grievances which soon became a challenge to the state itself and was met with serious state-sponsored repression. A year after independence Nehru was convinced that he could not delay much longer and in September 1948 the Indian army went in to restore order in the name of the nation state, and Hyderabad's pretensions to separate status were ended. As Nehru noted to his provincial premiers, the gains for India as a nation were significant. Now the whole of the country was under the control of one government, and no part of it could challenge the centre's authority. Further, it had helped to lessen the 'communal atmosphere' and this was highly significant. 'It relieves our minds of the continuing burden and allows us to concentrate on the work of building of the new India.'[16]

The problem of Kashmir, the other princely state whose status was in doubt, was not so easily resolved. Here a Hindu maharaja ruling a state bordering Pakistan had a majority of Muslim subjects. As he, too, wavered about accession, 'tribesmen' from Pakistan invaded, precipitating a hurried accession to the Indian Union which enabled India to send in regular troops to protect what it saw as now a part of its national territory. When Pakistani regular troops also joined the conflict it was clear that this was war. Mountbatten, as a personal friend of Nehru and in his role of governor-general of a Dominion within the Commonwealth, attempted, as he did in the case of Hyderabad, to dissuade the independent government from force and to urge negotiation. In the case of Kashmir he prevailed on Nehru to refer the issue of Pakistani 'aggression' to the fledgling United Nations. This was to prove disastrous, involving the world community with all its political cross-currents in a local dispute, giving both parties an international stage on which to parade their claims and counter-claims, and thereby prolonging a dispute which cost both countries dear in prestige and in scarce resources which had to be channelled into defence rather than badly needed development projects.

To Nehru, Kashmir was a much-loved ancestral homeland. But, even more important, the future of Kashmir as part of India was a vital part of his project of creating a non-communal nation in which Muslims would be secure. If Kashmiri Muslims became Pakistanis under duress then India's claims about her own secular national identity would be a hollow mockery. As he said to his old friend, Sir Stafford Cripps, in December 1948, Kashmir was vital for India's internal relations with its Muslim citizens. Its presence within the union was a challenge to the 'two-nation theory' that Hindus and Muslims were two distinct and separate nations; if it went then the position of India's remaining Muslims would become much more difficult and Hindus would become in turn more 'communal'.[17] For Nehru the identity of the Indian nation was at stake, not just the future of a particular piece of border territory. As the conflict wore on, despite a formal ceasefire at the start of 1949, it generated deep popular bitterness against Pakistan. This in turn served to make the issue a non-negotiable one for any Indian government, and deepened Hindu anxieties about the identity of their nation and suspicions about the loyalty of their Muslim fellow-citizens. Kashmir, the touchstone of Nehru's envisaged nation, thus became a source of national instability through his life and beyond.

.   .   .

MAKING THE STATE

Forging the nation was inextricable from the more mundane task of making the new state, as nationalists turned themselves into rulers and administrators. This less glamorous aspect of their work has often received comparatively little historical attention, but it was as vital as the task of anti-colonial struggle. The making of nations is an ongoing business, and central to it has always been the nature and functions of the state and the state's relationship to those within its authority. Nehru and his colleagues in the new Indian government proceeded with two main assumptions about the state they wished to construct. First, there had to be a different relationship between government and people compared with the raj's relationship with its subjects: the new regime had to gain a legitimacy based on a new relationship. Government, its institutions and its personnel, had to be representative of and responsive to its citizens. This meant not only that the structure should be made fully democratic, but that there should also be a different ethic and ethos informing government action – compared with the imperial one of paternalist care and control. Secondly, they assumed that the nation state had, in contrast to the imperial state, a vital function to perform in many aspects of the country's life, for which the raj had had neither the will nor the resources – from social reform to the provision of health and education, to the management of the economy. The directing role of a strong state was deemed essential if India was to develop socially and economically, and also to be strong in relation to the wider world.

Nehru appreciated the new role the state would have to play, and argued that it could not 'function in the old way with a few politicians at the top passing laws'. The willing dedication and cooperation of citizens was also vital in achieving real change, and here he echoed Gandhi's insistence on the importance of constructive work.[18] However, he and his colleagues effectively discounted Gandhi's views on the desirable shape of Indian society and on the nature of the state itself. The Mahatma had hoped for a social order based on India's villages, where change would come from the heart of individuals rather than through state planning and legislation, where the economy was geared to sufficiency rather than growth and greater consumption, and where the institutions of governance became progressively decentralised. As independence approached he was painfully aware of the gulf which was opening wider between his views and those even of his closest colleagues.[19] Their concern for a strong and centralised authority had been at the root of their acceptance of the need for partition. For Nehru state power was essential for his project of national regeneration, and in the first three years of independence much of his energy was devoted to setting in place structures which would enable the use of state power democratically to this end.

Partition of the land had necessitated the partition of government assets and personnel. Out of this division India emerged far stonger than Pakistan. In spite of the violence which engulfed parts of India she had a viable structure for administration and the maintenance of internal and external security, as she to a very great extent inherited the raj. The ICS stayed in place at the apex of an administrative structure which was also retained, stretching from the division down through the districts to the lowliest levels of tax collection. So did the Indian army and the Indian police service, the one retaining its proud all-India and apolitical traditions, besides the ceremonial associated with the imperial army, the other still plagued by low status, poor pay and ambiguous relationships with the locally powerful.

Nehru was deeply concerned in his early years in office about the minutiae of government functioning, knowing how the ethos and style of government officials was the interface between state and citizen and was the touchstone by which Indians would judge and accord legitimacy to the new regime. His papers for the late 1940s are full of his worry about the fact that there was not sufficient change from the time of the raj. He commented on the hordes of lowly messengers who still thronged the corridors of government buildings, wrote strongly about the need for confidentiality and honesty among government servants, and deplored the delays and slowness he observed in dealing with important issues. He also became increasingly worried about what he saw as their reliance on the coercive apparatus of government – deeply uncomfortable to one who had suffered and criticised the coercion exercised by the imperial raj. In 1948 he told his colleague, G.B. Pant, chief minister of UP, that he was concerned about what he saw as the deterioration of morals and ideals in public life, and also increasing reliance on government and on the coercive apparatus of government. He felt these trends were threatening to imprison them – just at the point when they should be making freedom a reality. His intrusive concerns over police use of arms caused tension between him and Patel, who as home minister argued forcefully that the machinery of administration could not function if there was a continual threat of inquisition hanging over them.[20] But Nehru insisted to Patel that he feared the representatives of free India were behaving like their predecessors.

I think there is a tendency for our officers to behave in a manner which does not fit in with a democratic structure. They tend to revert to the days of British rule, when they looked upon the public as some kind of enemy or opponent which had to be put down. This is a dangerous development, because it undermines the prestige of Government with the people, apart from making our Services disliked. In the ultimate analysis we can only carry on with a large measure of public approval. We cannot function as the British Government did, nor can our officers or police function in the old way.[21]

Although Nehru argued that reform of government machinery was one of the big questions facing India, in fact he did virtually nothing to change the administrative system and in effect relied on an imperial administrative structure to achieve the new goals of a free government. The most striking case in point was the ICS itself. Nehru, the nationalist, had shown great hostility to the ICS as elitist and anti-democratic. His criticisms had included Indian members of the service who were much like their British colleagues in social status and education and had been socialised by them in the conventions of the service. By 1946 his views were mellowing as he set his sights on a smooth transfer of power, and he advised against any campaign against officials except those who could be proved guilty of extreme misconduct or corruption. He was also clearly working to encourage competent Indian civil servants to realise that they had a significant role to play in the new India if they could adapt to the new situation.[22] It was Vallabhabhai Patel, skilled in the arts of organisation from his role in the pre-independence Congress party, and now home minister, who saw most clearly how India needed the remnants of the ICS and their successors in the IAS (Indian Administrative Service). He argued to Nehru in 1948 that the service must have constitutional recognition and protection, and that appointments to it must be made on merit without political interference. 'I need hardly emphasise that an efficient and disciplined and contented service, assured of its prospects as a result of diligent and honest work, is a sine qua non of sound administration under a democratic regime even more than under an authoritarian rule.'[23] Subsequently he argued successfully for such a constitutional guarantee in the Constituent Assembly which was debating the new constitution. Nehru was absent from the relevant debates and let Patel's plan come to fruition. Within a year he was acknowledging the importance of the service in the making of state and nation, in the context of a dire shortage of trained people and of persistent communalism.

So India retained and reconstituted its main administrative service on lines which bore a deep resemblance to the imperial service, with its elitist and generalist philosophy of gentlemanly service, and its recruitment from an educated, social elite. In retrospect it is clear that Nehru did not have sufficient dominance in government to overrule his powerful home minister, nor indeed the resources to make radical change in the structure and style of administration. This led to a profound ambiguity in his task of making a state which would contribute to the regeneration of the nation. Through the rest of his premiership he was to face the recurring question whether instruments fashioned by the raj, whose primary concerns were stability and control, could perform the tasks required by an independent government with a programme of wide-ranging change; and whether the successors of the ICS (and lower levels of the bureaucracy and the police, whose nature and role changed equally little) could forge new relationships with those who were now citizens rather than subjects.

Perhaps the biggest task in the making of the state, though it was less urgent than stabilising the administrative structure, was the fashioning of the new constitution, a process which took until late 1949. The body charged with this was the Constituent Assembly, elected in mid-1946 by the members of the provincial legislatures under the terms of the plan proposed by the ill-fated Cabinet Mission. It functioned after independence as India's parliament and as the constitution-making body.[24] Much of the constitutional work was done by a range of committees, which were effectively dominated by about twenty influential members of the assembly, including Nehru and Patel as prime minister and deputy respectively, Rajendra Prasad as assembly president, and A.K. Azad, who was like the others on the Congress Working Committee and also a minister. Nehru chaired two of the eight major committees, but he tended to leave much of the basic work to others. His major role was in drafting and moving in the assembly in December 1946 the so-called Objectives Resolution, which laid down the basic principles which should guide the formulation of the new constitution. He saw this as no ordinary resolution, but as more like a pledge to the millions of their fellow Indians: he urged members to rise above party and think of the nation and with wisdom and broad-mindedness produce something worthy of India and also capable of enhancing India's repute and role in the wider world as a new independent nation of great size and with significant resources. The objectives laid out were straightforward and clear. India was to be a sovereign republic, whose component parts would be united in a federal structure. All power was derived from the people, who would all be guaranteed 'justice, social, economic and political, equality of status, of opportunity, and before the law; freedom of thought, expression, belief, faith, worship, vocation, association and action, subject to law and public morality', while special safeguards would be provided for minorities and backward groups. India would maintain its national integrity but would conduct its foreign relations according to international law and in pursuit of world peace and welfare.[25] The new constitution was adopted by the assembly on 26 November 1949. So the world's largest democracy came into being, grounded in a document which represented many of the hopes of the nationalist leaders for freedom and unity and for a nation built on articulated ideals, and which provided a framework for the management of public life and for the continuing development of the nation's society, polity and economy.

For Nehru the constitution was particularly important. It spelt out many of the ideals which he felt should be the purposes underlying the exercise of power. It also created the structures through which he would personally have to exercise power. The guiding ideals of the constitution were laid out in the preamble, which closely mirrored Nehru's objectives resolution, and in the sections on fundamental rights and directive principles. Citizens had rights of equality and of various freedoms, including freedom of religion, freedom to hold property and freedom from exploitation; and minorities were specifically protected. The state had the duty of promoting the welfare of the people, and of endeavouring to ensure that national life and society was informed by social, economic and political justice. Thus the new state was to be grounded in a new relationship with its citizens which would never have been possible for a state which served imperial interests. That new relationship carried over into the structures for governance. There would be an adult franchise for men and women, through which legislators would be chosen for the legislatures in Delhi and the state capitals, and from whom governments at the centre and in the constituent states of the new union would be constituted. There the novelty ceased. The role of the central government and that of the states was laid out, bearing a striking resemblance to the relationship between centre and provinces under the 1935 Government of India Act, from which about 250 clauses were adopted. The centre was to control all major matters of national importance, including defence, foreign affairs, currency, and banking; while the states had control of public order, police, welfare, health, education, local government, agriculture and industry. Some powers were to be shared, for example criminal and civil law, and social and economic planning. But residual power rested with the union government, and the whole thrust of the federal arrangements was towards a powerful central government. Reinforcing the constitutional division of powers, the centre also had greater financial resources from taxation than the states. A further likeness to the imperial regime was the retention by the national government of considerable emergency power, which could be invoked in the country as a whole, or in a particular state, enabling the president to suspend ordinary constitutional government.

Once India ceased to be an imperial dependency and then a dominion, there was need to find a replacement for the British monarch (and his representative) as head of state. This office was to be vested in a president, elected for a fixed term of office by the legislators of the state and central legislatures. Although the president has considerable power spelt out in the constitution, he is expected to act on ministerial advice and to be more like a constitutional monarch. At the time parallels were overtly drawn with the role of the British monarch within British political life. Real power lay with the prime minister as head of the executive, though not of the state itself, who was to be appointed by the president when it was clear that he or she could command a majority in the Lok Sabha, the all-India parliament based in Delhi.

Thus by the end of 1949 Indians had created a structure for decision-making and for the use and control of executive power in the nation's public life. They would soon embark on the first fully democratic election in their history, making India the world's largest democracy. This was deeply significant in terms of the pathways to power now open to aspiring politicians, much as in imperial days the 1919 reforms had been significant, albeit on a smaller scale, in enlarging the political arena. At the apex of the political system the prime minister's position offered the leader of a party successful in elections potential for power far greater than even the viceroy had wielded, particularly if his party had a significant majority. For he would have national legitimacy, a degree of genuinely popular support in the country, and the backing of his legislative colleagues. However, there were circumstances which might severely curtail a prime minister's power – if he was unable to rely on the support of his party in the legislature for controversial measures, if he found himself opposed by interests in the states who controlled the legitimate powers of the state governments, if there were insufficient resources to carry though policies, if the administration proved weak or obstructive, or if public opinion was to work against government policy. The problems faced by the British in Delhi in governing such a large and diverse country were now compounded by the requirements of mass democracy, as Nehru was to find in the 1950s.

To Nehru the conduct of foreign affairs was a vital aspect of the creation of the new state. Foreign policy was its face to the world community and must reflect the reality of the country's new freedom. As prime minister he was his own foreign minister, and devoted considerable time and energy to the details of constructing a new foreign service for the nation, whose members and their life-styles would appropriately represent their country abroad, and to laying the foundation for a new foreign policy which would make India a player on the world stage, displaying both her independence in world affairs yet also her ideals for international life.

Several major threads ran through Nehru's thinking on world affairs, often maintaining continuity with his meditation on India's place in the course of world history while he was a nationalist leader. One was the importance of the Asian region and the potential role of India within it. For years Nehru had argued that India's problems were part of the international problem of world capitalism, and that to resolve them they must discard narrow nationalism and work towards an international vision of cooperation. By the time the war ended he was saying that Europe was no longer the dominant world power and that Asian nations were increasingly going to be significant for human progress; and that in the context of Asian cooperation India would find its proper place.[26] Throughout 1946 he returned to the theme of Asia renascent, not in a military sense but in terms of creative vitality, forging a new unity and playing a new role in world affairs. This vision lay behind an Asian relations conference he organised in Delhi in March 1947. It was typical of what was to be a persistent aspect of his life in office – the gulf between his great ideals and practical reality. He was delighted with this conference, yet it produced no practical results. Nehru's vision of the unity of Asia and the common interests of its peoples was to come back to haunt him in the actions of the new People's Republic of China, which India formally recognised at the end of 1949.

The second great idealistic thread running through Nehru's foreign policy was that of non-alignment with any world bloc, and Indian commitment to work for world peace and decolonisation. This was a natural development from his commitment to Indian freedom being genuine in international terms. He was determined, particularly as the strains of the Cold War sharpened, to prove India's integrity and independence in international relations, although the Soviet Union initially refused to recognise this and assumed that India was a British puppet in foreign affairs. Speaking to the country through All-India Radio just after taking up office in the interim government in 1946, he enunciated India's future stance of non-alignment.

> We propose, as far as possible, to keep away from the power politics of groups, aligned against one another, which led in the past to world wars and which may again lead to disasters on an even vaster scale. We believe that peace and freedom are indivisible and the denial of freedom anywhere must endanger freedom elsewhere and lead to conflict and war. We are particularly interested in the emancipation of colonial and dependent countries and peoples, and in the recognition in theory and practice of equal opportunities for all peoples.

After independence, when laying down the basic principles of India's foreign policy he repeated the necessity for non-alignment, for practical as well as ideological reasons. 'This policy fits in with our basic principles and is at the same time beneficial even from the narrow opportunist point of view. Indeed there is no other policy which we can pursue with any advantage.' He also saw the danger that if India became aligned then it would be the more difficult for other countries to keep out of such 'lining up', and that would bring another world war nearer.[27] From the perspective of the end of the twentieth century, after the ending of the Cold War and the period of decolonisation, it is hard to perceive just how original and creative a stand this was for a country emerging from colonial control; and how, despite criticism at home and abroad, it enabled Nehru subsequently to become a world figure on the international stage.

Although Nehru's foreign policy is remembered primarily for his stance of non-alignment, of even more long-term practical significance was his government's position on India's relationship with the British Commonwealth. In 1948 as the constitution was formulated and it was obvious that India would soon become a republic, as outlined in Nehru's objectives resolution, the issue of India's future ties with the Commonwealth became urgent. There was no precedent for a republic within the Commonwealth, for its very essence was unity of the dominions who shared the British monarch as head of state. Burma had left the Commonwealth at the beginning of 1948 when on independence she became a republic. Even the ambiguous Irish position within the Commonwealth was known to be about to end as the government prepared to put the Republic of Ireland bill before the Irish parliament late in the year. Moreover in India there had for decades been a hostility to continuing dominion status as less than true independence, and there was an assumption that when India became a republic it would automatically leave the Commonwealth. Nehru shared this assumption and in April 1947 told Baldev Singh, who held the defence portfolio in the interim government and was concerned about the effect on India's armed forces of a complete break with Britain, 'India must go out of the British Commonwealth. Apart from our own personal views in the matter, there is not the least shadow of a doubt that any other proposition would be rejected completely by the Indian people.' He reiterated within days his sense that 'Any attempt to remain in the Commonwealth will sweep away those who propose it and might bring about major trouble in India.'[28]

However, in 1948 there were signs that some experienced Indian politicians were considering the advantages of retaining close ties with the Commonwealth, even membership, particularly as Pakistan was clearly going to remain a member. In April, for example, Sir T.B. Sapru, old friend of Nehru's father and respected moderate Indian politician, strongly advised that India should remain within the Commonwealth, not least because of Pakistan's continuing membership and the strain that would put on British attitudes to India in the event of war between the two neighbours if India was outside the Commonwealth.

Nehru agreed when he was shown this advice. Patel, as deputy prime minister, also made it known to Attlee's government in July that he felt India's interests lay with the Commonwealth. 'I have no doubt that with a careful handling of the situation at your end it would be possible for us to make the ties even closer.'[29] Even earlier Attlee had made a personal request to Nehru to consider whether there was a way India could remain within the Commonwealth with the Crown as the linkage. Nehru had replied that there had been a great change in Indian attitudes to ties with Britain: a year earlier there would have been unanimous refusal in India to countenance any link with the Commonwealth, but now he wanted to tread warily, though himself hoping it would be possible to associate India with Britain and the Commonwealth by means of 'close and intimate' ties.[30] There followed a year of intensive negotiation between London and Delhi and within the Commonwealth to see how such intimacy could be achieved. By November 1948 Nehru was writing to his premiers saying that although India would become a republic he would like close association with the Commonwealth for the sake of India's own interests and of world peace:[31] he had already formally asked that India as a republic could stay within the Commonwealth. In December at Jaipur Congress resolved that it would welcome free association with the independent nations of the Commonwealth for their common welfare and the promotion of world peace. At last in April 1949 at a Commonwealth conference specially convened in London to discuss India's position it was agreed, in the words of a declaration released on the 28th, that India would remain a member of the Commonwealth, for, despite her impending status as a republic, her government had affirmed a desire to remain a member and 'her acceptance of the King as the symbol of the free association of its independent member nations and as such the Head of the Commonwealth'.[32]

So was accepted a formula for membership which was to enable the transformation of the former British Commonwealth, predominantly an association of old Dominions peopled by those of British origin and dominated by the former mother country, into the new Commonwealth — a free multiracial and multinational association of countries which would be dramatically enlarged as Britain handed over her imperial power to national governments in Asia and Africa and new independent states came into being. Nehru was clearly a crucial figure in this momentous development, though only one of several whose commitment to a new mode of relationship and whose hard work achieved this end. Attlee, Cripps, Mountbatten and Lord Ismay on the British side were primary players, as were several Indian politicians and civil servants who took far less public credit than their prime minister. However, if Nehru had not thrown his weight behind the enterprise of finding the means for continued membership of the Commonwealth, and had he not argued for it and justified it at home as in India's interests and as a step towards world peace, then it is unlikely that it would have come to fruition. His stance greatly enhanced his repute in the Commonwealth community, secured India's place in an important international forum and assisted in the evolution of a unique international association which still bridges so many of the gulfs and differences which can sour international relations and precipitate conflict.

. . .

On 26 January 1950 India's new constitution came into effect, and she became a republic; the lengthy process of transferring power from imperial to national control, and making a new nation state was thereby formally completed. Within her borders a significant measure of stability had been achieved and externally India had established a distinctive position in the international community. During these years Nehru was desperately overworked. He dealt with great issues which challenged the roots of his convictions and assumptions about the new India. He also worried over and involved himself with much smaller problems – such as the number of messengers in government offices, what sort of tractors India should buy, the issue of prohibition or whether India should permit horse-racing. (Where such comparatively minor issues were potentially contentious he showed a robust moral sense, arguing that people were to come first, and that governments should not risk revenue, for example in the case of prohibition, which was badly needed for housing, education and health.) He felt weighed down by his responsibilities and frustrated at other people's pettiness, as well as the restricting official life he was forced to lead in New Delhi. His most personal and honest letters indicated that he was by 1948 weary and dispirited, oppressed by all that was wrong with the country and wondering where and how to begin to change things. He felt that politics had become opportunistic and that there had been a collapse of morals and ideals in public life.[33] However, by mid-1949 he had rediscovered his fighting spirit. 'I am just going to fight my hardest against all this sloth and inertia and corruption and self-interest and little-mindedness that we see around us.' Even so, he still felt uneasy in his new role, as if he was a prime minister by accident rather than by choice. He looked back on his days in the nationalist movement as the most significant part of his life, when he had found real fulfilment.[34]

It is easy to overestimate Nehru's power at this stage, particularly as he had come to symbolise so much of the nation's aspirations, struggle and achievements. But he was one of a group of senior politicians who had worked together closely in congress and had now come to power. Although he was the one who enunciated the great principles and made the memorable speeches, his effectiveness as prime minister rested on their routine work, as, for example, in the preparations for India's continuing membership of the Commonwealth, in the integration into India of the princely states, and of course particularly in the immense detail and range of work which went into the drafting of the new constitution. Nehru's relationship with his close colleagues was often not an easy one. He and they were learning on the job the conventions of cabinet government and of allowing colleagues space and authority in the performance of their governmental roles. Nehru was known for his passionate convictions which could manifest as arrogance or irritation with those who did not share his views or whom he considered inefficient. He also possessed a fierce temper which could erupt in dramatic bursts. The reverse side of his own energy and conviction could therefore be a tempestuous relationship with people – a relationship in which he appeared autocratic and interfering. In February 1948 Mountbatten told him in no uncertain terms that he thought he was treating his ministers, principally Patel, in a roughshod manner, and that even Churchill at the height of his powers would not have dared to treat his ministers in such a way.[35] Nehru's strained relations with Patel had come almost to breaking-point at the start of the year. Patel felt that Nehru was acting in such a way as would make him a virtual dictator, rather than appropriately for a democratic and cabinet style of government. He also acknowledged that they were very different in temperament, and that they differed in their views on socio-economic developments and communal relations. Gandhi was well aware of the problems which might ensue if these two senior figures ceased to cooperate or if one of them resigned from government, as Patel was thinking of doing, and wanted them to work together. His death at the height of their personal crisis brought the two together, and Nehru with great magnanimity mended fences with Patel, who responded similarly, saying he was overwhelmed with Nehru's affection and warmth and would cooperate with him, and that he hoped that in future they would have more time together and would be able to resolve difficulties as they arose.[36] Nehru's position of influence thus rested on the cooperation and hard work of his colleagues, as well as on his own capacities and reputation. But the attitudes and priorities of his fellow Congressmen in government and in the party would come to constrain him, as would the fact that he had inherited the raj and its instruments of governance, with all their limitations, as part of the transfer of power.

. . .

NOTES AND REFERENCES

1. Nehru's independence speech, *SWJN(2)*, vol. 3, pp. 135–6.
2. 22 December 1945, *SWJN(1)*, vol. 14, p. 503.
3. 31 December 1946, P. Moon (ed.), *Wavell. The Viceroy's Journal* (Oxford: Oxford University Press, 1973), p. 402. On the need for a breakdown plan see his note, 29 June 1946, *TP* vol. VII, pp. 1084–9; the plan, 7 September 1946, is in *TP* vol. VIII, pp. 454–65.
4. See A. Jalal, *The Sole Spokesman. Jinnah, the Muslim League and the Demand for Pakistan* (Cambridge: Cambridge University Press, 1985); I. Talbot *Provincial Politics and the Pakistan Movement* (Karachi: Oxford University Press, 1988); M. Hasan (ed.), *India's Partition. Process, Strategy and Mobilization* (Delhi: Oxford University Press, 1994).
5. 21 September, 28 December 1943, *SWJN(1)*, vol. 13, pp. 244, 324.
6. Press conference, 17 July 1945, speech to Sikhs, 16 August 1945, *SWJN(1)*, vol. 14, pp. 49–50, 65.
7. Documents relating to this phase are in *TP* vols V–XI; *SWJN(1)*, vol. 15–*SWJN(2)*, vol. 2. See also R.J. Moore, *Escape from Empire. The Attlee Government and the Indian Problem* (Oxford: Clarendon Press, 1983); B.R. Nanda, *Jawaharlal Nehru. Rebel and Statesman* (Delhi: Oxford University Press, 1995), ch. 7.
8. Nehru to R. Prasad, 17 September 1947, *SWJN(2)*, vol. 4, p. 83.

9. For example, note by Nehru, 14 November 1948, Nehru to V. Patel, 27 October 1948, *SWJN(2)*, vol. 8, pp. 104, 287.

10. Nehru to Liaquat Ali Khan, 24 September 1948, *SWJN(2)*, vol. 7, pp. 90–1; speech at Congress, 18 December 1948, *SWJN(2)*, vol. 8, pp. 6–7.

11. Undated note from Patel to Gandhi, D. Das (ed.), *Sardar Patel's Correspondence 1945–50* (Ahmedabad: Navajivan), vol. 6, pp. 21–4.

12. Nehru's 30 January 1948 broadcast, *SWJN(2)*, vol. 5, pp. 35–6; Nehru speaking to the Constituent Assembly, 2 February 1948, ibid., pp. 39–42; Nehru's speech at a public meeting, 2 February 1948, ibid., pp. 42–5.

13. Nehru to M.C. Khanna, 6 June 1949, *SWJN(2)*, vol. 11, p. 81.

14. Report, 11 July 1947, *TP*, vol. XII, p. 99; see I. Copland, *The princes of India in the endgame of empire, 1917–1947* (Cambridge: Cambridge University Press, 1997).

15. Article, 27 November 1933, *SWJN(1)*, vol. 6, pp. 29–30; speech as president of All India States People's Conference, 30 December 1945, *SWJN(1)*, vol. 14, pp. 406–16.

16. 4 October 1948, *SWJN(2)*, vol. 7, pp. 371–3.

17. Nehru to Stafford Cripps, 17/18 December 1948, *SWJN(2)*, vol. 8, p. 338.

18. Speech, 25 July 1948, *SWJN(2)*, vol. 7, pp. 411–13.

19. Gandhi to Nehru, 5 (?2) October 1945, *CWMG*, vol. 81, pp. 319–21.

20. Nehru to G.B. Pant, 6 May 1948, *SWJN(2)*, vol. 6, pp. 438–9; V. Patel to Nehru, 21 February 1950, Das (ed.), *Sardar Patel's Correspondence*, vol. 10, pp. 84–7.

21. Nehru to V. Patel, 4 March 1950, *SWJN(2)*, vol. 14 i, p. 462.

22. Nehru as Congress president to prime ministers of Congress-ruled provinces, 22 July 1946, *SWJN(1)*, vol. 15, pp. 469–71; Nehru to G.S. Bajpai (ICS since 1914), 5 December 1946, *SWJN(2)*, vol. 1, pp. 549–50.

23. V. Patel to Nehru, 27 April 1948, Das (ed.), *Sardar Patel's Correspondence*, vol. 6, pp. 324–6. On the continuities between the ICS and the IAS see D.C. Potter, *India's Political Administrators 1919–1983* (Oxford: Clarendon Press, 1986).

24. The details of constitution-making are in G. Austin, *The Indian Constitution: Cornerstone of a Nation* (London: Oxford University Press, 1966).

25. Speech in Constituent Assembly, 13 December 1946, *SWJN(2)*, vol. 1, pp. 240–51.

26. Speech, 13 July 1945, *SWJN(1)*, vol. 14, pp. 39–40.

27. Broadcast, 7 September 1946, *SWJN(2)*, vol. 1, pp. 405–6; note on basic principles of foreign policy, 12 September 1948, *SWJN(2)*, vol. 7, pp. 609–14.

28. Nehru to Baldev Singh, 8 and 14 April 1947, *SWJN(2)*, vol. 2, pp. 369–72.
29. V. Patel to Arthur Henderson, Under-Secretary of State for India and Burma, 3 July 1948, Das (ed.), *Sardar Patel's Correspondence*, vol. 6, p. 386. On Sapru's views see his letters of 16 and 19 April quoted in N. Mansergh, *The Commonwealth Experience* rev edn (Basingstoke: Macmillan, 1982), vol. 2, pp. 147–8.
30. Attlee to Nehru, 11 March 1948, Nehru to Attlee, 18 April 1948, quoted in R.J. Moore, *Making the New Commonwealth* (Oxford: Clarendon Press, 1987), pp. 128–30. (This contains a detailed study of the negotiations which enabled India to remain within the Commonwealth.)
31. Nehru to provincial premiers, 16 November 1948, *SWJN(2)*, vol. 8, pp. 223–4. See also his speech in Subjects Committee of Jaipur Congress, 16 December 1948, ibid., pp. 333–4; Nehru to provincial premiers, 16 April 1949, *SWJN(2)*, vol. 10, pp. 311–12.
32. Declaration quoted in Moore, *Making the New Commonwealth*, p. 192.
33. Nehru to V. Patel, 27 April 1948, to C. Rajgopalachariar, 6 May 1948, to G.B. Pant, 6 May 1948, *SWJN(2)*, vol. 6, pp. 374–5, 367, 438–9.
34. Nehru to M. Asaf Ali, 2 July 1949, *SWJN(2)*, vol. 12, p. 470; talk in the USA, 27 October 1949, *SWJN(2)*, vol. 13, p. 359.
35. Record by Mountbatten of interview with Nehru, 5 February 1948, *SWJN(2)*, vol. 5, pp. 480–2.
36. Undated note from V. Patel to Gandhi, V. Patel to Gandhi, 13 January 1948, V. Patel to Nehru, 5 February 1948, Das (ed.), *Sardar Patel's Correspondence*, vol. 6, pp. 21–4, 25–6, 30–1; Nehru to V. Patel, 23 December 1947, *SWJN(2)*, vol. 4, p. 539; note by Nehru for Gandhi, 6 January 1948, Nehru to V. Patel, 3 February 1948, *SWJN(2)*, vol. 5, pp. 471–5, 479–80.

Chapter 4

THE VISIONARY AS
PRIME MINISTER

Nehru was prime minister of India until his death in 1964. The man who had grown to maturity in the disciplined and idealistic context of a nationalist movement under Gandhi's leadership now had the opportunity provided by the highest political post in the nation state to put into practice something of his vision of a new India once the structures of the new state had been put into place. In the early 1950s he was at the height of his powers and reputation. Although he was a man in his sixties he was exceptionally vigorous intellectually and physically, capable of hard and intensive work which would have daunted a much younger man. Not only did he take care of his health, but his daughter, Indira, now lived apart from her husband and became his companion and hostess, looking after and protecting him. With her two small sons, Rajiv and Sanjay, she provided him with the novel luxury of a stable home base at Teen Murti House in New Delhi, with its gracious rooms and lovely gardens. These were the years when he was established as undisputed leader in the country at large and in the Congress party, to the extent that by mid-decade people were already voicing the fear, 'After Nehru, who?' Moreover, he had become an international figure of influence, not just on an Asian stage, but more widely, as world leaders courted him and India in the context of the Cold War.

Now, if ever, Nehru was a figure of power. This chapter seeks to explore his achievement of such a unique dominance in Indian public life, in contrast to the years immediately after independence. It then asks what he tried to do with that dominance. Here themes appear which were to become even clearer in the later 1950s and up to his death, particularly the constraints on the extent of his power and his influence, although they were not so obvious in years given over idealistically to the making of key decisions and the putting of new policies, laws and institutions into place. In retrospect it is possible to discern impending problems which were to beset so much of his attempt to put ideals into practice, to make vision into reality – the restraints caused by the working of the federal constitution, the deep-rooted dynamics of Indian society, the persistent strands of ideological and social conservatism, and the weaknesses of the instruments at his disposal to effect radical change.

As crucial to any individual's position of leadership and use of power as external opportunity and office is an inner dynamic – the particular self-image of that person, and his or her unique sense of vocation or will to exercise power on the public stage. Nehru was remarkably reflective and articulate about his inner response to the public position in which he found himself. Despite his passionate struggle for independence and the power to create a new India, and his acknowledgement of his own attraction to personal influence and public acclaim, he was still in a sense perplexed by his position and never totally comfortable with it. While visiting the United States in late 1949 he told a Chicago audience that the most significant time of his life, and the phase when he had felt most fulfilled, was during the nationalist struggle. He did not see himself as a conventional career politician, or his current position as the natural peak of his career.

> I am prime minister accidentally if I may say so, or in a sense in a non-political way. I was thrust into politics because of the force of circumstances, and not because of any free will. And there I remain because the circumstances continued, and there I suppose, I shall remain for some time more because it is difficult to leave.[1]

Within several months he was in fact seriously considering resignation. He felt he might be able to serve India better, and particularly to do battle against communalism, by a more active and on-the-spot role: he was clearly thinking about the teaching and example of his great mentor, Gandhi, in the dark months of violence before independence. His whole temperament rebelled against sitting in an office in New Delhi when he felt he should be up and doing, as he told his sister, Mrs

Pandit.[2] By May of 1950 when he had decided to stay on in office he still recognised that the business of government was not his *forte* temperamentally and at times could depress him. But he still had a sense of vocation, wanting to give all his energy to things that he counted valuable, and he felt he could not escape responsibility and the burden of people's trust.[3] His ambivalence over political life and high office never left him. But even when he confessed later to being deeply dispirited over the state of India's politics and social life his faith in her future and his powerful inner drive to play a role in shaping that future sustained him.[4]

While Nehru was in office Gandhi's teaching and leadership remained a powerful and abiding influence. But he realised that although Gandhi's inspiring presence and style of moral leadership had suited the time of nationalist struggle, now a new kind of leadership was required to encourage a dynamic and positive attitude to the nation's future. Moreover, as he wrote in a foreword to a major biography of Gandhi in 1951, his generation of leaders (and presumably he thought of himself in particular) had to function in a democratic context, and that made their task much more complex than Gandhi's had been. How could he walk the fine line between compromising on ideals in order to accommodate himself to the majority and sticking to ideals and cutting himself off from those he was trying to lead?

> The average leader of men, especially in a democratic society, has continually to adapt himself to his environment and to choose what he considers the lesser evil. Some adaptation is inevitable. But as this process goes on, occasions arise when that adaptation imperils the basic ideal and objective. I suppose there is no clear answer to this question and each individual and each generation will have to find its own answer.[5]

Nehru remained an intellectual and an idealist, painfully self-aware and analytical about his personal role, with those aspects of his personality in constant debate and often conflict with the practical politician in him. This led to considerable inner tension and hesitation, as he strove to be a prime minister who was both a realist and a creative leader attempting to solve some of the formidable problems facing the new India.

. . .

THE ESTABLISHMENT OF DOMINANCE

Nehru's humorous description of himself as an 'accidental' prime minister had an element of truth in it. He was not a regional leader who had risen to all-India leadership through a local power base. Nor had he worked his way to the pinnacle of the political system by service in the ranks of a political party, or by growing prominence and expertise in the legislatures. Rather, he had become a national figure with influence in the Congress party and in the country mainly by virtue of his special relationship with Gandhi. In the immediate post-war period his skills as a negotiator and spokesman for Congress had confirmed his position. After independence he had retained a particularly important role in government because there had been no dramatic break in the country's political life and institutions in 1947, and because there was considerable continuity between the interim and new governments. At this juncture he was still only one member of a powerful composite Congress leadership.

However, in the 1950s this changed, and he established himself in a personal and unique position of dominance in India's politics and government. This involved a significant expansion of his influence in the Congress party, in the country at large, and over the institutions and processes of government. Moreover, this had to be done in a new situation, that of a fully democratic political system once the new constitution had been put in place. Voters and political activists now expected much more of their government as it was in a new sense 'theirs' rather than a colonial regime, and the nationalist movement itself had done much to create a wide range of rising expectations. It was by no means automatic, in India and elsewhere in the post-colonial world, that nationalist leaders who had come to prominence as opponents of government had the skills required for governance, or that they could retrain and adapt themselves to a new role and setting. Indian politicians had often had more experience of legislative and administrative work than politicians in other parts of the British empire, following the constitutional reforms of 1919 and 1935. The experience of being in office in provincial governments between 1937 and 1939 had been an important training time for a whole generation of Congressmen who took up governmental roles after 1946. But Nehru himself had never held governmental office until 1946 except briefly at civic level twenty years before.

The first area of India's political life within which Nehru consciously strove to establish his authority was the Congress party. But why was the party important to him? Gandhi for one had argued that once independence had been attained its role had ended, and that its members should disband and organise themselves for constructive national work rather than political activism. Nehru himself admitted in late 1949 to his old Congress colleague, Rajendra Prasad, his deep disquiet at the state of Congress, particularly its indiscipline, lack of common effort and internal feuding. But he could see no alternative all-India body which could be used as an instrument of governance.[6] For anybody who aspired to creative all-India leadership it was a highly significant element in the political system. As the party of nationalism for over seven decades it had huge public legitimacy, reinforced by its connection with the revered name of Gandhi. Moreover, the majority of political activists still found it their natural home and arena of activity, and the main political structure through which they could hope to forge political careers. It was thus a powerful institution for incorporating and controlling the country's political community. It was also the most effective mechanism available for attracting voters and vetting candidates for election to the central and regional legislatures. As such it was vital for the formation of governments in Delhi and the state capitals as well as for major changes in the country's life which required legislation. Its committee structure and particularly its plenary sessions were an arena for major ideological debate and the forging of political commitment to big ideals and policies which, once debated and agreed, could be handed over to the legislatures and administration for enactment.

If Congress was vital for Nehru and for others who aspired to all-India leadership, it none the less had its limitations and weaknesses. It was not a tightly knit and well-disciplined party fashioned to pursue a clear programme. Nor was it a cadre-based party with dependable local activists. Throughout its existence it had been a loose, inclusive and accommodating party, striving to incorporate as much of the potential nation as possible, masking or compromising over serious ideological rifts within it, and often shelving potentially divisive issues. The result had been the growth of a pan-continental umbrella party which

contained under its shelter people of different ideological per-
suasions and political priorities, with very different levels of
commitment to political work. But party organisation, beneath
the all-India level, was still often weak or dominated by local
notables who ran it as their fiefdom. It was therefore of limited
use as an agent of social and economic change, or as a means
to pursue clear ideological goals, and its weakness in these
respects and the lack of an alternative were an ominous sign
for Nehru with his vision of a renewed and much-changed
India. He was well aware of this and in 1951, in the months
before the first general election on an adult franchise, bewailed
the party's lack of internal discipline, the dominance of small
groups within it and its growing distance from the grass roots
of India's polity.[7] Even after its success in the election of 1952
(in which it polled 45 per cent of the votes for the Lok Sabha
and won 74 per cent of the seats) he maintained that it had to
change, to reform its organisation and re-establish its popular
base if it were to perform its essential role of social and economic reconstruction of the nation.[8] Although he insisted that
it still had an important and unique role in such reconstruction, he did not spell out precisely what that role included, and
probably never worked it out in his own mind. For, unlike
Patel, he was not naturally at home in the realm of institution
building and management.

Nehru's struggle for dominance in Congress reached a crisis
in 1950–51, when the impending elections made control of
the party machinery and the selection of candidates vital for
the different groups within it. In this phase two issues crucial
to him were intertwined. One was the whole ideological thrust
behind the government of the new state, and the persistence
of a strong streak of conservative thinking within the Congress
which spread over economic and social issues to the importance of Hindu identity in the new nation. This conservatism,
with its tendency to support Hindu communalism, was the
antithesis of Nehru's driving ideals, and had lain beneath the
uneasy relationship he had had with Vallabhbhai Patel even
after Gandhi's death had prevented an open rupture between
them. To Nehru it seemed that this tendency was threatening
to become dominant in Congress and thus in the main political
forum in which India's identity could be articulated. Inter-
locked with this was the second issue of the relationship between
the Congress as a party organisation and the government itself.

Nehru believed from the point of independence onwards that the party had a junior role – that of laying down broad lines of policy. Government had the task of working out the details, in which process the prime minister would have a decisive directing and coordinating role.[9]

As a result of his stance on these two issues Nehru had a profoundly uneasy relationship with the Congress president elected in August 1950, P.D. Tandon, a UP Congressman who was an orthodox Hindu and a henchman of Patel. However, Patel died at the end of the year. Loss of him both weakened the position of the conservatives and forced Nehru to involve himself more closely in Congress's organisational affairs, which had been largely Patel's domain. Months of internal conflict ensued and at first Nehru tried to achieve unity between the competing groups. Finally he was prepared to stand his ground on both the central issues at stake and in September 1951 the conflict ended with Tandon's resignation and Nehru's election as Congress president by the All-India Congress Committee by a vote of 295 to 4. The strength of support for him reflected sympathy for his views and also the sense within Congress that he was indispensable to them. Not only had he won the battle for what he called 'the soul' of Congress:[10] he had affirmed the pre-eminence of the government and prime minister and showed how limited a role in policy-making would be expected from the Congress organisation and its president. In August, as the conflict was nearing its climax, he told an old Congress colleague how he saw the two issues as intertwined, and how he wished he had taken this stand even earlier.[11]

Tandon later complained that the party had become 'the slave' of the government.[12] This was an exaggeration. But from the crisis of 1951 the Congress party organisation was increasingly neutralised as a potential challenge to the government and to Nehru himself. In 1952 he reiterated to the chief ministers of the states that the general principle guiding relations between the party organisation and government was that matters of high policy and principle should be discussed in and with the party, but that the party should not interfere in day-to-day government.[13] But this was still a matter of debate within Congress and he felt constrained to remain president until November 1954, during which time it was effectively managed for him by two general secretaries. Thereafter (until early 1959) the president was U.N. Dhebar, who took care of party matters for Nehru and kept him informed about them, and was in no doubt that his was a subservient role to that of the prime minister. Not only did Nehru increasingly not have the time for this sort of work, but he recognised that, unlike Patel, he was not fitted for it. As he remarked wrily to a close friend, 'I am not a political boss and I cannot function as such. . . . I cannot run a political machine.'[14] For their part, most Congress activists were happy to work in and for the party on these terms as Dhebar evolved a congenial consultative pattern of relations between the party and the prime minister and his government, and because under Nehru Congress continued to be ideologically embracing and more than any other political party or group an arena for personal political advancement.

One aspect of Nehru's value to the Congress party was his repute in the country at large. In a real sense Congressmen needed him as much as he needed the support and facilities afforded by a loyal and genuinely nation-wide party. After Gandhi, Nehru was one of the most well-known and revered leaders within the national movement. But now informed public support for a party leader and prime minister was even more important within the political system because of the democratic processes set up by the new constitution, and the imminence of the first general elections on a universal adult suffrage. For Nehru public support was also important because he needed to get across to the country at large his messages of national identiy and the need for change.

Increasingly in the 1950s his personal repute and authority in India were confirmed and widened – to a remarkable extent given the lack of mass communications at the time. This was partly the result of his considerable personal effort to make contact with the Indian public. He was always accessible to ordinary people when he was at home in New Delhi, careless of his own security, and welcoming to those ordinary people who gathered to catch sight of him or present a petition to him. He toured the country, made innumerable speeches and particularly at election-time threw himself into the business of making mass contact. In the weeks before the first general election he confessed that he hated much of the pre-election business, particularly having to choose candidates. But he revelled in meeting people and expounding to them his vision of a new India. By late January 1952 he reckoned that in the past two and half months he had been continuously on the move, living like a nomad, and had spoken to 35 million people. He had given the work all his energy and was exhausted, but at the time exhilarated.

His country-wide reputation did not only rest on his personal actions. It was also derived from the very nature of the Congress party and the way his name was inextricably associated with it. Congress was the one truly dominant political party on the Indian scene, yet it was open and accepting to many ideological groups. Further, it was pan-Indian yet accommodated itself to the social and political patterns of dominance in each locality, giving those who aspired to political influence a place in its organisation and deliberations. It was never a party of the prime minister's cronies and 'yes-men' (as it was later to become under his daughter), but was a genuinely open environment with elections to posts within it every two years. Moreover, at election-time candidates were carefully chosen to represent the social complexion of each constituency, a strategy which saw the incorporation of men and women of an increasingly broad caste and socio-economic background, and even in some places members of former princely and landholding families if they were deemed still important in attracting local support.

Nehru knew the importance of forging new types of connections between the rulers and the ruled if a government based in Delhi was to be secure and capable of leading the country in great processes of change. He also saw the importance to a prime minister of maintaining authority over the processes of governance. Here, however, there were limits on what a Delhi-based leader of government could do. All rulers of India had experienced serious problems of controlling a country so large and diverse, and had to achieve a balance between modes of control from the centre and delegation of power to people and institutions in the regions. The federal constitution of the new Indian state formalised this balance, leaving demarcated areas within the control of the state governments and legislatures. Thus Nehru was never able to exert formal authority over state matters, and this was to become a real problem when there was a clash between the priorities and policies of Delhi and the state capitals. However, the severity of the problem and the chance of destructive clashes between centre and periphery were under Nehru somewhat restricted by the fact that Congress not only formed the central government during these years but also dominated state politics.

In Delhi, Nehru's authority over parliament, the Lok Sabha, was unchallenged. His authority lay in part in the large majorities Congress won while he was prime minister. But he also valued parliament greatly and took care to nurture what he saw as good parliamentary behaviour, and to assert its significance by his own regular attendance and by explaining and consulting within its forum. He used a system of sixteen whips under a minister for parliamentary affairs with cabinet rank, who liaised with parliamentarians, organised attendance, speeches and voting, and made sure that he was alerted to opinion within parliament. Moreover, he never attempted to sidestep the authority of parliament or undercut its role, as occurred after his death with the expansion of the prime minister's private office, which became a sort of court of those considered trustworthy servants of the premier and increasingly an alternative mechanism for making policy. It was a sign of his parliamentary authority that only once in his premiership did he face a motion of no confidence in parliament – in 1963 after Chinese forces had attacked India.

Over other institutions of central government Nehru sought to exercise closer control. Such was his personal standing in his party and the country that he towered above his cabinet colleagues after the death of Patel, the only long-standing colleague who could have challenged his position. When a Planning Commission was created in 1950 to deal with India's economic problems he was its chairman. Initially it was a purely advisory body, but from the mid-1950s it became virtually as important as the cabinet in moulding Indian policy, and a further mechanism through which Nehru and trusted associates could influence government. However, such unchallenged dominance had its negative implications. Nehru's heart and talent were not in administration. Although he worked phenomenally hard and drove himself and his secretaries mercilessly, he was not good at coordinating the work of others or at delegating tasks. So the central bureaucracy functioned only as fast as he could manage the papers that came to his desk; and when he was travelling abroad decision-making virtually stopped. Moreover, he was prone in his position of isolation to trust individuals who had no significant national standing or proven record of efficiency, with disastrous results, as in the case of a head of his small personal office, or of Krishna Menon, a brilliant but erratic friend who was partly responsible for the defence débâcle of 1962.

Nehru's dominance over the processes of central government did not reflect any simple personal will to power. He was, however, committed to a 'statist' model of change for his country, envisaging that change in society and the economy would be inspired and directed from above.[15] A political elite of educated visionaries, primarily himself and like-minded colleagues, would articulate the principles and strategies of desirable change, and the people would be led and educated by those with experience. Hence it was essential that he and others of the visionary elite should secure the commanding heights of the state's structures. But, as he himself had recognised immediately after independence when he accepted the need to retain the ICS despite its 'imperial' antecedents, there could be a great gap between vision and policy and actual implementation, if lower levels of the administrative structure were hostile, inept, corrupt or in the pocket of those with vested interests. He saw both the need for an administrative revolution and the seeming impossibility of achieving one when resources were so scarce and existing administrative structures were so entrenched and self-perpetuating. What he seemed not to have contemplated was that 'the people' might not wish to be led in certain directions, or that significant segments of society might capture the structures of decision-making and administration, particularly in the states, and thereby nullify policies emanating from Delhi.

Nehru's contemporaries sometimes joked that he was 'the last viceroy'. Despite his impeccable nationalist and democratic credentials this was in some ways uncomfortably near the truth. Not only did his personal position of authority recall the autocratic centralisation of the imperial order under the monarch's representative and the social deference accorded to the head of the imperial government: in attitude he was elitist and paternalistic, as the viceroys had been, the difference being that for him the new visionaries and guardians of the Indian people were an educated, modernising Indian elite rather than an imperial elite. Moreover, for him as for them the state's structures, authority and prestige were vital, though he saw the state's goal as planned change rather than stability. More serious, given his vision of a more equal, prosperous and modern India, was the similarity between his problems of policy implementation and theirs. The size and diversity of the subcontinent remained, as did the administrative structure his predecessors had evolved for their own purposes rather than for enacting policies which meant addressing deep issues of attitudes, social structures and entrenched interests and attempting to generate great sea-changes in society and the economy. The British had found India increasingly difficult and 'political' to rule in the first half of the century. Now Nehru was to use his unique dominance to attempt to achieve tasks far greater than they had undertaken.

. . .

THE USES OF POWER

Nurturing democracy

Among Nehru's fundamental priorities was the nurturing of India's new democracy. His commitment to democracy had been forged by his intellectual training and also by his long fight against autocratic imperial government in the name of the Indian people. For him it meant not only a particular framework of political institutions and relationships, but also a set of cultural norms which would affect ordinary life as well as politics and the style of government. He recognised that more authoritarian regimes might appear to achieve quicker 'results' but believed that democracy was ultimately and more deeply creative. As he wrote to his chief ministers in 1952, 'I firmly believe that it is a better way than a dictatorship or authoritarianism . . . it is very doubtful if the essential quality which underlies human progress, that is the creative spirit of man, can develop adequately under an authoritarian system.'[16]

The strength of his commitment to the nurturing of democratic norms was remarkable. It was also profoundly influential for India's political future when it is compared with the erosion or failure of democratic forms of government in Pakistan or in many other states which emerged in Africa out of the processes of decolonisation. In practice he helped to sustain democratic ideals and processes by a constant vigilance and by personal reminder and exhortation; and also by cherishing Congress as an inclusive party which could accommodate widely different views and be an effective vehicle for political careers.

The strength of Congress and its deep social roots made India's emerging political system a 'dominant party system', compared with a two-party system as in Britain. But it was none the less democratic for that, for it enabled the articulation of public opinion and of considerable dissent, while its members in the legislatures were able to influence legislation to a very considerable degree.

Most obviously Nehru accorded great significance to general elections, to that periodic calling to account of the ruling party which became such a major feature of India's democratic practice. No other democratic state had such a large and geographically dispersed electorate or had to manage the business of registering and counting votes in circumstances of poor communications and mass illiteracy. In 1952 the electorate was 173.2 millions, casting their votes in 132,560 polling stations. Nehru hated the bartering that went on in the pre-election selection of candidates to suit the social makeup of each constituency and to maintain party and factional loyalties. But he revelled in the opportunity elections gave him and the party for contact with huge numbers of ordinary people. Not only were elections a means of gathering votes and gaining legitimacy for the government and its policies. They were also a powerful educational mechanism in the meaning of democracy and citizenship, as voters were exposed to party manifestoes, political speeches and the new habit of voting. Nehru wrote triumphantly to Mountbatten in 1952, 'The elections have been a tremendous experience for hundreds of millions in the country. They have taken a very active interest in them. On the whole large numbers have voted, including women, who often came in their fineries, especially the village women.'[17] Nearly 47 per cent of the enfranchised actually voted in this first election, and the figure rose significantly thereafter. Democratic elections became a great public and political rite, affirming India's freedom and identity, and were constantly remarkable for their high turnout among both men and women.

Nehru also respected the institutions of democratic government. Such were the powers of a prime minister and of the central government under the constitution that had he not thrown his personal authority behind these structures they could have been seriously weakened or bypassed, as occurred under his daughter two decades later. He treated the Lok Sabha in Delhi with utmost seriousness, making a point of being there for prime minister's question time, using it as a theatre for important policy announcements, valuing it as a forum for genuine discussion, and respecting its opinions even when it seemed to block reforms he considered essential for the country. Similarly, he respected the federal structure of the Indian Union, recognising the autonomy of the states and the right of voters to elect their own state governments. Of course it was easier for him to respect the autonomous political life of the states because at this stage the Congress was dominant in most states as well as at the centre. As a result the party itself could be used to discipline local Congress politicians at odds with the Delhi government, while in most states it was unlikely that local governments would be elected who owed allegiance to non-Congress parties.

Nehru recognised that this was a very sensitive area, where an over-dominant centre might set precedents which would seriously weaken the democratic nature of the constitution by exploiting the reserve and emergency powers available to the central government. In 1951, for example, after twenty months of instability in the Punjab, where rival Congress leaders battled for control of the state, the Congress leadership in Delhi attempted to sort out the local confusion, using the mechanism of the party's central parliamentary board. When the incumbent chief minister refused to obey its directive Nehru's patience gave way and he argued that the centre must restore order and stability to the state. He eventually advised the president, Rajendra Prasad, to impose president's rule – the first time this reserve power was used – though he said he had tried to avoid the step for three months. He was clearly uneasy, however. 'I think it is certainly possible to criticise, from the democratic point of view, the action that we have taken in the Punjab. At the same time I am convinced that this action was necessary in order to stop the progressive rot that was setting in and to give the province and its people a shock.'[18] In 1952 he was adamant that he was not prepared to countenance president's rule in Madras just because Congress had failed to gain a majority in the state legislature, and that other constitutional avenues had to be explored to achieve a viable government.[19] It was only towards the end of his life, in 1959, that he was party to the toppling of a non-Congress regime because of pressure from within his party to get rid of the properly elected communist regime in Kerala.

Nehru as a democratic prime minister was also most uneasy about the use of coercive force in relation to a free citizenry which was so reminiscent of the behaviour of the imperial regime. His letters to his colleagues show how he looked back on ways the British had tried to control opinion and action, and how they, as nationalists, had responded on the receiving end of such measures. Not only had they loathed the imperial regime: they had positively thrived on coercion. Now he disliked the uncomfortable likeness to actions of the current state governments. He thought coercion to be wrong in itself as well as counterproductive, and he feared how it would damage India's reputation abroad. He recognised that only state governments could judge the merits and dangers of particular circumstances, but he warned his chief ministers of the fundamental dangers of 'repressive measures':

> These measures unfortunately become inevitable sometimes and we have to use them. But always we must remember that repression has never crushed an idea or solved a problem. It is a temporary expedient for special occasions. There is [a] tendency sometimes to get used to the repressive apparatus and try to meet every problem by its means. That is a dangerous trend and we must always pull ourselves up.[20]

Eighteen months later the issue was still on his mind when he told his old colleague, Rajagopalachariar, of his anger at a recent circular from the Intelligence Bureau about controlling students.[21]

However, he recognised that the new democratic state needed to arm itself to deal with actions which threatened its stability and integrity; and it must be remembered that domestic peace was often threatened in the early years of India's independence by the upheavals following partition, and by a concerted communist strategy of insurrection. In October 1951 he was thus prepared to argue for a press bill as a necessity, though he admitted to great reluctance in agreeing to limit the freedom of the press.[22] He was similarly prepared to back provision for preventive detention largely because of what he saw as open and brutal war waged by groups in the country. But he warned that it must only be used in special circumstances and feared that some officials might get into the habit of locking people up.[23]

Nehru's understanding of democracy was far more than the holding of elections and the functioning of the constitution with a proper regard for people's constitutional rights. He believed that at its deepest it was the release of a creative and responsible spirit among the citizens. Here surely there were echoes of Gandhi's understanding of *swaraj* as 'self-rule', and his commitment to the reconstruction of society and polity at the very roots by the actions of ordinary people in quite humdrum circumstances. He had been convinced that lasting change could only come 'from below' on the initiative and commitment of ordinary Indians. These themes were reinforced by Nehru's deep distrust of an imperial-style civil service designed primarily to maintain order and to control rather than enable people to reach unknown potential. He therefore tried to open up debate about the decentralisation of government and ways of making people more responsible for their own lives.

While the new Planning Commission was discussing the content of a first Five-Year Plan for India's economic development, he told his chief ministers in July 1952 how concerned he was about nurturing organs of representation and decision-making at village level, although he recognised that in the modern world there had to be a large measure of centralisation. The first practical signs of this concern were the establishment in October that year of fifty-five Community Projects under the supervision of the Planning Commission, aimed at tackling problems of poverty and low agricultural productivity, but which also encouraged village communities to help themselves. When the final version of the plan recommended a 'national extension scheme' to involve village people in rural development he wrote again enthusiastically, 'I attach the greatest importance to the new national extension service which is a development of our community centre scheme. It has in it the seeds of a great revolutionary change in India. If we succeed that way, we can really change the face of India peacefully and without conflict.'[24]

At the same time Nehru was also concerned with the idea of 'democratising' the administrative apparatus and making the civil servants more responsive to the wishes and needs of the people rather than remaining close cousins of their imperial predecessors, concerned for stability rather than for dynamic change. This had concerned him since independence. But now he reverted to the theme as a result of a visit to India in 1952, at the invitation of the government, of Dr Paul Appleby, a prominent American academic expert on public administration. Appleby made detailed suggestions about civil-service recruitment and training and suggested the need for new levels of administrators, for he argued that the central government was gravely hampered in its pursuit of change by the constraints imposed by state, district and municipal control. He noted how little change there had been in the manner of administration since independence, despite the new goals of the state, and argued that India would have to tackle such issues as the hierarchies within the administration, the wasteful and dilatory nature of administration and the need to find new ways of ensuring where responsibility actually lay. Nehru sent the report to all his chief ministers and corresponded with them about it, urging them to recognise its importance, while the cabinet also discussed it. In the end little was done to effect major change in attitudes or procedures. A few months before his death Nehru is reported to have said privately to friends that his greatest failure as prime minister was his inability to change the administration. He thought it had remained a colonial administration and that it was one of the main causes of India's failure to solve her pressing economic problems.[25]

There can be no doubt of Nehru's commitment to democracy. Ironically, however, the evidence suggests that instead of liberating the spirit of creativity as Nehru had hoped, India's developing democracy only served to entrench those who were not so committed to radical change, in the civil service and in the various levels of decision-making, and that it failed to generate tools for social and economic transformation.

Fostering national cohesion

As important to Nehru as the nurturing of democracy was his commitment to throwing his personal influence and prime-ministerial power behind the cause of a new national unity. The deep fissures in society which had horrified him at partition had forced him to see the need for the ongoing work of constructing India as a unified nation once the common 'enemy', the imperial regime, had gone. In 1956 he was reported as saying that his profession was to foster the unity of India.[26] He recognised that India encompassed great diversities of many kinds – cultural, linguistic and religious, and he urged that a tolerant and accommodating pluralism was the surest route to a new and deeply rooted sense of commonality. This was to him one of the most valuable aspects of 'Indianness' in the past. Now he argued that in the new situation of their own free nation state Indians must cast off narrow social and sectarian identities in order to create a modern Indian national identity and a community where minorities would be welcomed for their contribution to the whole, and where the weaker and disadvantaged would be nurtured and accepted. These were constant themes in his public rhetoric and private exhortations. Some of his fiercest argument was against the continuing strands of 'communalism' he feared were still powerful in the subcontinent. Writing to the chief ministers of the states in 1953, six years after partition, he warned of the domestic dangers of a narrow nationalism which were even greater than outward national aggressiveness witnessed in Germany and Japan in the previous decade.

> But a more insidious form of nationalism is the narrowness of mind that it develops within a country, when a majority thinks itself as the entire nation and in its attempt to absorb the minority actually separates them even more . . . Communal organizations are the clearest examples of extreme narrowness of outlook, strutting about in the guise of nationalism. In the name of unity, they separate and destroy.[27]

In the early 1950s Nehru faced a number of severe challenges to his vision of an Indian unity founded on pluralism, which tested both his ideological commitment and his political skills. The first, urgent from the very birth of the new nation, was the treatment of India's religious minorities. Despite partition Muslims remained a sizeable minority of about 11 per cent in India, and there were other significant minority groups such as the Sikhs, now clustered in Indian Punjab, and Indian Christians (around 7 million in 1941). Although religious freedom was written into the constitution and Indian citizenship was accorded to people of all religious beliefs, India's minorities were often deeply fearful of the Hindu majority after independence, particularly those who had looked to the British for protection through special constitutional provisions and patronage. Moreover, there were persistent assumptions among many Hindus that India was really a Hindu country and that minorities were not to be trusted.

Nehru threw his weight against a narrow Hindu interpretation of Indian identity and argued that the welfare and integration of the religious minorities was essential for India's progress. He was particularly sensitive to the confusion and dilemmas of Muslims remaining in India after partition, and condemned Hindu tendencies to question their loyalty.

> But I think it is wrong to lay stress always on the loyalty . . . of the Muslims of India. Loyalty is not produced to order or by fear. It comes as a natural growth from circumstances which make loyalty not only a sentiment which appeals to one but also profitable in the long run. We have to produce conditions which lead to this sentiment being produced. In any event, criticism and cavilling at minorities does not help.[28]

This emphasis led to his persistent concern for a variety of aspects of the situation in which Muslims found themselves. He worried about the lack of Muslim office-holders in Congress and urged his party men to consult informally with prominent local Muslims to make up for this defect. He sensed a potentially dangerous decline in the representation of Muslims in the armed and civil services by 1953 and argued that the central and state governments had a special duty to encourage minorities and ensure that all the communities which made up India had a fair deal and an assurance of their future prospects in the country. However, despite these exhortations there was little change in the situation, and his writings and speeches at the end of the decade still stressed the problems of minority weakness and of prejudice against them in the administration and police.

Another aspect of Nehru's concern for Muslims was his personal championship of Urdu as an important language which must be nurtured and allowed to flourish alongside other regional vernaculars. Coming from the old United Provinces Nehru himself regarded Urdu as his mother tongue although he was a Hindu. But he was well aware how significant it was for Muslims in India as a language particularly associated with their culture and history. Hostility to Urdu in matters of education or administration, he argued, would only hurt large numbers of the Muslim minority just when India needed to produce 'a sense of fulfilment' in their minds.[29]

India's Christians also concerned him. Even before independence he had reassured them of their future religious freedom as Indian citizens and written publicly that they were an integral part of India with long traditions and were 'one of the many enriching elements in the country's cultural and spiritual life'.[30] Early in the 1950s he learned of harassment of Christians and discrimination against them in some areas and warned his chief ministers that this was contrary to India's basic principles. In 1953–54 when there was considerable controversy about the presence of Christian missionaries in India he refused to treat the issue as a religious one, and argued that as a secular state they should judge the matter on political grounds, particularly that of security in border areas.

Religious differences were only one of the forces which challenged Nehru's vision of a new national cohesion. He also became embroiled in matters relating to India's tribal populations, distinguished from the Hindu majority by their ethnicity and their social and economic traditions. These were to be found on the north-eastern frontier, in a belt stretching across the continent from Gujarat to Orissa, and in isolated hill areas in the south. By mid-century all tribal groups were facing increasing pressure on their older life-styles from the diminution of the wild areas which had sustained their hunting tradition and from the social and economic expectations of their settled Hindu neighbours. Some were being assimilated into Hindu society and tradition, while in the north-east groups such as the Nagas had become Christian in large numbers following the religious and social work of missionaries. In relation to tribal peoples Nehru's elitist upbringing and his strong streak of paternalism combined with his vision of national unity based on diversity. He would describe himself as being very fond of the tribal people and after a visit to the north-east in 1952 he had the grace to admit that he had previously categorised them all as primitive and backward, but now realised how different the various groups were, and how considerable were the achievements of some of them. India's policy should be one of giving them confidence in their future within the nation (just as it was for the religious minorities) and then allowing them to develop at their own pace and retaining such of their cultural distinctiveness as they wished.[31] What he hoped for was a 'middle way' – between treating them as isolated anthropological specimens and treating them just as any other citizens. The latter might sound democratic but he felt they were 'unsuited to compete with the acquisitive economy of other regions and other persons who exploit and oppress them'.[32]

However, in the north-east such a policy proved impossible to achieve because of a singular combination of circumstances. This was a border area where security was vital for the nation state. But the Naga population's sense of distinctive tribal identity, reinforced by their conversion to Christianity, was threatened by perceived pressure to assimilate into Hindu society from the state of Assam and its Hindu population, and by the threat of absorption into the regular state administration. A group of them led by A Z Phizo of the Naga National Council began to demand total independence from India, a demand which Nehru described as absurd and unacceptable. He hoped to persuade them of his government's acceptance of their need for a measure of autonomy and was anxious to avoid any punitive measures against them.[33] In the early 1950s he spent considerable time and energy on the problem, conferring with the Assam government, urging the need to appoint sensitive officials in the tribal area, visiting the area and even meeting Phizo in early 1952. Despite his personal commitment to finding a peaceful solution and to reassuring Nagas that their identity would be respected and protected the controversy degenerated into armed conflict – between a section of the Nagas and the state's considerable coercive apparatus, including the army and the police. The conflict persisted for nearly a decade, only ending with the flight of Phizo from India and the agreement of the Delhi government in 1960 to the formation of a Naga state within the Indian Union, after negotiations with those Nagas who had maintained a non-violent and non-secessionist stance.

Similar tensions between the need to maintain the unity of India and the desire to respect diversity erupted on the issue of language. Here again Nehru faced challenges to his vision of a new national identity and unity which in the early 1950s threatened to tear the country apart in violence in a way which was incomprehensible and irritating to his sophisticated and urbane conception of a composite, mutually tolerant nation.[34] India was and is a land of great linguistic diversity. The constitution recognised fourteen languages; and beyond that were many smaller dialects, some spoken by many thousands, and English, the major shared language among the educated and the principal international language through which Indians interacted with the wider political, cultural and intellectual world. But language is not just a means of communication: in India as elsewhere it is an aspect of culture and shared identity, and a means of economic and social achievement through education and administrative employment. It was therefore bound to become an explosive issue in the new state as linguistic groups reassessed their position in the new India and worked to secure their interests in relation to the new political structures and employment opportunities.

Nehru's own concern was that India's vernacular languages should flourish as languages of communication and education and enable the creative powers of those who spoke them. It was partly for this reason that he championed the cause of Urdu as the natural language of many of India's Muslims. However, he believed that India should be realistic and retain English as a means of national and international communication, while fostering Hindi as a pan-Indian vernacular language. As the constitution was being fashioned controversy was fierce between Hindi-speakers who wanted to abandon English and establish Hindi as the national language, and non-Hindi-speakers, particularly from the south, who feared the advantages this would give in government service to native speakers of Hindi. Nehru backed a pluralist compromise which provided for Hindi as the country's official language but retained English for a transitional period as the official language of the union and inter-state communication, while elevating the major regional languages to the status of national languages which would be used in their own areas. In the eyes of non-Hindi-speakers he was the champion and safeguard of linguistic diversity. But he was evidently irritated by what he had no hesitation in calling childishness and immaturity in relation to language, and in 1952, for example, he scolded audiences for this, insisting that there was no question of Hindi being imposed on anyone but that they needed it as a common language, just as they could not do without English in universities as their commitment had to be to high standards.[35]

Far more difficult to resolve was the demand for the redistribution of India's former provinces into states based on language boundaries. This had been developing in the final decades of British rule as the revitalisation of many of India's vernaculars had dovetailed with the increasing British devolution of power to Indians, thereby making the language of regional administration increasingly significant for aspiring vernacular-speakers. Congress had accepted the principle of linguistic boundaries and had organised itself on linguistic lines after the First World War as part of Gandhi's drive to popularise its work. But in the turmoil of independence, partition and the making of a constitution Nehru argued that India's security and stability were more important issues and that they should not divert their attention to what he saw as petty problems by comparison. He steered both a Constituent Assembly committee (the 1948 Dar commission) and a subsequent Congress committee consisting of himself, Patel and another prominent Congressman, P. Sitaramayya, towards rejection of any immediate tampering with existing boundaries. The 'JVP Committee', as the latter was known, after its members' initials, recognised that the primary consideration must be the security, unity and economic prosperity of India, and that linguistic provinces could only be created after very serious thought in each case and great care for the country's stability and unity. But it did recognise that public demand might make such consideration inevitable.[36] What evidently worried Nehru was not just the administrative upheaval and expense which boundary-changing might involve, but the encouragement any discussions might give to other potentially divisive tendencies in India as well as the opening up of a Pandora's Box of linguistic loyalties. The unity of India had been second only to freedom in his mind as the British had prepared for their departure, and one of his worst fears had been the possible 'Balkanisation' of India in the process of decolonisation. Now as prime minister he was determined not to sacrifice that unity to sectional interests.

However, events overtook him. The demand for a linguistic state had been strongest among the Telugu speakers of south India, who wanted an Andhra state in which they would thrive, apart from the well-educated Tamil speakers who had dominated the old Madras Presidency. This demand continued to escalate, despite the warnings of the JVP Committee, and reached flash-point with the death of one of its most vocal exponents late in 1952 following a fast on the issue. Nehru loathed the strategy of fasting – just as he had when Gandhi had fasted. But within days of the death he had announced in parliament that the government was prepared to set in motion the creation of an Andhra state It came into being in 1953, and in its final shape, including Telugu-speaking areas of former princely territory, was inaugurated by Nehru himself in 1956. During 1953 he also accepted that the process could not stop with Andhra and that public demand now necessitated a commission to consider the reorganisation of state boundaries. The Commission on States Reorganisation was set up late in the year and reported in September 1955 after a process of public hearings and reception of thousands of documentary submissions. It recognised that comparatively few of these were seriously considered and constructed, and Nehru himself was

> deeply distressed at the turn the linguistic states controversy is taking. In spite of all our attempts to keep this controversy within the bounds of reason and good sense people tend to become more and more passionate and aggressive . . . I do not know what we can do about it except to impress upon our people and, more especially our Governments, that we should deal with this problem in a friendly and dispassionate way.[37]

Following the States Reorganization Act of 1956 boundaries were re-drawn to conform more closely to linguistic boundaries, and the only further change during Nehru's prime-ministership was the division in 1960 of the old Bombay Presidency into Gujarat and Maharashtra. Nehru had been pushed towards a conclusion which he personally had deemed unnecessary and distasteful, but despite the controversies his government had achieved a resolution of the problem which eventually gave India considerable internal stability and confirmed the ideal of a national unity which respected and drew strength from various kinds of diversity.

Nehru's responses to these different but very serious challenges to India's unity show him to be a visionary, battling to go on building in people's hearts and minds as well as in institutional structures a sense of an India which was tolerant and plural, and he threw his personal prestige and authority behind this vision. On two issues he would tolerate no compromise. One was the essential political unity of the nation state. It was for this reason that he would not negotiate with Nagas who demanded independence, but equally if reluctantly was prepared to accept public demands for linguistic provinces when he saw that a refusal would accentuate rather than heal divisions. The other was his refusal to countenance communal challenges to an inclusive and secular Indian citizenship. It was for this reason that he refused to consider the claims of some Sikhs in the Punjab, led by Tara Singh, for a Punjabi-speaking state which was in essence a Sikh homeland. As early as 1948 he was saying that such Sikh demands were like the communalism of the old Muslim League and that there was nothing to choose between Tara Singh and Jinnah. Nehru believed it was a demand of astonishing futility and profoundly unpatriotic, and tried to persuade other leading Sikhs to dissociate themselves from it.[38] No change was made in Punjab's boundaries until after his death, and even then not on communal grounds. Where these two fundamentals were not at stake Nehru and his government engaged increasingly in management of potential conflict and mediation between opposing groups.

At least in his early years as prime minister Nehru exhibited some of the characteristics of an irritated schoolmaster in relation to his more volatile and tempestuous compatriots, whose concerns he considered minor compared with weighty matters of state and foreign affairs. However, his 'learning curve' was steep, as he discovered that a prime minister had to do more than expound visions of a new future and urge 'rationality' in decisions and relationships. The exercise of power in Delhi had to involve realism, sensitivity to public opinion and the skills of a manager. Although his government resolved many of the challenges to India's unity in the 1950s, and gave the country valuable time to sustain its political structures and conventions, there remained a delicate balance between all-India and particularist identities. The latter were ready to flare into aggressive demands and even violence in times of economic competition and deprivation or when later, after Nehru's death, a Delhi government played with fire and exploited such particularisms for its own advantage.

Encouraging social change

When Nehru spoke of India's minorities he often emphasised that they must be given a stake in the new India and a psychological sense that it was worth being part of the nation. The same theme occurred in his work in these early years of his prime-ministership to lay the foundations of what he saw as essential social change. Those who had traditionally been undervalued and deprived, particularly women and those at the base of Hindu society, had to be given justice and the capacity to participate in the life of the new nation: this was vital not just for them but for the country as a whole. As he told his chief ministers in 1954,

> We cannot go ahead if women do not play a full part in national progress. In fact, we cannot build up the unity of India unless there is this emotional awareness of not only political, but economic and social equality. When we talk about a secular state, this does not simply mean some negative idea, but a positive approach on the basis of equality of opportunity for everyone, man or woman, of any religion or caste, in every part of India.[39]

He reiterated to them the theme that political, economic and social progress had to proceed together. In his insistence on the need for social change Nehru was drawing on Gandhian and socialist strands within Congress's own traditions, and the commitments it had given for equality in the future, as in 1931 at its Karachi session or in 1932 after Gandhi's fast on the issue of untouchables. But he also had an acute personal sense of the history of societies and their possible fate if they ceased to be dynamic, as he had shown in writing *The Discovery of India*. He returned robustly to this theme in a speech to women in 1951 when he urged them to agitate for their rights: Indian society must change or else it 'will decay and whither away . . . and it will be thrown into the dustbin of history'.[40] Therefore another of his priorities at this stage was to use the authority of his government, and his personal influence, to initiate social changes which the imperial government had never dared to contemplate, and to begin to make real the declaration of equality among citizens placed within the constitution.

One of his major concerns was to give women a more equal status in critical domestic areas such as inheritance, divorce and adoption, and to facilitate women's participation in national life. He believed that the nation would suffer if it was deprived of their potential contribution in all fields, and that India (like any nation) would be judged by its treatment of women. He therefore threw his personal influence behind this issue, in his public rhetoric and in his private manoeuverings and exhortations. Immediately after independence, for example, he worked to ensure that women would be admitted to all public services, including the prestigious foreign service and the IAS. He told his chief ministers in mid-1952 after the first general election how shameful it was, and how damaging to the future growth of the country, that so few women had been elected to the country's legislatures. A year later he returned to the theme, telling them that it was 'the height of unwisdom' to ignore half the electorate and not welcome and encourage women into politics.[41]

His main legislative initiative on behalf of women's equality was his attempt to put through the Delhi parliament a package of legal reforms known as the Hindu Code Bill. Consideration of such a codification and modernisation of Hindu law had been initiated as early as 1941, but once it came before the Constituent Assembly after independence it encountered a broad spectrum of bitter opposition, despite the themes of equality which were being enshrined in the constitution at the same time. Even the country's president, Rajendra Prasad, threw the weight of his office against it. Nehru believed that the reforms were vital for India's progress and was surprised and dismayed at the reaction against them. As in the case of the demand for linguistic provinces, which he had similarly not anticipated, he rapidly learned that negotiation and management of the issue was essential. His law minister was Dr B.R. Ambedkar, an untouchable by caste who had risen to most unusual eminence and was a key figure in the making of the constitution To him Nehru said that it might be better to give up parts rather than risk the sabotage of the whole.[42] He pressed on, trying to find ways of achieving broad agreement, despite the president's opposition and Ambedkar's resignation in despair in September 1951. At the end of that year, after four years of struggle on the issue, he decided to break the reform up into separate parts in order to salvage something, and recognised that his initial strategy of a complete package had been misguided. Once the general election had yielded Congress a substantial majority in the legislature, and with Nehru's own increasing authority over the party, he was able to achieve four separate pieces of legislation on marriage, divorce, succession and adoption between May 1955 and the end of 1956.

Nehru's personal influence and persistence was critical for the survival and passage of this reform initiative, as Amrit Kaur, one of his women ministers (and a Christian), admitted. Although the laws as actually passed were much delayed and somewhat weaker than originally intended they were of great significance as a public sign of the new nation's ideals and expected standard for the treatment of women. They also demonstrated how broad was the interventionist and reforming role the national government had adopted in contrast to its predecessor. Nehru, however, had learnt painfully the limits of his personal influence in the context of democratic decision-making, and the need for a visionary to compromise if he was to realise at least a part of his vision in the context of politics and of wide social conservatism. And this was even before it had become possible to see whether legislation, once on the statute book, could be made effective in practice in the homes and courts of the subcontinent once its loopholes became apparent and in view of the fact that frightened and ignorant women were often unable to take up the 'rights' the law had given them.

Nehru's other social priority at this stage was to begin to make good Congress's commitments to end the deep-seated discrimination against the untouchables, those at the base of Hindu society. As in the case of women, what was done at this stage was to set in place structures and public expectations to enable longer-term social change. The most important aspect of this was legislation passed in 1955 to give legislative backing to the 'abolition' of the practice of untouchability declared in the constitution, through the Untouchability Offences Act. This made illegal discrimination 'on the ground of untouchability' in public places in such situations as access to shops, temples and wells and educational institutions, and made resulting offences punishable by a range of penalties including fines and imprisonment. It also prohibited wider social support for the practice of untouchability, for example the boycott of those who tried to use the act or the caste excommunication of those who refused to observe untouchability. Later it was to become clear how powerful local people and clever lawyers could circumvent the legislation, and how powerless and illiterate untouchables could seldom avail themselves of the law's protection.

Nehru's government recognised that empowering the untouchables was just as important as the passage of legislation and therefore set in motion a range of programmes to help them, to fulfil the directives written into the constitution. It thus embarked on one of the earliest and most outstanding attempts at 'positive discrimination' as a means of social engineering in this century. Provisions included reservation of seats in the various legislatures for the untouchables or 'Scheduled Castes', reserved places in government service and higher education, and a wide range of scholarships, loans and other protective services. The actual effects of these provisions on the lives of former untouchables and their capacity to embark on the long processes of socio-economic improvement took time to become apparent. The comparative poverty of the state at this early stage, however, made it impossible to invest the amounts of money which would have been necessary to create very rapid social change.[43] Moreover, the weight of social conservatism was still a powerful barrier to change in social relations and socio-economic opportunity at the base of society.

From the perspective of the end of the twentieth century the actual progress of India's disadvantaged in the early 1950s may still look small, and Nehru himself may seem a man of huge ideals but considerable weakness in practical implementation. Yet in the case of women and of untouchables he initiated the most remarkable use of the political arena and of state structures to pursue goals of radical social change and to spell out expectations of equality as part of the public ethos of the new nation state. In contrast to the revolutionary changes imposed with considerable violence on Russian or Chinese society, at the time Nehru's was an unprecedented attempt to change a society moulded by deeply rooted traditions by the peaceful and non-coercive means of persuasion, demonstration and democratic processes of law.

Initiating economic change

Nehru also used the prime minister's office and his personal prestige to initiate centrally planned and wide-ranging economic change. This he believed was the way to generate the resources which would in turn enable the state to engage in social investment (in health, education, programmes for the relief of poverty and discrimination, and basic infrastructure), as well as enabling individuals to improve their own quality of life and the expectations of their children. At a deeper level he argued that economic development and the fairer distribution of resources was the solid core of real independence for India and genuine democracy for its people. The 1951 Congress party election manifesto, which he prepared, stated, "The time has come for our struggle for emancipation to enter into the second phase of realising those objectives [of Congress and the constitution], without which political freedom can have little meaning for most of us. Economic progress must therefore be given first priority, subject only to the maintenance of the freedom and integrity of the country.' Five years later, discussing the country's proposed Second Five-Year Plan, he saw no contradiction between democracy and planned development towards a more socialist economic structure. 'Indeed, I would say that there is an ultimate conflict between a democracy and an economic structure which does not lead to economic democracy.'[44]

In the early 1950s Nehru was determined to set in place structures of planning and decision-making at the centre of the polity, and structures of ownership and socio-economic relationships which would be the foundations for sustained economic growth and the redistribution of resources. For him this was using his power and that of the new nation state to create the very antithesis of the imperialism he had fought and criticised – to replace the international economic priorities of an imperial regime and undermine the entrenched and privileged groups in India's socio-economic structures which he believed had been sustained by the British raj. Initially he spoke of India's goal as the creation of a 'cooperative commonwealth' based on equality of opportunity and equal political, social and economic rights, in which people would cooperate with each other for their own and the public good. It was a vision of a new type of society aimed at the welfare of the people which had to be achieved by finding a middle way between the obvious dangers of authoritarianism and of unregulated private enterprise. But by 1954 – as he saw the dimensions of India's poverty and her people's needs, and as he became more secure in his leadership of the Congress party and of the Lok Sabha in Delhi – he began to define the goal in the more radical terms of a 'socialist pattern of society'. He told his chief ministers that this was the only ideal which would suit India's particular problems and conditions: 'our various differences and disruptive tendencies such as communalism, casteism and provincialism can only be countered effectively by this wider approach which leads to a socialist basis of society. But I equally believe in a peaceful and democratic approach.'[45] In December 1954 the Lok Sabha passed a resolution in favour of a socialist pattern of society and a month later Congress accepted that this should be its goal. Nehru believed this to be a considerable advance in policy and was considerably heartened by the Congress meeting at Avadi which had accepted the new goal. But Nehru's government was the prime mover in this shift, and it is doubtful whether to other Congressmen it meant much more than a form of words.

One of Nehru's major commitments – and achievements – in the early 1950s was the development of structures through which India's economy could be planned. He had been involved with preparations for national planning from the late 1930s, believing this to be the only way to tackle India's problems as a whole rather than by tinkering and patchwork. At a personal level he found it immensely exciting, and where others might have seen dry statistics he saw processes which could affect millions of his countrymen, and a unique experiment in planned socio-economic change by democratic methods. However, there was opposition to the idea of planning towards major socio-economic reform within Congress and the cabinet and it was only after acrimonious debate that Nehru was able in March 1950 to achieve the establishment of a Planning Commission.[46] From the outset he was its chairman, and through it he exercised increasingly unchallenged authority over the making of economic and social policy. Although it was an advisory body, with decision-making powers remaining vested in the cabinet and parliament, it became increasingly powerful, particularly in the mid-1950s. The functions and boundaries between it and the central government became blurred, and a small group of the prime minister's hand-picked sympathisers dominated it under his leadership, with the assistance of an elaborate secretariat of technical experts who gathered detailed information on which policy could be based. Outside it, in Congress, in parliament and in the states, few had the expertise to challenge it.

The First Five-Year Plan, approved by parliament late in 1952, was modest in its scope and built mainly on existing development projects. Nehru accepted that it was cautious and moderate, but believed that it was the start of the process of building a new India and that they should work at it with missionary fervour and try to involve and enthuse ordinary people with it. However cautious by comparison with Nehru's aspirations, it set India on the road to state direction and increasing control of the economy with the intent of reducing poverty and ensuring that ownership and control of resources were distributed to achieve the common good. Over Rs 20 billion were to be spent under the Plan. Eventually 27 per cent went on agriculture, 18 per cent on transport, but only 12 per cent on industry and mining.

It was only with the preparations for the second plan in 1954 that the longer-term strategy espoused by Nehru and the Planning Commission became clear – as the conservative challenge within Congress diminished and he had established the dominance of the Commission in the processes of policy-making. A more ambitious approach was also possible because the first plan, aided by good monsoon rainfall, appeared to be achieving considerable success in creating badly needed economic stability and a clear 18 per cent growth in national income. Not only were the social goals of policy more radical after the 1955 Avadi Congress: now Nehru and his planners, principally advised by the economist Professor P.C. Mahalanobis, put forward a strategy which placed far greater stress on the dominant role of the state and on the importance of encouraging capital-goods industry. Planned investment would be more than double that of the first plan, while the proportion spent on agriculture would decrease and that on large-scale industry would rise significantly.

It was from this time that the main lines of India's subsequent economic policy under Nehru became clear, with the development of a strategy which emphasised the importance of heavy industry to lessen India's reliance on imports, and a dominant role for the state both as owner of basic and strategic industries and as director of private capital within the framework of the plan by a range of licensing and import controls. India was still a basically agricultural society and economy, but it seemed clear to the planners, looking at European and other examples of rapid economic development, that industrialisation was the only strategy which would eventually generate the resources to alleviate mass poverty, increase national wealth for a wide range of desirable expenditures, and also end India's reliance on exports of raw materials which had in living memory put the country at the mercy of erratic international price levels and might open the way to external influence which looked like 'neo-imperialism'. One small strand of Gandhian thinking only remained – encouragement of cottage and small-scale industry. But the rationale here was not a Gandhian one of simplicity and local self-reliance, but rather that of providing for consumers' needs and combating unemployment. Consequently spending was boosted in this area but was still only a third of that allocated for larger industry under the second plan. For the first time Nehru and his planners had to think seriously about the resources for expenditure under the plan. They turned to taxation, domestic borrowing, foreign aid and deficit financing. The long-term economic and social results of this ambitious programme of socio-economic management and engineering only became apparent in the later 1950s when Nehru had to face the issues of implementation.

In spite of the increasing emphasis on rapid industrialisation Nehru and his policy-makers were aware that in a country where the vast majority remained agriculturalists it was essential to tackle problems of agricultural productivity – not just to grow food but to liberate surpluses which could be reinvested. The multiple problems of the Indian countryside, with its manifestations of poverty, debt and lack of dynamism, had been issues the British had recognised but never tried to tackle except in piecemeal fashion when necessity drove them on. Congress as a body came to power committed to abolishing large-scale landlords, *zamindars*, and intermediaries who drew rents from land but contributed little to agricultural productivity. The party of course needed to confirm its standing among its rural voters, and also remembered how large landlords had supported the British and helped to create deep rural distress in the 1930s. Nehru came from the old United Provinces, one of the areas where there was a sizeable landlord class. *Zamindari* abolition was one of his personal priorities and he believed it to be an essential preliminary to tackling the problems of the countryside and enabling the fairer redistribution of land. Soon after independence most Congress state governments moved to abolish *zamindari* in their areas by local legislation. However, in Bihar state legislation was challenged in the courts on a number of grounds, including the allegation that it contravened Article 14 of the constitution which gave equality before the law and the equal protection of the law to all citizens. Nehru was deeply concerned about this setback, believing that the Bihar problem threatened the policy of abolishing large landlords throughout the country; and by 1950 he recognised that they might have to resort even to an alteration of the constitution to prevent such challenges. In a note to his home minister in July 1950 he wrote, 'I have long felt that this agrarian problem is far the most important of all our problems and the stability of any Government of India depends upon the manner of solving it.'[47] Later evidence shows how exasperated he was that even the constitution could stand in the way of urgent reform. Eventually in mid-1951 parliament amended the constitution and made it impossible for *zamindari*-abolition legislation to be challenged in the courts.

Although this battle had paved the way for a more equitable distribution of land Nehru and his planners recognised that much more needed to be done to help those at the base of rural society, many of whom had no land or whose holdings were uneconomic. The first plan urged a solution through village cooperatives which were to manage schemes of joint farming. But these were to be voluntary. It was to facilitate local moves to self-help that the Community Development programme was begun in 1952. Of the money laid aside for agricultural development in the budget for the first plan more than a quarter was assigned to this programme, with a third as much again ear-marked for the cooperative programme. However, as the planners contemplated a second plan it was evident that little had been done in practice to set up village cooperatives,and they now turned to the strategy of encouraging peasant agriculture by placing 'ceilings' on individual landholdings. Detailed proposals were not ready until 1956, and it was only in the years immediately before Nehru's death that the states eventually began to pass 'ceiling legislation'. Nehru was forced to return to agrarian problems with growing concern in the later phase of his prime-ministership as change on the ground proved far more difficult than changes in policy or even in law.

None the less in these critical and turbulent years after independence Nehru had gone a considerable way towards setting up the institutional and policy framework for socio-economic change of the sort he had envisaged as a nationalist leader when jail had allowed him to write at length about his vision of a new, egalitarian and more prosperous society and the way the state would take on a creative role in its making. Unlike many later leaders of movements for political independence he had never lost his vision or been content just with political freedom. Nor had he used the resources of the new state for his own personal benefit or that of his family in ways which later became familiar in the wake of decolonisation. Rather, he had striven to make freedom a socio-economic reality for a broad swathe of Indians, regardless of the difficulties such a stance created for him as an individual, and the struggles with his own countrymen into which it had plunged him.

Foreign affairs

The pursuit of these domestic priorities was hugely demanding in terms of vision, energy and time, particularly given Nehru's insistence on personal involvement with issues he thought were crucial for India's integration and development. The way they piled up in the early 1950s, making it impossible to deal with them one at a time, would have defeated a less robust individual. It was hardly surprising that at times Nehru confessed to exhaustion. However, he also had to deal with foreign affairs. Ironically this was the area where the structures of governance gave him the freest hand and the most power to determine policy. He continued to be his own foreign minister, and there were few colleagues who had the knowledge and position to challenge him on international matters, while in the country at large there was comparatively little discussion of foreign policy. He faced a rapidly changing world, particularly in the Asian region, where there was considerable turmoil and the potential for dangerous conflict, and was personally equipped with no diplomatic training and assisted by a foreign service he had had to build up from scratch at independence. As he looked out from Delhi in the early years of the decade he saw instability on India's borders, created by the running sore of the Kashmir conflict with Pakistan compounded by internal political difficulties in the Indian part of the state, by domestic conflict in Nepal, and by Chinese military movement into Tibet from 1950. Beyond, in Asia, there were conflicts generated by the contested endings of the British, Dutch and French empires, by the emergence of communist China as a regional power, and by the growing impact on the region of the developing Cold War. Moreover the United Nations, a new international institution and forum to enable cooperation and peaceful resolution of disputes, increasingly seemed to him to be dominated by the USA and manipulated for that nation's own interests.

Nehru had set out the main priorities of India's foreign policy immediately after independence. Beyond the most obvious priority of defending India's own territorial integrity, they included continued opposition to world-wide imperialism and the development of a creative role for Asia in world affairs, commitment to world peace, and on India's own part a stance of non-alignment with any great power bloc. (See Chapter 3.) In Nehru's pursuit of these goals several threads of achievement become clear. Though it would be inaccurate to call him a figure of 'power' in the international arena in the sense that one could use that term of the leader of a world power or the head of a major international organisation, by the mid-1950s he had become a figure of considerable international influence, as a result of his travels, for example to the USA, England and China, his presence at the Commonwealth and other international conferences, and his commitment to an Indian contribution in major international debates. His stature was clear, for example, when in 1954 Chou en-Lai, prime minister of the People's Republic of China, asked to visit him on his way home from Geneva, or when in 1955 Churchill put their past differences on Indian independence behind him and told him of his unparalleled role in making India the leading exponent of ideals of freedom and democracy and his outstanding part in world affairs.[48]

Even more than the development of personal stature as an international figure, Nehru had also achieved for India the standing of a significant player on the world stage, yet one whose policies and influence were independent of the former colonial power or of either of the two emerging world powers, the USA and the USSR. This was clear, for example, in Nehru's determination not to waver on Kashmir or give way to what he saw as UN pressure manipulated by America and Britain: at this stage discussions with the UN mediator became bogged down on the issues of demilitarisation and the appropriate conditions for a plebiscite. India's distinctive and growing role was also clear in the timing of her recognition of 'new' national governments, as in the case of China, in her argument that China should be admitted to the UN, and in her considerable mediation to bring the Korean war to an end. Even the Soviet leaders, who had initially presumed that India's foreign policy would merely follow that of Britain after independence, recognised in the early 1950s that India's policies were her own, and that she was worth cultivating. Meanwhile the American leadership was increasingly worried about its inability to mould India for its own Cold War policies and turned to a military alliance with Pakistan as part of its strategy to contain communism. But Nehru refused even then to alter the country's stance. As he explained to his chief ministers at the end of 1953,

> Some people think that this new danger would make us think again about our foreign policy, and that the pressure and fear of coming events might induce us to give up our attitude of non-alignment to power groups. This is a complete misreading of the situation. The policy that we have been pursuing has not been based on temporary advantage or fear but has grown out of our national way of thinking with its roots in the long past. It is the inevitable result of the state of affairs in Asia and in the world. That policy we are going to adhere to, even though our frontiers may have to face a new threat. It would be unfortunate that Pakistan should gradually lose her independence and become a satellite and almost a colony. That would be a reversal of the great process of the liberation of Asia which is one of the striking developments of the modern age.[49]

This letter also demonstrated Nehru's idealistic approach to foreign affairs and his reading of history. He believed passionately that the righting of old wrongs would flow from the destruction of imperialism and the resurgence of new nations, and was determined to try to ensure that these new nations threw their weight behind international peace as well as domestic reconstruction, rather than becoming entangled with the Cold War calculations and alliances of the two great powers. It was for this reason that he threw himself behind the idea of a conference of the independent nations of Asia and Africa to be held at Bandung in Indonesia, in April 1955. Twenty-nine countries were eventually represented, and the gathering demonstrated the significance of those areas of the world which were now striving to build new identities for themselves, free both of western imperialism and of dominance by western power blocs. It was also a demonstration of new hopes for peace, international cooperation and the fostering of human rights. Its purpose was largely symbolic, rather than the pursuit of a specific agenda, and there remained considerable differences between participants, particularly on issues of international organisation for defence. But Nehru believed that despite such differences the participants had in a totally new way come together, got to know each other and discovered how much they had in common:

> we have gone some way towards helping the creation of this common feeling among these countries. What is even more important is the psychological impact of this Conference on the peoples of Asia and Africa and also in Europe and America. This impact, though imponderable, will have far-reaching consequences . . . Everyone present at the Conference had a sense of participation in a historic process . . . The Conference has opened a new chapter not only in Asia and Africa, but in the world.[50]

In his idealistic hopes for a new and non-aligned world of cooperation to be built by countries newly freed from the burdens of imperial rule Nehru was dangerously blind to other possible sources of violence and coercion. His fears of entanglement with the power blocs in process of construction during the Cold War reinforced this attitude. Consequently, and despite his remarkable international stance and achievements, he failed to recognise the potential danger of a resurgent China for India's territorial integrity. His own understanding of the common cultural heritage of all Asian peoples and their common need to assert their national and regional independence of the western world predisposed him to offer a cautious welcome to the new leaders of China after the communist revolution of 1949. It should also be recognised that China's internal politics and decision-making structures were almost a closed book to outsiders, and therefore all international leaders were to an extent working in the dark in their relationships with China. However, in 1950 Chinese troops began to move into Tibet and some of Nehru's colleagues expressed their disquiet. Vallabhbhai Patel wrote to Nehru on 7 November and argued that they had gone out of their way to assuage China's feelings on a range of international issues, but now China was behaving as a potential enemy of India and had expanded virtually to India's gates. He urged Nehru to recognise that communists could be imperialists, too, and that communist ideology in fact made Chinese irredentism and imperialism even more dangerous than the imperialism of the western powers. He expanded on the troubles India already had on its borders – troubles which the Chinese could exploit – and urged that they must assess the danger realistically and build up their potential for armed defence, as well as strengthening their communications

and intelligence. Nehru had obviously been worried and surprised by the Chinese advance, and had not understood what
lay behind it. None the less, on reflection, within ten days of
Patel's broadside, he argued that the main danger to India still
came from Pakistan. He thought it was 'exceedingly unlikely'
that China would invade India in the foreseeable future, though
he was concerned about possible Chinese infiltration and believed that they must take precautions against this. Further, he
had accepted that China was likely to become politically dominant in Tibet now, and that India could do nothing to stop it.[51]

Nehru persisted in thinking that there was little danger
to India's north-east frontier, and argued that India's policy
towards China should be friendliness combined with the firm
protection of India's interests. The culmination of this policy
came in 1954, when the two countries signed an agreement
on Tibet, and later in the year Chou en-Lai visited Delhi and
Nehru went to Peking. The agreement provided for the withdrawal of India's remaining influence in Tibet, effectively trust-
ing Indian security in the region to a positive relationship with
China rather than the presence of a buffer zone. In it also
were enshrined five principles of that relationship, the so-called
Panchsheel which were increasingly present in Nehru's thinking
about Indo-Chinese relations. (These were mutual respect for
each other's territorial integrity and sovereignty, mutual non-
aggression, mutual non-interference in each other's internal
affairs, equality and mutual benefit, and peaceful coexistence.)
Nehru also seems to have been convinced that there were no
problems with the Indian border and declined to push for
direct discussions on the border issue and clarification of it
as the agreement on Tibet was being formulated. At the time
of Chou en-Lai's visit to India he reiterated his policy towards
China to his chief ministers, emphasising the importance for
Asia and the world of their two countries building up a positive relationship. He clearly found he could do business with
the Chinese leader and liked his apparent freedom from the
slogans and clichés of 'the average Communist'.[52] At the end
of 1954, after his visit to China, he wrote in the same positive
tone about China's peaceful intentions in international affairs,
his own lack of concern about their common border because
he felt it was quite clear and not a matter for argument, and
their common problems and concerns for domestic economic
development. Despite their different ideologies, 'We entirely

agreed that we should respect each other's viewpoints and without interference co-operate in dealing with our problems. More especially we should co-operate in the maintenance of peace in Asia and the world at large.'[53] In his own mind Nehru was content with the apparent impact of his own vision of Asia and its importance for the future, and certainly in China saw nothing which might deter him from his commitment to non-alignment.

.   .   .

In the early 1950s Nehru's dominance over policy-making in India was seldom challenged, either on domestic or foreign issues. He showed himself to be a human dynamo, capable of working on a huge range of issues, and a visionary who saw the multiple aspects of the reconstruction of his country as necessary in order to make political independence a living reality for the vast majority of his countrymen. He was also, ironically, an authoritarian figure committed to democracy and the development of popular involvement in the processes of change. However, the singular importance of one man was to prove deeply problematic in the long run. In foreign affairs so much had come to depend on his vision and his reading of other nations and their policies. In domestic affairs his energy and influence helped to put new policies and ideals into place, but these alone were no guarantee of self-sustaining change without also ensuring that the instruments for policy implementation were also in place and that public opinion was behind them. Moreover, the long shadow he threw over the political system inhibited the flourishing of other younger men and their training as potential leaders who could help him with the growing burden of national leadership as he aged. His enduring presence undoubtedly did much to maintain India's stability and democracy, but it delayed the necessary processes of creating legitimacy for a new generation of potential national leaders who did not have the cachet of nationalist leadership or the connection with Gandhi.

.   .   .

NOTES AND REFERENCES

1. Speech in Chicago, 27 October 1949, *SWJN(2)*, vol. 13, p. 359.
2. Nehru to V. Pandit, 20 March 1950, *SWJN(2)*, vol. 14 i, pp. 132–3; see also Nehru to V. Patel, 20 and 21 February 1950, ibid., pp. 47–9, 49–51.

3. Nehru to J. Matthai, 4 May 1950, *SWJN(2)*, vol. 14 ii, p. 232.
4. Nehru to Sri Prakasa, 11 November 1951, *SWJN(2)*, vol. 17, pp. 629–31.
5. Foreword by J. Nehru to D.G. Tendulkar (ed.), *Mahatma. Volume 1 1869–1920* ([1951] Delhi: Government of India, 1960), pp. x–xi.
6. Nehru to R. Prasad, 8 December 1949, *SWJN(2)*, vol. 14 i, pp. 427–31.
7. Nehru to chief ministers, 10 April and 17 May 1951, *LCM*, vol. 2, pp. 369–70, 393–4.
8. Speeches on 27 November and 12 December 1951, *SWJN(2)*, vol. 17, pp. 48–54, 54–60; notes by Nehru for Congress Working Committee, 31 January 1952, and to PCC presidents, 8 February 1952, ibid., pp. 100–6, 131–5.
9. See S.A. Kochanek, *The Congress Party of India. The Dynamics of One-Party Democracy* (Princeton: Princeton University Press, 1968), pp. 7–8.
10. Nehru to P. Tandon, 9 August 1951, *SWJN(2)*, vol. 16 ii, pp. 157–9. This volume has key documents relating to this crisis, pp. 131 ff.
11. Nehru to B.C. Roy, 17 August 1951, ibid., pp. 160–1. For a detailed account of this episode see Kochanek, *The Congress Party of India*, pp. 27–53.
12. Cited in R. Jeffrey, 'The Prime Minister and The Ruling Party', in J. Manor (ed.), *Nehru to the Nineties. The Changing Office of the Prime Minister in India* (London: Hurst, 1994), p. 165.
13. Nehru to chief ministers, 22 September 1952, *LCM*, vol. 3, pp. 621–2.
14. Nehru to Krishna Menon, 25 August 1950, *SWJN(2)*, vol. 15 i, p. 101.
15. B. Parekh, 'Jawaharlal Nehru and the Crisis of Modernisation', in U. Baxi and B. Parekh (eds), *Crisis and Change in Contemporary India* (New Delhi, Newbury Park (Calif.) and London: Sage, 1995), pp. 21–56.
16. Nehru to chief ministers, 16 June 1952, *LCM*, vol. 3, p. 18.
17. Nehru to Mountbatten, 22 January 1952, *SWJN(2)*, vol. 17, p. 95.
18. Nehru to C. Trivedi, 24 June 1951, *SWJN(2)*, vol. 16 i, p. 306.
19. See, for example, Nehru's firm letter to the very senior Congressman C. Rajagopalachariar, 17 February 1952, and his 3 February 1952 note on the proper constitutional procedure in Madras, *SWJN(2)*, vol. 17, pp. 333, 323–6.
20. Nehru to chief ministers, 3 February 1949, *SWJN(2)*, vol. 9, p. 304.
21. Nehru to C. Rajagopalachariar, 11 September 1951, *SWJN(2)*, vol. 16 ii, pp. 469–70.
22. Nehru to chief ministers, 4 October 1951, *LCM*, vol. 2, pp. 502–4.
23. Nehru to chief ministers, 2 March 1951, ibid., p. 349; 25 July 1952, *LCM*, vol. 3, pp. 60–2.

24. Nehru to chief ministers, 5 July 1952, 28 September 1953, ibid., pp. 38–9, 394.
25. Cited in D. Potter, 'The Prime Minister and the Bureaucracy', in Manor (ed.), *Nehru to the Nineties*, p. 85. Letters to chief ministers, 1953–54, on the Appleby Report, are in *LCM*, vol. 3, eg. pp. 296–7, 392, 402–3, 413–14, 424–31, 482–3, 539–40.
26. *National Herald* 10 February 1956 cited in R.D. King, *Nehru and the Language Politics of India* (Delhi: Oxford University Press, 1997), p. 132.
27. Nehru to chief ministers, 20 September 1953, *LCM*, vol. 3, p. 380.
28. Nehru to chief ministers, 1 March 1950, *LCM*, vol. 2, p. 41.
29. Nehru to chief ministers, 20 September 1953, *LCM*, vol. 3, pp. 377–9.
30. Interview to the *Catholic Herald* (London), 1946, *SWJN(1)*, vol. 15, p. 171.
31. Enclosure, 29 October 1953, in Nehru to chief ministers, 30 October 1952, *LCM*, vol. 3, pp. 147–165.
32. Nehru to B. Medhi, 2 February 1951, *SWJN(2)*, vol. 15 ii, pp. 183–4.
33. Ibid., pp. 182–7.
34. On Nehru and issues relating to language see King, *Nehru and the Language Politics of India*.
35. Speeches on 25 September and 9 October 1952, *SWJN(2)*, vol. 19, pp. 27, 66–7.
36. Draft of JVP report, accepted by the committee on 26 March 1949, *SWJN(2)*, vol. 10, pp. 128–37.
37. Nehru to chief ministers, 15 June 1954, *LCM*, vol. 3, p. 568.
38. Nehru to G. Bhagarva, 24 November 1948, *SWJN(2)*, vol. 8, p. 152; Nehru to chief ministers, 15 July 1950, *LCM*, vol. 2, pp. 149–50.
39. Nehru to chief ministers, 15 August 1954, *LCM*, vol. 4, p. 21.
40. Speech by Nehru, 31 January 1951, *SWJN(2)*, vol. 15 ii, pp. 194–5.
41. Nehru to chief ministers, 18 May 1952, *LCM*, vol. 2, p. 64; Nehru to chief ministers, 20 September 1953, *LCM*, vol. 3, p. 381. (In this election nineteen women had been elected to the Lok Sabha and eighty-two to state legislative assemblies.)
42. Nehru to B.R. Ambedkar, 8 June 1949, *SWJN(2)*, vol. 11, pp. 207–8. A detailed study of this episode is R. Som, 'Jawaharlal Nehru and the Hindu code: A Victory of Symbol over Substance?', in *Modern Asian Studies*, 26 (1) (February 1994), pp. 165–94.
43. In 1951–6 under half a rupee was planned as per capita government expenditure on scheduled caste uplift. M. Galanter, *Competing Inequalities. Law and the Backward Classes in India* (Delhi: Oxford University Press, [1984] 1991), p. 57.

44. Congress election manifesto, July 1951, *SWJN(2)*, vol. 16 ii, p. 4; Nehru to chief ministers, 16 January 1956, *LCM*, vol. 4, p. 337.
45. Nehru to chief ministers, 9 December 1954, ibid., pp. 101–2.
46. On planning see F.R. Frankel, *India's Political Economy 1947–1977. The Gradual Revolution* (Delhi: Oxford University Press, 1978); B.R. Tomlinson, *The Economy of Modern India 1860–1970* (Cambridge: Cambridge University Press, 1993), ch. 4.
47. Nehru's note to home minister, 22 July 1950, *SWJN(2)*, vol. 14 ii, p. 223.
48. W. Churchill to Nehru, 21 February and 30 June 1955, cited in S. Gopal, *Jawaharlal Nehru*, 3 vols (London: Jonathan Cape, 1973–84), vol. 2, pp. 256–7.
49. Nehru to chief ministers, 1 December 1953, *LCM*, vol. 3, p. 455.
50. Note on Bandung conference, 28 April 1955, sent to chief ministers, *LCM*, vol. 4, pp. 159–71.
51. V. Patel to Nehru, 7 November 1950, D. Das (ed.), *Sardar Patel's Correspondence 1945–50*, vol. X, pp. 335–41.
52. Nehru to chief ministers, 1 July 1954, *LCM*, vol. 3, pp. 580–601.
53. Note by Nehru, 15 November 1954, sent to chief ministers, *LCM*, vol. 4, pp. 76–89.

Chapter 5

THE LIMITS OF POWER

In the mid-1950s Nehru embarked on what was to be the final phase of his prime-ministership and of his long and varied career. He was by this time well on into his sixties, and at a time in his life when many people naturally contemplate a slowing down of professional work if not formal retirement. It is remarkable, however, that virtually no Indian politicians of his own or his father's generation withdrew from active public work. Motilal and Gandhi had both died in harness, as had Nehru's nearer contemporary, Vallabhbhai Patel. Far deeper than the material rewards of public influence or office, they seemed never to lose the drive originally generated by the heady days of involvement in the nationalist movement and association with Gandhi. Nehru had been in public life for nearly four decades, and had shown himself capable of considerable adaptation and responsiveness to new situations and challenges. He had turned himself from a disenchanted young lawyer into nationalist activist, ideologue and opponent of government, and in 1947 into the leader of a new state with all the attendant demands of administration and policy-making, for which he had little prior training.

In his early years in the prime minister's office he had had to deal with urgent issues central to the very existence of the new India, ranging from external defence, to internal stability and cohesion, to the construction of institutions and procedures of democratic government; and simultaneously had become visionary and apologist for a new type of national community and society. Now from the mid-1950s he faced the longer-term problems of the implementation of policies, and of determining how government should respond to the wishes and felt needs of an increasingly demanding citizenry. He still had a unique status in the country, and was buoyed up by his vision of a new India and by remarkable physical stamina. But in what might have been expected to be the final flowering of his career it became evident that there were severe limits to his power to control events in the country at large and indeed to shape and inform the actions of governmental agencies. The later commentator can also discern how his particular style and skills proved increasingly dysfunctional, and how he failed in these final years to develop new attitudes and techniques to meet the challenges of a changing environment.

There is evidence that Nehru himself was in these years more prone to periods of exhaustion and despair, and sometimes of ill-health, before his final and mercifully brief illness. Moreover, he could be sharply imperious towards and critical of Indians, in ways which echoed the discourse of earlier British rulers about their divided and narrow-minded subjects, who were deemed to be incompetent in public work. On 1 August 1957 he wrote to his chief ministers of his fear that 'we are succumbing to our old and corroding disease of lack of unity, disruptive tendencies and narrowness of outlook'. They seemed to have lost the vision which had once inspired and strengthened them, were miring themselves 'in petty controversies and conflicts', and were lapsing into complacency and parochialism. In October he returned to this theme: 'When I think of the high mission that India is supposed to have, and then of what one finds in India today in the way of conflict over petty matters, caste and language, and the degeneration of our public life, I am a little disheartened. The gap between what we proclaim and what we do is terribly wide.'[1] In March 1958 he admitted to being stale and tired, and taking little pleasure in his work. He was aware that this was not a proper state for one called to bear the responsibilities of high office, and began to wonder about leaving what he admitted was the daily drudgery of office for a while, to rest and give himself time for serious thinking. The Congress party, not unnaturally, did not allow him to pursue this idea, and the leaders of the world's two superpowers also worried about such an absence. All Nehru achieved in the way of a recuperative break were two short holidays in May and June in Manali, in the Himalayan foothills. Although these clearly did him good, a year later he was admitting that he found it difficult even to keep pace with just the urgent demands of each day.

It was not so much the range of domestic and international problems which depressed him. He was temperamentally a romantic and a fighter who rose to challenges. What distressed and dragged him down was frustration at his inability to achieve real change even in response to glaring domestic problems. For example, in 1961 he said that one of the things which disheartened him most as prime minister was the failure over so many years in office to find a real solution to India's problem of slums, primarily because of vested interests and of the amazingly slow functioning of municipal government. Such was his 'utter sense of frustration' that he thought power should be given to competent individuals or small committees who had authority to go ahead without being held up by people objecting to change.[2] Here was a man who, at the end of a life dedicated to achieving a democratic and self-governing India, was contemplating an administrative solution by experts in place of the messy business of self-governance, and attempting to escape from the bargaining and management of interests and groups essential to democracy. In old age the paternalist element in his character was very evident, reflecting the sense of constraint he increasingly felt, despite his office and reputation, on his ability to use power for what he saw as manifest public good.

This chapter focuses on the last phase of Nehru's life, and seeks to explore issues of the implementation of Nehru's vision of a new India and her place in the wider world. The evidence underlines the constraints on the prime minister's exercise of power and freedom to manoeuvre. Three intertwining themes will emerge. One is the issue of the depth and spread within India of a will for change, or whether the persistence of deeply rooted social structures and attitudes and of vested interests meant that Nehru was out of step with the majority of Indians and indeed with many of his own colleagues and party members. Another recurring theme is the weakness of the instruments available to achieve change and whether the instruments of government could indeed work to thwart Nehru's hopes and policies. Finally there is the issue of available resources with which to pursue the reconstruction of India's economy and society as envisaged in the public rhetoric of the Congress party and the state, particularly financial resources given the need for major investment in a wide range of economic and social programmes.

Exploring the limits to Nehru's power raises even longer-term questions about the Indian state and political system. Nehru achieved the highest political office in a unique way, at the culmination of a nationalist movement led by Gandhi and the peaceful withdrawal of an imperial ruler. As he aged, people increasingly wondered who or what could replace him. No subsequent national leader would come to prominence in the same way as he had done, and the political system had been profoundly changed in the meantime by the coming of adult franchise and the forming of the new federal constitution. For the political analyst this poses problems of new pathways to all-India leadership, while Nehru's experiences in office raise the question of what kind of leadership at the national level would be effective in so vast and diverse a democratic society. India had in 1949 rejected the model of an authoritarian national government, which was the only type of government which had at that time embarked on radical domestic change. Instead her constitution-makers had commited their country to democratic and federal government. In such a political system what sort of individual or composite leadership in Delhi could emerge which would be effective and built on solid foundations? Moreover, what skills would be required of aspiring national leaders in such changed political circumstances? Nehru always hankered after the heady days of anti-imperial struggle. He was increasingly depressed and constrained by the realities of democratic politics and government. Would subsequent leaders try to cast off such constraints or would they have the skills to manage the diverse interests within India and draw sustenance from them while building up a national sense of identity and purpose? Since Nehru's death India has struggled to find answers to the questions which began to be raised by his own experience of an office which appears to offer to its holder great power over one of the largest societies and states in the world.

.　.　.

STATE AND SOCIETY

An investigation of Nehru's ability to implement his vision of a new India, and to use the power which his office seemed to offer, must focus first on the nature of the Indian state and its relationship with society. To Nehru, the role of the state was paramount in the achievement of change; and it was for this reason that he had fought so hard to wrest it from imperial control and to refashion it for new purposes after 1947. In this he was quite unlike his mentor, Gandhi, whose vision of truly radical change had little role for the state and its organised structures of politics. For him India's transformation, and true *swaraj*, could come only from below, being rooted in the transformation of individual lives and achieved by self-help and self-control. Nehru, by contrast, belonged with the vast mass of Congressmen who had given little credence to Gandhi's 'constructive programme'. His intellectual training in a western radical tradition and his awareness of the magnitude of India's problems and needs made him turn to the state as the primary motor, planner and coordinator of change. In his view it alone could summon the sort of resources needed for the task, and its structures and rhetoric were the most truly national in spread which could be used to inculcate a new commitment to change. Such a new role for the nation state should, moreover, be possible because it had gained a new legitimacy at independence, subsequently reinforced by the first general election on a mass franchise.

However, by the later 1950s the Indian state was barely a decade old, a decade which had seen profound crises and threats of major instability. Was it by this stage sufficiently stable and endowed with legitimacy to perform the radical and intrusive functions which Nehru envisaged for it? Compared with its earliest years, marked by the turbulence and challenge of the aftermath of partition, the integration of the former princely states and latterly the issue of linguistic provinces, the state was comparatively stable. There were still sources of opposition to it as constituted, but these created localised turbulence and were not linked up into a generalised challenge to its legitimacy. Naga opposition in the north-east persisted throughout the decade, and the problem was only resolved with the creation of a separate state of Nagaland, divided from Assam in 1963. The violent resistance to the state had in the mean time elicited a violent response, including deployment of an entire army division and other paramilitary forces, and draconian administrative action. Meanwhile another tribal revolt in the same area, by the Mizo people, began to develop into similar resistance to incorporation into Assam, and this was not resolved until well after Nehru's death. These explicit challenges to the state stemmed from the intersection of ethnic and linguistic conflicts between groups peculiar to Assam and its patterns of settlement and migration. In the north-west, another challenge to the integrity of the state came from the demand of a section of the Sikh community for special political status. In Nehru's eyes this was not a legitimate cultural or linguistic demand for recognition but communalism again rearing its head, and it received short shrift, leaving over 21,500 militant demonstrators in Punjabi jails when demand turned into organised resistance.

By contrast linguistic differences and demands, though on occasion disruptive of public order, posed less of a threat to the state and its legitimacy than in earlier years. The worst incidence of public violence occurred in Bombay among speakers of Gujarati and Marathi over the bifurcation of the old presidency and the fate of cosmopolitan Bombay city, with all its skills and resources. Eventually Bombay was divided into the states of Gujarat and Maharashtra in 1960 and Bombay city went to the latter. The capacity of the state, and of Nehru himself, to soothe fears about language and to achieve compromise and contain difference was also clear when southerners began to feel that Hindi might soon be imposed on them as the transitional period earlier agreed to began to run out. In 1963 the Official Languages Act declared that Hindi would indeed become the sole official language of India, as envisaged in the constitution, but accepted that English would remain indefinitely as an additional official language. Nehru also gave his personal assurances in parliament that no state would have Hindi imposed on it. He was sensitive to the fears of non-Hindi-speakers, aware of the divisive potential of the controversy over the status of Hindi and English, and also realistic about the significance to India of English as a world language.[3]

Other sources of discontent led to violence between citizens, but not directed at the state itself. These included riots on religious grounds, as in Madhya Pradesh in 1961, conflicts between lower and higher castes, student 'indiscipline', and agrarian and industrial unrest. Taken over all, these were not a severe threat at any time to the state's ability to preserve public order; nor were they as numerous or destabilising as in later years after Nehru's death.

In the longer term and a far deeper challenge to the state itself was the growing politicisation of individuals and of a whole range of pressure groups, who, because of the new centrality of the state in public life and the distribution of resources, began to make more demands of it. Not only did students, teachers and a range of other interest groups turn to government for the redress of their grievances: even voluntary organisations came cap in hand to government and appeared to want to model themselves on official lines. Nehru reacted with a mixture of contempt and despair.

> Quite apart from the fact that government cannot pour out money everywhere, and it has not got limitless resources, this conversion of self-reliance into dependence is thoroughly bad. Thereby we are sapping at the roots of our work and bringing in State interference and control in place[s] where it should be least needed and where it may well be harmful.[4]

He harked back to the ethos and style of the nationalist movement when all they did was in spite of and in opposition to the government of the day. Increasingly he deplored what he saw as the persistence of narrow loyalties of caste, region and community, even among younger people, and criticised this as evidence of India's 'backwardness'. Yet the enduring legitimacy of the new nation state would depend on the state's ability to recognise and manage such loyalties and identities (as it had done in the case of language), and to use its resources to convince people that the new India was worth belonging to. Nehru seems not to have recognised the significance of political management in the ongoing work of building the nation, or the importance of the political skills associated with ensuring state responsiveness to sectional demands. Rather, as he aged, he fell back on the rhetoric of the nationalist movement and on reminiscence of that earlier struggle which in retrospect could be portrayed as pure and ideological when compared with contemporary politics.

During this last phase of Nehru's life the main link connecting state to society was the Congress party. It was the means through which the state was firmly rooted in the structures and interests of Indian society, and through which demands were often mediated and satisfied. The dominance of Congress over the political system, and its peculiar nature, made it at this stage a powerful force for national integration and the legitimation of the state. Its dominance was displayed in the general elections held under Nehru in 1952, 1957 and 1962. Compared with elections held later in the century these were almost totally peaceful and without violent incident. (In 1952 in seven polling stations the poll was adjourned because of a breach of law and order; in 1957 the number was four, and in 1962 none.) Congress was far and away the largest party in India. In each of these three Lok Sabha elections it put forward nearly 500 candidates, won just over 360 of the available seats (just under 500), and polled between 45 per cent and nearly 48 per cent of the votes. In the state assembly elections at the same time it polled a somewhat lower percentage of the votes and won a lower percentage of seats, but was still the major political player, coming through the ballot box to form both national and most provincial governments.[5] It was thus unquestionably the dominant party in the political system. Not surprisingly success fed support, and the vast majority of aspiring politicians wanted to be within its ranks in order to reap the benefits which accrued to them and their own supporters from being within the ruling party.

Further evidence, over and above election results, of the way Congress connected state structures to society, and particularly to significant social groups, is to be found in the types of people who became Congress members, legislators and office-holders.[6] By the end of Nehru's life Congress at its base was no longer an elite, urban party, but reflected the diversity of Indian society, and particularly the numerical and socio-economic significance of substantial rural caste groups. Aspiring groups were being incorporated into the party, continuing a process which had begun before independence, thus rooting it more firmly, particularly in rural society. However, for most of Nehru's time as prime minister the decision-making organs of the party, the AICC and the Working Committee, were still dominated by older, professional men; though this began to change towards the end of the 1950s when a cohort of younger people began to rise in the party hierarchy, bringing with them experience not so much of the nationalist movement but of competitive state politics and of the power in the states of local elite groups with a more traditional outlook than many of the early generations of secular, westernised politicians. The growing social breadth of the party is also clear from the background of those who became legislators at different levels within the political system, with a gradual decline in the numbers drawn from a professional background. In the second parliament (1957–62), for example, over 40 per cent of legislators drew their main income from land, and nearly 14 per cent from professional fees. Of the landholders, most owned small or medium-sized holdings. It is also significant that almost half of the Congress members of this Lok Sabha had never been to jail – an indication that Congress was now recruiting from a spread of politically active people who had skills and power bases rather different from those who had been the core of the old nationalist Congress with its commitment to civil disobedience.

Although this subtle but clear process of change in the relationship of Congress to Indian society was vital in sustaining the legitimacy of the political system and the state structures Congressmen came to dominate, it also suggested that Congress would be unable to generate the commitment to change in the socio-economic order which Nehru's vision of a new India required. As the dominant party in Indian politics, and the only one which was truly pan-Indian in spread and support, it could have been the ideological motor for change. Nehru indeed tried to drive it on to perform this role, using its sessions and policy committees to gather support for his plans. However, it became apparent that there was a gulf between the rhetoric of the party, particularly in the later 1950s, and the actual interests of those who were its core. Commitments to the imposition of ceilings on land holdings (1953), to a socialist pattern of society (1955) or to cooperative joint farming (1959) were to prove little more than platitudes, and were certainly not among the majority of party members' genuine convictions for which they were prepared to sacrifice their own positions and interests and those of their supporters and clients. Further, the structural nature of the party meant that it was not an instrument which could be used to achieve radical change in the country at large. It was still an alliance of local groups bound together by a wish to gain access to the legislatures and the powers of decision-making and patronage which went with access to ministers and to organs of government, rather than by ideology. Nor was it a cadre-based party with a clear structure of discipline and direction, which could send its members out into the towns and countryside to spread the message of change, alert people to their rights and organise them. Thus the Chinese model of local-level change was not available to Nehru.[7]

In the closing years of his life Nehru became increasingly aware of the feebleness of Congress for his larger purposes. He regretted its lack of clear thinking on vital economic and social problems; and lamented that Congressmen seemed lacking in both idealism and 'moral fibre'. As he wrote late in 1962,

> We have, therefore, to pull ourselves up in our personal lives as well as in our organizations and, of course, in our governmental activity. This conviction is growing upon me more and more. It is right that we should think clearly and put our policy and programme before the public. But, even more so, it is necessary for us to create the impression of a certain unselfish service of the nation.[8]

These were the words of a patrician and a nationalist, schooled in a Gandhian moral ethos, not of a political leader who recognised the bargains and compromises inevitable in politics and saw a leadership role in the management of them.

Two incidents in Nehru's relations with Congress at this time particularly indicated his unease with it but also its power to constrain him and compromise his ideals. One occurred in 1959 in the southern state of Kerala. A communist state government had come legitimately to power two years earlier in the elections of 1957, a development of which Nehru himself was tolerant as to him it was a sign of the vitality of Indian democracy. But the new state government began to attack substantial vested interests in land and education, which provoked agitations in which the local Congress was implicated. Nehru was deeply reluctant to intervene in a state matter but recognised how dangerous the conflict had become and how intractable the opposing positions. Eventually in mid-1959 the central government dismissed the state government and took over the administration, as it was empowered to do under the constitution. Nehru's own party had undoubtedly forced his hand, putting its own local interests first. Its leverage over him was strengthened by the fact that his daughter, Indira, was at that time the party's president and determined to defeat the communists, and was far less scrupulous than her father about democratic procedures.

The other episode which displayed Nehru's ambivalence about the party and his ambiguous relationship with it was what became known as the Kamaraj plan to revive it in 1963. The plan bore the name of one of the senior Congressmen from southern India though it came out of discussions between several important party leaders and was eventually accepted by Nehru as a way of strengthening the party's organisation and reviving its public repute. Under its terms, adopted by the Working Committee in August, leading Congressmen in government would resign their posts and offer themselves for fulltime work in the party organisation; and Nehru was to decide on a list of those holding ministerial posts in Delhi and in the states whose resignations were to be accepted. The list of twelve eventually included six chief ministers, including Kamaraj himself. Whatever the motives of the movers of the plan, conscious as they must have been of a not-too-distant and inevitable succession struggle once Nehru ceased to be prime minister, Nehru himself saw it as a way of stressing the importance of work in the party organisation as opposed to ministerial office, and thus of reviving the party and equipping it to perform a more significant role in the country at large, more in the tradition of his great mentor, Gandhi.

As the Congress party was a weak instrument with which to achieve major change in the economy and society Nehru had little alternative but to use the existing instruments of government and the administrators who were already in post. But it was clear that they were no more dynamic or committed to change than when the new government had inherited them from the British raj. Despite his earlier concerns for an overhaul of the administration and changes in its ethos and relationship with society, nothing had happened. In this later phase he was still expressing anxiety – about the attitude of superiority towards ordinary people and particularly rural folk taken by higher officials, which worked against popular cooperation and the solution of large social problems; about the slowness of the governmental machine; and about inefficiency, nepotism and corruption at lower levels. He was painfully aware that these problems stemmed in part from their imperial inheritance, writing in 1960 that they were

> checked at every step by the old procedures and institutional methods which have come down to us from the past. Those institutions had been built up, with a large measure of success, under a different type of Government and economy. There was no urge to deal with a rapidly changing situation in the social and economic sphere, such as we have to face today. It is no good blaming those institutions because they were meant for a different purpose.[9]

146

Despite his clear understanding that many of the structures inherited from the imperial British and the style and attitudes of those socialised in the administrative services were at odds with what he saw as the purposes of the new India, he did not engage in major administrative reform or set up any monitoring or directing agency to modify what was in place or check on government functionaries. Moreover, in some outstanding cases his judgement about individuals and their fitness for office was flawed.[10]

Nehru placed his main hopes in processes of decentralisation, which he thought would encourage self reliance. This was essentially a recognition that in the Indian context the apparatus of the state was failing in the function he thought it could perform, and that one of the insights Gandhi had emphasised had greater relevance than he had recognised in the Mahatma's own life-time. The Indian constitution had envisaged some measure of decentralisation and the devolution of power to village *panchayats* or councils; and in Article 40 had provided that the state should organise such *panchayats* 'and endow them with such powers and authority as may be necessary to enable them to function as units of self-government'.[11] The power to do this was vested in the state governments, but in 1958–59 the central government stepped in to encourage a nation-wide scheme of local self-government, following a report on existing community development projects which was prepared by a team under the chairmanship of Balvantray Mehta, who had been a member of the Lok Sabha and was later to become chief minister of Gujarat. The team was worried at the lack of popular initiative so far evoked by the community projects or the National Extension Service, and argued that it was vital to create democratic local institutions with real power and adequate finance: without this 'we will never be able to evoke local interest and excite local initiative in the field of development'.[12] Early in 1958 the National Development Council accepted the broad outlines of the scheme suggested by Mehta – a three-tier system of elected committees reaching down to village level with the bottom tier representing a group of villages – and resolved that each state should work out the structure best suited to its local conditions.

Rajasthan was the first state to inaugurate *panchayati raj* late in 1959, and under pressure from the centre most states had a system at least partially in operation by the time Nehru died. However, Nehru's hopes were not entirely fulfilled. Development continued to be a 'top-down' process and the new bodies were not given the powers or funds which would have enabled them to be really creative. Moreover, the low levels of education in the countryside meant that initiative normally rested with the staff allocated to the system. These tended not to be a new breed of administrator committed to new relationships with ordinary people or possessing a new ethos of empowering them and facilitating their wishes, but officials recruited in the same way as existing government officials, or indeed existing officials on secondment. Moreover, political control of the new institutions and resources tended to fall into the hands of those powerful groups who could see that they offered buttresses to their existing local power and who had the political skills to manipulate elections to them and the flow of resources through them. A government report in 1978 spelt this out: economically and socially privileged sections of rural society had come to dominate the new system which had 'facilitated the emergence of oligarchic forces yielding no benefits to weaker sections'.[13] In the much longer term it became clear that *panchayati raj* was a powerful means of politicisation of the countryside, eventually helping to empower the most disadvantaged and to enable them to articulate their wishes. But as a means of popular involvement in social and economic development it was of limited use in Nehru's life-time.

Structures of administration and expectations of careers in government service were undoubtedly a barrier to change or dynamic leadership by officials. But an even more basic problem was that of material resources. The scale of India's needs was vast – whether it was a case of providing such basic essentials as clean water and food for her expanding population (which had risen from 357 million in 1951 to 439 million in 1961), or investing in schools and hospitals, building roads, providing modern power supplies or beginning the task of building modern factories. Once the new rulers had turned their backs on the Gandhian vision of a simple rural life-style built on self-sufficiency they had need of huge sums of money. But the country was too poor to sustain tax levels which could have yielded up such sums. Probably half the people lived at a level of bare subsistence or under, and for political reasons to do with the support for the ruling party, Congress governments did not tax agricultural incomes. By the late 1950s India had exhausted the sterling balances she had built up in London during the war, was encountering severe food shortages, and was now increasingly dependent on foreign aid both to feed the people and to sustain investment in planned economic growth. In 1960–61 she received US$ 514.5 million in aid, with the biggest share coming from the USA, followed by West Germany and the UK. Food imports in 1961 stood at 3.5 million tonnes, and had more than doubled by the year after Nehru's death. Moreover, India needed to sustain considerable defence forces, not just on her border with Pakistan but increasingly with a view to countering Chinese incursions in the north-east. After the 1962 Chinese invasion defence spending doubled, and in the last year of Nehru's life was equivalent to 40 per cent of central government expenditure. Thus examination of Nehru's ability to pursue his vision of a new India, and the constraints on his power despite his standing as prime minister and unchallenged national leader, must turn to the twin problems of the economy and India's resources, and foreign relations.

. . .

THE PROBLEM OF RESOURCES

For Nehru significant and rapid economic development was central to making real his country's independence. He had long held that industrialisation and reform of the agrarian sector were vital – in order to generate the material resources necessary for the defence of national integrity; and within the country for investment in infrastructure, economic development and broader social needs, as well as to alleviate poverty and deprivation through a 'trickle-down' effect from overall increases in the standard of living and levels of income. By the mid-1950s he had in place national institutions to plan and attempt to manage the economy in an unprecedented way, for what he and his expert advisors saw as the national good. The final phase of his life saw the period of the Second Five-Year Plan (1956–61) and the making of the third, which ran from 1961 until after his death. Now came the crucial questions about whether the national state could implement the policies set in place, and whether the policies themselves were appropriate or adequate for the task envisaged.

Under the brief of creating 'a socialist pattern of society', endorsed by parliament late in 1954 and the Congress at Avadi in January 1955, Nehru and his experts embarked on an economic strategy which put a major emphasis on industrial development, particularly on heavy industry and the production of capital goods and steel. Only 12 per cent of investment under the first plan had gone into industry. The figures for the second and third plans were up to 27 per cent and 25 per cent. Investment in transport also rose very considerably. In contrast, investment in agriculture dropped across the three plans from 27 per cent to 19 per cent and then 18 per cent.[14] Not only did the national state plan where investment should go: it also reserved for public investment strategic and basic industries. Private capital was permitted to function elsewhere either in conjunction with the state or alone, but now subject to the targets of the national plan and under strict licensing and import controls. This was the origin of what later became known as 'licence-permit raj'. Not surprisingly domestic resources could not fund the lion's share of this ambitious strategy and under the second and third plans deficit financing and external resources came to provide over 40 per cent of the necessary funding. In the later 1950s the plan financing ran into considerable difficulty, particularly its foreign-exchange requirements. India had now spent its sterling balances accumulated in wartime, while her exports were losing their competitiveness in the world market. This included commodities for which she had been famous, such as jute and tea. As a result, from 1957 tough foreign-exchange controls were imposed to protect the key areas of investment in steel, coal, transport and power; and from 1958 India needed increasing amounts of foreign aid, particularly from the Aid-India Consortium dominated by the USA.

During Nehru's period of office Indian industry made significant advances. Between 1951 and 1965 total industrial output increased at an average annual rate of 7.4 per cent; and the share of manufacturing in national product rose, too, from 10 per cent in the early 1950s to 16 per cent in the mid-1960s. Progress was most marked in the strategic areas ear-marked by the planners and protected by them when foreign-exchange problems threatened projected levels of investment. For example, finished steel goods production rose from 1.0 to 2.4 million tonnes between 1950–51 and 1960–61, aluminium goods from 4 to 18.3 thousand tonnes, coal from 32.8 to 55.7 million tonnes. There was major growth in the production of various types of machinery – from electric motors and machine tools (up in value from nearly Rs 4 million to Rs 70 million in the period) to automobiles and bicycles. In the consumer industries sugar production more than doubled, production of paper goods tripled, while cotton yarn and jute textile production rose more modestly. In the same decade there was a marked increase in many aspects of a modern economic infrastructure – such as the generation of power, the electrification of towns and villages, the growth of railway freight (which almost doubled) and the length of surfaced road, which went up by almost 80,000 km. Availability of a whole range of goods which indicated a raised quality of life, including food and clothing, also rose; though this availability was, of course, no guarantee of an equal distribution of such goods.

However, such progress did not mean that India was becoming an industrial economy or society. Although employment in industry grew (at around 3 per cent per year) the share of the industrial sector in total employment was only about 11 per cent in the early 1960s. Moreover, there were very real problems in implementing the industrial strategy outlined in the second and third plans, quite apart from problems of funding. It was clear almost from the start that return on investment in the public sector was consistently and substantially lower than in the private sector, and that public enterprises were very inefficiently managed. Moreover, high rates of protection permitted sections of Indian industry to remain profitable despite low efficiency and productivity; and there was no close and expert monitoring and rationalising of industrial capacity and performance. There were several reasons for this – including deficiencies at planning stage for particular projects and developments, political pressures at state level for a share in major projects regardless of national economic 'rationality', and the nature of the bureaucracy given the unprecedented task of planning and management. The professions of management and engineering were still in their infancy in India, and the brightest of young men had tended to go into law and the civil service. Civil servants were generalist administrators subject to frequent transfer, and not dependent on commercial 'success' and proven performance for career advancement. They were hardly the people to manage efficiently such an unprecedented enterprise. It has been estimated that every major industrial project in the public sector took two years longer and cost 40 per cent more to set up than had been anticipated; even when completed, at the level of day-to-day operation there was not the skilled workforce or managerial staff to run them properly. It was hardly surprising that both the second and third plans failed to achieve their targets in industrial production by a sizeable margin. Thus serious questions soon came to be asked about the appropriateness and realism of the plans themselves in the political context of a federal structure where the centre did not control all subjects and resources; and in the context of low levels of managerial and technical expertise.

In the later 1950s it also became clear that a further and damaging brake on economic development, and on the planned industrialisation, was the nature and performance of the agrarian sector itself. Agriculture was in fact still vital to India's economic well-being. Its flourishing was essential to feed the population, to generate high enough incomes so that there were adequate numbers of consumers for India's industrial products, and to produce sufficient surplus in the form of tax and savings to help fund the broader development strategies conceived by the planners. To an extent the planners (and Nehru himself) had assumed that India's farmers could perform these multiple functions, once unproductive 'intermediaries' were removed by *zamindari* abolition. However, the 1950s saw a steadily rising population, which needed food and employment and expected from its government provision of social facilities such as improved education and health. Although the population had been growing steadily since the 1920s the rate of growth began to quicken in the 1950s to an annual rate of almost 2 per cent, and this rose to about 2.25 per cent in the 1960s. (By contrast the Second Five-Year Plan had been based on the assumption of a much lower annual growth rate of about 1.4 per cent.) In the 1950s the urban population grew by 16.5 million, and by 1961 almost 20 per cent of the population were classified as urban people. This meant that 80 per cent of Indians were country people and needed not only to be fed in the rural areas but to find work there.

But Indian agriculture was based on low capital investment and simple technology, and consequently did not have the dynamism to rise to the food and employment requirements of an expanding population and the savings expectations of the planners. Expansion of output took place in the 1950s in practically all sectors of agriculture. The figure was about 30 per cent in foodgrain output, and was largely the result of more intensive labour on a larger area of unirrigated land. Only 17 per cent of this growth resulted from an expansion of irrigation and by 1961 less than one-fifth of the area cultivated was irrigated. The fragility of India's food supply became devastatingly apparent in 1957 when poor rainfall in northern India damaged the wheat crop, leading to an 8 per cent drop in foodgrain production and a sharp rise in food prices. Monsoon failure could in the absence of widespread irrigation bring about a major short-fall in food grains, a slump in rural incomes and consequently a break on overall economic development. Indeed by 1958 it was becoming apparent that not only could India not feed herself: the states, which drew their revenue very largely from the agrarian sector, were failing to meet their targets for contributions to the funding of the second plan.

The government in Delhi responded to the increasingly obvious problems of agriculture with long- and short-term measures. In the immediate crisis of the late 1950s it began to import food (3.7 million tonnes in 1957, and remaining at that annual level). It also started to intervene in the markets and in price levels. However, the Planning Commission's more radical suggestions about controlling prices by wide-ranging intervention to meet the needs of consumers rather than farmers met stiff opposition from the states and indeed from the food ministry in Delhi. The union food minister, A.P. Jain, demonstrated a deep hostility to this potentially aggressive and managerial state style of intervention, even when such a basic necessity as food was at stake, which was to block the hope of the planners and of Nehru himself. In the Lok Sabha in July 1957 Jain attacked the planners' strategy of fixing low prices for food and agricultural products as paying insufficient attention to the vitality of the rural economy and to the need to give farmers incentives to grow more; later he noted the interventionist and redistributive powers which would have been needed to pursue such a policy.[15] It was hardly surprising that with such opposition and obstruction at the heart of government in Delhi and from the states themselves, the planners' strategies were blunted in practice, and that the food at the disposal of government came almost entirely from imports rather than from domestic redistribution.

Longer-term strategies to dynamise the agricultural sector were equally problematic. Despite the abolition of large-scale landlords at the start of the decade, and the acceptance in

principle from 1953 of 'ceilings' on land holdings, the implementation of these strategies was in the hands of state governments and few of them had passed ceiling legislation until
the 1960s. In the mounting economic crisis of the late 1950s
Nehru and the National Development Council saw the prospect
of the failure of the second plan. Nehru returned to one of his
major hopes for rural society – the development of cooperative
farming – and proceeded to pursue it in the decision-making
structures of the Congress party, despite the agrarian vested
interests in the party. In January 1959 at its meeting in Nagpur
the Working Committee endorsed Nehru's strategy for raising
agricultural output by structural change in agricultural society.
The crucial section in the Nagpur resolution argued for an
agrarian pattern

> of cooperative joint farming, in which the land will be pooled for
> joint cultivation, the farmers continuing to retain their property
> rights, and getting a share from the net produce in proportion to
> their land. Further, those who actually work the land, whether they
> own the land or not, will get a share in proportion to the work put
> in by them on the joint farm.[16]

Although the idea of cooperatives had been accepted in principle under the five-year plans, now there was a definite time-
table for major change within three years and no apparent
loopholes for those who wished to continue with substantial
family farms. A storm of opposition broke out – in the party at
large, in the press and in parliament – and within three months
Nehru was forced to retreat, and both party and parliament
accepted the attenuated strategy of creating service cooperatives as a first step towards joint farming. It was clear that there
would be no serious attempt to bring about joint farming until
after the third plan.

These years of economic crisis demonstrated not just the
fragility of the resource-base on which Nehru's strategy for
economic development was built but also the systemic barriers
to the implementation of his vision of a modernised economy
and a transformed society. For him as much as for Gandhi true
swaraj seemed to be out of reach. In Nehru's case the main
problem lay in the nature of the Congress party and in the
Indian constitution itself. Entrenched and conservative interests
in Congress were its immediate political strength, but they were

also its great weakness as a force for radical change. Under the terms of the constitution so many of the issues which were keys to Nehru's vision and strategy were within the power of the states within the Indian Union, where again local elites often held the reins of power, dominating the state legislatures and governments. Nehru was himself deeply aware of these problems, particularly as they impinged on agriculture; and his letters from the later 1950s demonstrate his growing despair at his inability to solve the problems relating to the agricultural sector or even to persuade his colleagues in government and party of the urgency of the situation. In the critical year 1957 he wrote to his chief ministers that agricultural production was the keystone of planning and that there was not genuine and urgent realisation of just how vital this was and how destructive were deficits in food production. It shamed him that after ten years of independence India, an agricultural country, could not feed itself.[17] He was also becoming increasingly aware that failures here reflected attitudes in the state governments and failures in the states' administrative efficiency. He exhorted chief ministers to galvanise their governments and to recognise how vital was agricultural change, and particularly increased food production.[18] Despite his exhortations he still felt early in 1958 that one of the major problems lay in the state agricultural departments which were of comparatively low status in the official pecking order and moved in leisurely ways along old routine paths, totally lacking in any sense of urgency; and he urged his chief ministers to shake up these departments and even take charge of them themselves.[19] However, by the end of the decade he had learned painfully that he could not cajole or bully the states and their administrations. Nor could he, despite his position in the Congress party, persuade his party colleagues of the wisdom of his own vision of a transformed rural society. He wrote somewhat plaintively in July 1959 of his bewilderment at the 'ferocity of attack' on the Nagpur resolutions, and his 'astonishment' that 'in the modern age' anyone should oppose cooperatives.[20]

By the time Nehru died it was plain that, despite his personal vision and commitment, the problems of the countryside and of the agrarian sector of the economy had scarcely been tackled. Although production had risen, as had cropped and irrigated areas, India could not feed herself, rural savings were very low as was the contribution through taxes of the rural sector to plan funding, and there continued to be extreme levels of poverty and underemployment as well as low demand for consumer goods. Little had been done to address the fundamental lack of dynamism in Indian agriculture, despite the importance of the Planning Commission and Nehru's own dominance in policy-making. It was not until after his death that fundamental reappraisals of agricultural policy were taken, once it was abundantly clear that the whole planning process for economic development would stall without such major reconsideration. It was to be nearly a decade until parts of India saw a 'green revolution', based on high-yielding seeds of wheat and rice, which enriched a rural bourgeoisie and eventually enabled the country to feed its citizens without importing food.

Clearly there had been a failure of planning in a technical economic sense, in relation to the industrial and economic sectors and in particular with respect to the crucial relationship between them. There had also been a political failure – to recognise and deal with the power of political forces at work in the party and in the states which could nullify or at least impede central policy at the point of implementation. Nehru himself had taken refuge in cajoling and criticism, and ultimately in grudging accommodation. This was particularly damaging because of his position at the apex of the political system. The appearance of power as he aged proved ultimately and deeply dysfunctional to the political system and the economy, because it masked the vital need to encourage creative politics and to welcome new and younger people into government and decision-making.

Over and above these problems of planning and political management there loomed the inexorable increase in the population. It was not until after the taking of the 1961 census and the clear evidence of an unexpectedly high growth rate over the previous decade that the planners recognised that population would have to be stabilised – by artificial means, now that modern medicine had defeated many of the old killers which had limited population growth for centuries. From then increasing stress was laid on a comprehensive national family-planning strategy, and ever larger sums were invested in the service. During his life this was not for Nehru an urgent issue. Although he believed birth control was desirable, he felt India was not an overpopulated country and that broad economic progress would provide employment; while improved health care and education would naturally lead to individual control of fertility. For decades the contrary was to be the case. The rise in the number of Indians meant that scarce resources had to go further, and that there was not the surplus to enable the government to invest in health and education, and so to create the more modern and egalitarian society Nehru had envisaged.

. . .

RELATIONS WITH THE WIDER WORLD

For Nehru creating a new India was inextricably linked with her relations with the wider world – as a crucial part of her assertion of a truly independent character and a role as a leading player in international and particularly Asian affairs. But there was also the more mundane connection of foreign affairs with expenditure of scarce resources on arms. Nehru and his colleagues had accepted that independent India would need a modern army for defence and had rejected the Gandhian vision of non-violent means of defending a nation's integrity. Despite the inevitable weakening of the old imperial army by the processes of partition they had inherited a force which had been dramatically modernised by the imperial need to fight the Second World War. However, India's foreign policy was predicated on the ideals of peaceful coexistence with neighbours, abstention from military aggression, and non-alignment with any world power bloc. By the mid-1950s it seemed that Nehru had not only achieved a successful and workable foreign policy for India: he had also made a reputation for himself as a significant world figure who spoke a language of idealism in international relations which he genuinely tried to put into practice. The exception of course was India's troubled relations with Pakistan, particularly on the issue of Kashmir. However, by the time of his death in 1964 the ideals on which Nehru's foreign policy was built had been seriously undermined, as had the viability of his policies of peaceful coexistence and non-alignment. It was now debatable whether he could be seen as a figure of power in the international arena. He was challenged at home on foreign affairs more severely than at any time since he had established his dominance in government and party at the start of the previous decade. Moreover, India was increasingly encumbered with military expenditure which in turn limited the state's capacity to invest in both essential and desirable domestic programmes of economic and social development.

During the 1950s, as Cold War tensions became more acute, it seemed that Nehru's stance of non-alignment with either the western or the Soviet bloc was effective in serving India's national interests and enhancing his own domestic and international position. Both great powers had a serious interest in events on the subcontinent, and as the United States came closer to Pakistan (concluding a military alliance early in 1954) so earlier frosty relations between India and the Soviet Union began to thaw, and the new Soviet leadership after the death of Stalin in 1953 placed greater value on Nehru himself and on India. This enabled Nehru to turn to both blocs for vital development aid, and to seek to buy arms from a wider range of sources. It also gave him a position from which he could enunciate broad ideals and at times act as intermediary and interpreter between the opposing groups. Despite his undoubted international standing he remained, however, deeply sensitive about anything which he suspected as a reversion to an older 'imperial' attitude by Britain and her American allies. In 1955 he noted to his sister, now a major Indian diplomat, that the British Conservative government 'still live in a past age and imagine that they can treat India as some casual third-rate country'.[21]

One of the clearest examples of his own standing and India's non-alignment came in 1956, the year when French and British troops invaded Egypt in the Suez crisis, and when Soviet tanks crossed into Hungary. Nehru condemned both as acts of external aggression against a nation's integrity, and worked through the United Nations for solutions to both issues. He thought that there was nothing to choose between the two 'invasions'. However, his delay in outright condemnation of the Russian move as he waited for information roused suspicions in India and abroad that he was far more willing to criticise the former British ruler. Privately he told his chief ministers that the world had been close to a major war, but that the double crisis had demonstrated that neither old-style colonialism nor new-style international communism could be imposed on a nation from outside, not least because of the growing strength of world opinion which now increasingly reflected Asian opinion. However, he seems to have recognised the potential gulf between India's idealistic rhetoric and practical policies. 'It is easy enough to give expression to our views in brave language, condemning this country or that, but it is not easy to hold to the . . . path which leads to peace.' He admitted, 'I can offer no simple recipe. We may, however, lay down some broad considerations. The first one is that we should stand on our basic principles.'[22] These included opposition to all foreign aggression and fostering of genuine national independence for all countries. Further, the interlocking of the two crises confirmed his fears of all pacts and alliances (NATO, the Warsaw Treaty, SEATO and the Baghdad pact) as destabilising and threatening to world peace.

Apart from the principles of non-alignment and opposition to new and old forms of imperialism, Nehru had also for years articulated international ideals of peaceful coexistence and negotiation over contested issues rather than a resort to force. However, he was to find in the final decade of his life that even these apparently clear ideals provided no 'simple recipe' for his conduct of India's relations with other countries, even within the confines of Asia, where he assumed there was a natural affinity between countries and shared interests in relation to the international order. On the subcontinent itself no progress was made on the status of Kashmir, and consequently relations with Pakistan remained tense. Even more humiliating was the fact that there remained small pockets of foreign territory on the Indian landmass itself, notably Goa, still part of the Portuguese empire. By the mid-1950s there still seemed no peaceful progress towards the integration of Goa into India, although by 1954 former French territory had been amicably relinquished by France. However, Nehru set his face publicly against armed intervention, holding to the principle that armed action solved nothing and that if India gave up the principle of peaceful resolution of problems she would be seen as hypocritical, without moral anchors or principles for her foreign policy and unable to work for world-wide peace. However economic sanctions had little effect, nor did Nehru's hope that Britain, the USA or the Vatican might be able to put pressure on Portugal. In 1960, over a decade since independence, he was forced to admit privately that he really had no policy on the matter which looked like achieving success in the near future. However, increasing world condemnation of Portuguese colonialism began to strengthen Nehru's resolve and his leverage; in December 1961 Indian troops moved into Goa and the Portuguese governor-general, defying his masters in Lisbon, surrendered without a fight. Although the lack of resistance suggested that Goans were content to become fully part of India, the use of force was a betrayal of Nehru's proudly voiced principles, and many in the United States and Europe did not hesitate to say so publicly. He himself was sadly aware that he had compromised one principle to achieve another, and that, yet again, he could find no easy recipe for the conduct of foreign relations when opponents seemed not to be amenable to rational argument and negotiation.

Far more damaging – to Nehru as a world figure and to his principles, and to India as an aspiring regional power as well as a peace-maker – was the failure of his policy in relation to China. In the mid-1950s it seemed that he had stabilised relations with India's powerful neighbour and come to a mutual agreement about the principles which were to guide their relationship. However, the issue of their mutual border in the north-east of India had never been resolved, and early in 1959 China made it clear that she claimed a significant amount of what India regarded as her territory. Within weeks the tension was compounded by deepening unrest in Tibet and the flight to India of the Dalai Lama. Early in April 1959 the *Economist* commented with chilling perceptiveness: 'the independent India of 1947 tended to think of power politics as none of its business. As other newly independent nations have done before it, Mr Nehru's India may be emerging from the age of innocence. In later years, the republic of India may look back upon this month as its moment of truth.'[23] Nehru for his part recognised reality and saw that nothing short of an unthinkable war would give Tibet its freedom, and he declined to denounce Chinese 'colonialism', despite the wishes of the president, his old congress colleague, Rajendra Prasad.

However, Indo-Chinese relations were now seriously damaged and it was clear that the border was a major and disputed issue. But Nehru could not bring himself to believe that the Chinese could consider what he saw as the folly of armed conflict, as he told parliament in August that year. In October he told his chief ministers that although the tension between China and India was of great concern he did not fear serious consequences, and that their border was adequately protected. Further, he denied that the policy of peaceful coexistence and non-alignment had failed, and declared his determination to persist with it.[24] Despite the hopeful words, his actions spoke louder; and now the army was given general control of all the border areas. Looking back he recognised that more could have been done in terms of military preparation and border defence, but that this would have diverted money from social and economic investment, leaving India essentially weaker.[25] By the autumn of 1962 no solution to the border problem had been found, despite attempts at negotiation, and the situation on the ground had become extremely tense, with the Chinese and Indian armies perilously close to each other. Nehru at last recognised the gravity of the situation, but confessed himself perplexed by the Chinese stance and the reasoning behind it.[26]

For Nehru nemesis struck in mid-October when Chinese forces invaded in strength and subjected Indian forces to a humiliating series of defeats until a month later the Chinese leaders called a unilateral ceasefire and pulled back their troops. He reflected bitterly on the collapse of the principles which he had hoped would inform the Indo-Chinese relationship; but he was clear that the priority was now armed defence and the integrity of India. 'It is a tragedy that we who have stood for peace everywhere, should be attacked in this way and be compelled to resist attack by arms. But there is no help for it. No self-respecting nation can tolerate this kind of aggression, and we will certainly not do so.'[27] In his eyes the situation was the most dangerous India had faced since independence: he was prepared to call on massive American assistance and to place orders for arms from both America and Russia. Although the ceasefire averted a greater disaster, Nehru realised after months of ensuing verbal conflict and failed negotiation that there was little prospect of ever achieving the sort of relationship with China he had once hoped for.

The policy disaster compounded by the military débâcle raised major issues about Nehru's role as his country's foreign minister, about the underlying principles of his foreign policy and about India's military competence. Nehru himself admitted that the army had been ill-prepared for large-scale defence of India's borders in such difficult and high terrain. Moreover, he took on the role of defence minister at the peak of the crisis, thus effectively recognising that his old friend, the politician Krishna Menon, was inadequate in the post. But far deeper than technical military problems or personality conflicts and inadequate leadership in the defence ministry lay the basic issue of policy and of interpretation of foreign affairs. Here the onus lay squarely on Nehru's shoulders as he had been the source of India's foreign policy for nearly two decades, unchallenged by politicians or civil servants because of his formidable standing in the domestic political arena. As one of those civil servants later commented, 'with Nehru at the apex of the Government, there was a willing suspension of critical analysis on major issues of policies . . . the body of higher professional civil servants did not truly exert themselves to volunteer professional dissent on issues which eventually were to lead to grave damage to national interests and prestige.'[28]

What was now clear was that Nehru had seen China as in some sense a brotherly Asian neighbour with similar priorities and aspirations to India's own – to assert her independence of colonialism and her significance on the world stage, and to build up her own internal strength and modernise her society and economy. What he had not recognised was China's own persistent and aggressive brand of nationalism, and the dangers inherent in the growing rift between China and the Soviet Union from the late 1950s, leading to a situation in which an attack on India might be a tactic within a far broader Chinese strategy of national and ideological assertion. After the Chinese withdrawal he struggled to come to terms with the possible underlying reasons for the Chinese attack, which he now sensed were deeper and far more urgent than a mere concern for territory.[29] But the harsh truth was that he had not thought that China would ever attack India, and that as a result India had been totally unprepared for what befell her late in 1962.

The invasion undermined his authority at home, leading to the first ever no-confidence debate he faced in parliament. It also weakened his international status and cast doubts on the very principles on which he had built his country's foreign policy – non-aggression, peaceful resolution of conflicts, non-alignment, and solidarity among the countries of Asia and former colonial territories. Further, because of the drain on scarce state resources for defence, it had repercussions on his whole vision of a modernising India on the march towards a new society. Even in 1957, when the main cause of rising defence expenditure was the danger of conflict with Pakistan, he lamented, 'Few things have pained me so much recently as to spend large sums of money on the apparatus for Defence. I wish we could avoid it and spend this money instead for our

schemes of development and in bettering the lot of our people.'
Ironically in the light of 1962, he continued, 'in some matters,
and most of all, where the safety and security of the country
are concerned, there is no choice and no risks can be taken.'[30]
In the final year of his life, 1963–64, defence spending doubled,
and stood at about 40 per cent of total government expenditure. His interpretation of foreign affairs and his formulation
of India's international position and priorities had thus not
only eroded his personal standing as a world figure of influence and inspiration, and led to a threat to India's territorial
integrity. They had also jeopardised investment in the domestic
development of India which was at the heart of his vision of
the meaning of independence.

. . .

VISION AND REALITY

In this discussion of Nehru as a figure of power in the final
years of his life the focus has been on several broad issues
which had a profound bearing on his ability to wield power in
practice, and to implement his vision of a new India. Among
them were the complex relationship of the new state to India's
society, and the acute problem of resources, both material and
personal, with which to effect change. Now the focus shifts to
particular domestic problems, the resolution of which was central to Nehru's understanding of genuine independence for
India and his hopes for the creation of a dynamic, modern and
more egalitarian society – reform of landholding, the abolition
of the practice of treating those at the base of Hindu society as
untouchable, and improvement of the status of women as equal
citizens. By using these three problems as case studies one can
begin to see the extent to which Nehru was able to make his
vision into reality, and also to understand the constraints on
him despite his high office and unique authority, as well as
the formidable obstacles to the implementation of policies of
reform. These three problems are particularly significant for
they were in no sense Nehru's personal whims or idiosyncras-
ies. They had been part of Congress ideology and rhetoric for
decades and had often been the subject of specific commitments before 1947. Moreover, they were issues which touched
the lives of well over half the population, and particularly of
the most disadvantaged, precisely those for whom change was

essential – as Gandhi and Nehru had argued in their own ways – if independence was to be 'genuine'.

Land reform

Nehru and the Congress leadership had accepted when they came to power that reform of India's structure of landholding was essential, for the long-term health and vitality of the agricultural sector and in order to do away with some of the grossest inequalities in rural society. The means to this end were the abolition of the old landlord intermediaries between state and cultivators, the *zamindars*, and, somewhat later, attempts to place 'ceilings' on landholdings. However, these matters fell under the control of the states, not of the central government, under the new constitution. This immediately weakened the effective power of the prime minister and the planners to achieve change, giving influence instead into the hands of state legislators and state governments, many of whom (Congressmen or not) increasingly came from substantial rural backgrounds. The result was that in the processes of passage through the state legislatures reforms could be severely watered down, while the length of time taken to debate the issues and pass laws gave substantial landholders time to prepare to evade them.

A close study of the abolition of *zamindari* in Uttar Pradesh (the old United Provinces, Nehru's home province and an area of acute socio-economic tensions between the two world wars) has shown how even here the Congress government did not intend radical change in the countryside, but rather the abolition of a small number of the largest and most vocal *zamindars*. Preparation and discussion of state legislation, moreover, took over two years from the time a state committee had reported on the issue. As one of the key provincial Congressmen, Charan Singh, noted, the political consequences of land reform were crucial to those who drafted the legislation:

> Much thought was given to this matter since the drafters of the legislation were cognisant of the need to ensure political stability in the countryside. By strengthening the principle of private property where it was weakest, i.e. at the base of the social pyramid, the reforms have created a huge class of strong opponents of the class war ideology. By multiplyng the number of independent land-owning peasants there came into being a middle of the road stable rural society and a barrier against political extremism. It is fair to conclude

that an agrarian reform has taken the wind out of the sails of the disrupters of peace and the opponents of ordered progress.[31]

Later ceiling legislation followed very slowly, in practice often delayed well into the 1960s, despite the principle being accepted as national policy almost a decade earlier, as the states only reluctantly passed legislation which local Congressmen either opposed or viewed as irrelevant. As if these obstacles, stemming from the constitutional allocation of subjects to the states, were not enough, both *zamindari*-abolition legislation and ceiling legislation were challenged in the courts and required amendments to the constitution before they could be held as constitutionally valid.

The overall impact of the attempt at land reform by legislation was limited. The largest *zamindari* holdings were indeed dismantled. But overall throughout the country substantial farmers still controlled the bulk of the land, out of all proportion to their numbers. Moreover, many tenants were evicted during this period of change, lest they gained legal rights in land, and comparatively little land was redistributed to help those at the base of rural society. All-India figures suggest this trend clearly. In 1961–62 just under 5 per cent of households had operational holdings of 10 or more hectares, but they farmed almost 30 per cent of the land. At the other end of the scale just under 40 per cent of households had holdings of under 1 hectare, and they farmed about 7 per cent of the land. Particular state and village case studies tell the same story from many different parts of the country. In Uttar Pradesh, for example, before *zamindari* abolition 6.1 per cent of households held above 10 acres of land, controlling almost 35 per cent of the area owned. By 1953–54 that largest category of landholders was a slightly larger percentage of all landholders and owned nearly 40 per cent of the owned land. By 1961–62 the largest landholders owned nearly 60 per cent of the land and was nearly 12 per cent of households. By contrast at that last date just over 44 per cent of households fell into the category of the smallest holders (under 1 acre) but owned just under 1.6 per cent of the land in the state. Even the 'dispossessed' *zamindars* did not fare badly. The middle-sized ones in particular proved able to adapt economically and politically, often joining Congress as a matter of prudence, and becoming skilled agricultural managers and businessmen. In neighbouring Bihar land reform similarly did not radically change patterns of landholding. Twenty years after the passage of abolition legislation former *zamindars* could be found with estates of up to 5000 acres and more, while those at the base of society had tiny holdings or were landless.[32]

What were the main reasons for this failure to implement the sort of change in rural society to which Nehru had bent so much thought and effort? One major reason was the ambiguous attitude of state Congress parties which had within their ranks representatives of substantial rural people who battled (in the party and in the state legislatures) to limit the effects of land reform on all but the very largest holdings, often leaving considerable and legitimate ways in which landed families could retain sizeable holdings. Among these were, for example, the right to retain home farms and orchards. Moreover, these were just the people with the knowledge and money to use all possible loopholes in the acts and to hire lawyers to help them, and even before legislation was passed to prepare for it by devising ways to mitigate its effects – such devices as turning lands into orchards or distributing holdings into the names of a range of family members. By contrast, the administrative resources of the state governments were pathetically limited. Often there were not adequate records on which to base decisions, while there were inadequate numbers of civil servants to tackle the job. In Uttar Pradesh, for example, only seven officers at the board of revenue were assigned to the 'ceiling' enforcement programme, and in the districts no official was specially assigned to it. Not surprisingly enforcement was leisurely – at best.

Those at the base of rural society were precisely those who were too poor and often ignorant of their possible rights to help themselves, in the absence of proper governmental intervention. Research in Bihar, for example, conducted in the mid-1950s and 1960s, suggested that the purposes and provisions of land-reform legislation passed in 1950 were not well known in the villages of the state, and that the state government had made no attempt to spread such vital information.[33] Other unofficial sources of information and assistance were also lacking. For there were no radical parties with activist cadres at this time who might have helped tenants and the landless, neither was there a range of non-governmental agencies at work in the countryside. The only movement which attempted to help the landless was the Bhoodan movement inaugurated in 1951 by Vinobha Bhave, who attempted to persuade the landed to gift their land to their less fortunate compatriots, rather in the same way that Gandhi had favoured ideas of trusteeship and fraternity as means of reform, rather than legislation. But much of the land which was apparently donated under this scheme was poor or waste, and by the mid-1960s the movement had only redistributed under 3 per cent of its target set for 1957. Even when the Community Development projects came into operation they tended to benefit those with land, not the landless. As one official working in Bihar noted, 'The gap in standards of living between the landed and landless has increased as one result of government's development effort.'[34] In neighbouring Uttar Pradesh in one village which has been closely studied the untouchable landless labourers gained somewhat from opportunities for waged labour as agricultural development occurred: but the only direct result of the community development plan which reached them was the construction of improved wells in their residential quarters – and even for this they had to provide the labour.

Abolition of 'untouchability'

The weakness of the law as an instrument of socio-economic reform in the particular circumstances of India's polity and society was equally clear in relation to the so-called 'abolition' of untouchability. The ending of the degraded status of 'untouchables' within Hindu society, and of their humiliating daily social disabilities, had been stamped on India's nationalist rhetoric by Gandhi's campaigns for the uplift of those he called Harijans, or 'children of god', particularly after the Poona pact of 1932 which had ended his fast against the granting of separate electorates to untouchables. The constitution had thus declared in Article 17 that 'untouchability' was abolished and its practice in any form forbidden; and that the practice would be made an offence punishable under law. The 1955 Untouchability (Offences) Act was consequently passed by the central legislature in discharge of the duty laid on it by the constitution. As with the laws on land reform, so this was also challenged as 'unconstitutional' in the courts, but was upheld as not challenging other fundamental rights.

However, it is evident that the act has not been a significant instrument of change. The number of cases brought under it has been small compared with the size of the untouchable population, who probably comprised just under 14.5 per cent of the total population during the 1950s. The highest number of cases registered under the act was 693 in 1956, but from then until Nehru's death was more often between 400 and 500.[35] There was also a decline in the percentage of successful prosecutions – from just under 43 per cent during the first three and a half years the act was in operation to just over 31 per cent in the next four years. The reasons for the weakness of the law as a means for the protection of untouchables lie partly in the act itself and partly in the context in which it was supposed to work. As with the laws relating to land reform there were legal loopholes which the privileged with access to lawyers could exploit in order to escape prosecution for discrimination. These included the fact that the law only applied to public spaces and facilities, and so people could legally discriminate against untouchables, for example denying them access to wells or temples, if these could be proved to be 'private' property. Or there was the need to prove that a particular act of discrimination was 'on the ground of "untouchability"', which led to many loopholes such as 'tokenism' (for example, admitting one untouchable only to a temple) or the reverse of tokenism – excluding a range of specified groups including untouchables.

Given the significance of the reform in India's national rhetoric it might have been assumed that considerable resources would have been laid aside for enforcement of the legislation. But although it was a central law, enforcement lay with the states, and there was no central body or agency to oversee and coordinate enforcement. But nor were there any special agencies or staff to enforce the law at state level. (This lack was the more remarkable when contrasted, for example, with state resources given over to the enforcement of prohibition in 'dry' states.) Initiatives therefore had to come from untouchables themselves – just the people likely to be most ignorant of their new status and rights as equal citizens, unable to afford a lawyer, and most at the mercy of the locally dominant. Nor was it likely that police and magistrates would bestir themselves on behalf of the poorest and least significant socially, or that witnesses would willingly come forward to testify against the locally powerful. To compound the problem penalties for breaking the law were paltry – and no disincentive to offend again.

The existence of the 1955 act also had a negative effect on awareness of the persistence of the practice of untouchability and the plight of untouchables. Many educated and particularly urban people just assumed that the problem had gone away once the law was enacted. However, throughout the first two decades of independence it was abundantly clear that this was not the case. Untouchables still tended to be treated in the same way, denied equal status and access to a wide range of public facilities, and often subjected to humiliating treatment. As one chief secretary of Utter Pradesh put it in a letter to magistrates in 1959, there had been 'no appreciable improvement in the treatment given by members of the so-called higher castes to the persons belonging to the Scheduled Castes. The practice of untouchability continues unabated . . . The provisions of the Untouchability (Offences) Act are being disregarded on a large scale.'[36] Those untouchables who attempted to rebel against their status and treatment were often harassed, subjected to social or economic boycott, or even violently attacked. A measure of the despair felt by many of them of the prospect of ever being accepted into Hindu society was the mass 'conversion' following the notable untouchable leader, Dr B.R. Ambedkar, to Buddhism in 1956.

The problem in attempting to 'abolish' the practice of untouchability was not just one of formulating appropriate legislation or even of providing resources to help untouchables use the law and punish the discriminators. It was not even a question of changing entrenched attitudes about purity and pollution and inculcating ideals of fraternity, as Gandhi had thought, though this proved to be difficult enough. The untouchables' plight was compounded by the fact that they were the most disadvantaged in terms of their access to vital resources, such as land, and the most deprived in terms of the sort of education which would have enabled them to learn new skills and escape from dependence on the degrading manual jobs they had performed for centuries. Some statistics for 1961, just before Nehru's death, testify to this stark reality. Almost 35 per cent of the scheduled castes were landless labourers, compared with just under 17 per cent of the total population. Of the scheduled castes who did hold land just over 50 per cent of them had tiny holdings of less than 2.5 acres. Literacy rates among the former untouchables were just over 10 per cent compared with a general literacy level of 24 per cent, while only 3.6 per cent of their women folk were literate.

Law alone could clearly not tackle the degraded status composed of such multiple ritual, social and economic disabilities. Nor could the special programmes of aid and reservation of jobs in government service which the state embarked upon in the 1950s. Its resources, monetary and in terms of manpower, were inadequate to make more than a small dent in the problem. Moreover, without education, untouchables could not fill the quotas in government service allotted to them. It was only from 1962 that they were able to fill the reserved quota in the IAS, and they were still found in overwhelming numbers by comparison in the lowest classes of employees in central government, mainly as clerks and menials. Nor were the political parties, particularly the Congress party, disposed to work at grass roots for an issue which went against the conservative attitudes and vested interests of so many of their supporters. Untouchables themselves were unable to use their force of numbers as voters or their reserved seats in the legislatures to make their opinions and needs felt in the political arena. This failure was partly because they were scattered throughout the subcontinent, and often divided among themselves on ritual grounds rather than seeing themselves as a single deprived bloc; and partly because they preferred to shelter under the Congress party rather than to attempt to form their own political organisations. For example, in the 1957 general election 64 out of the 76 scheduled caste reserved seats went to Congress, as did 351 of the 469 reserved seats in the state legislative assemblies. Untouchable political assertion would only happen when a new generation of educated untouchables in the decade after Nehru's death saw what might be done with the vote and the weapon of organisation, and learned to challenge the patterns of acceptance and deference which had marked earlier generations. By the time Nehru died it was clear, to those few who wished to enquire into the fate of those at the base of society, that a strategy for uplift which relied on the law and the actions of the state had failed to achieve radical change, just as had the Gandhian strategy of a change of vision and sympathy.

Improving the status of women

The issue of changing the status of Indian woman was also, like untouchability, one with broad implications and ramifications which could not be resolved just by passing laws. Women's status in India varied markedly from region to region and between religious groups and socio-economic classes, and was not a single 'problem' which could be easily defined and addressed. Moreover, as with untouchables, women's roles and status were embedded in cultural patterns and in socio-economic structures, which legislation could not tackle. However, the constitution had given women the status of equal citizens and the vote, and Nehru was personally committed to making this status more of a reality by using the legislative power of the state. It was for this reason that he tried to push through parliament in Delhi the Hindu Code Bill. In order to achieve some measure of change in and through the law he was forced to accept piecemeal legislation instead. The most significant legal departures included giving Hindu women rights to monogamous marriage at a reasonably mature age, with a marriage age of 15 for brides and 18 for grooms, and rights to divorce, under the Hindu Marriage Act of 1955; rights of inheritance as daughters, widows or mothers under the Hindu Succession Act of 1956; and rights to adoption under the 1956 Hindu Adoption and Maintenance Act. Dowry was later forbidden under the Dowry Prohibition Act of 1961.

However, even these reasonably clear 'rights' for women could not be enforced in practice, as a National Committee on the Status of Women appointed in 1971, nearly a decade after Nehru's death, discovered. By 1971 in rural areas 13.6 per cent of girls between 10 and 14 were married, and in urban areas the figure was just under 4 per cent. However, a decade earlier in more than one-third of the districts which made up the states of India the average age for brides was under 15, despite the law. Similarly the legal abolition of dowry had done nothing to stop the practice: rather dowry was thought by the National Committee to be rapidly on the increase, while extremely few cases were brought under the act. The legislative attempt to ensure that Hindu women could inherit was also to a considerable extent abortive in practice, particularly in rural areas in northern India. Here the prospect of female inheritance, particularly of that most valuable resource, land, threatened traditions of marriage and residence where male descendants ensured a continuing hold over joint family property by bringing brides from outside close kin and locality, while daughters (being married out of the close kin and locality) brought no economic benefit. In such a cultural situation many women were reluctant to press their legal rights for fear of alienating their natal male kin and thus losing what might be their only refuge should their marriage break down or their husband die young. Male kin, fathers as well as brothers, often tried to 'dispossess' women by the terms of wills, forged wills, manipulated statements to the authorities, and even intimidation. Local government functionaries were mostly male, shared the cultural assumptions about the 'illegitimacy' of women's right to inherit land and made it hard for women to make claims under the law. Moreover, women were seriously disadvantaged in the public domain by cultural conventions about freedom to travel and work and by low standards of education, which made it difficult for them to know their rights or to press for them.[37] The National Committee, reporting in 1974 and entitling their document *Toward Equality*, noted the limitations of the constitution and of law in guaranteeing women equality and justice.

> The review of the disabilities and constraints on women, which stem from socio-cultural institutions, indicates that the majority of women are still very far from enjoying the rights and opportunities guaranteed to them by the Constitution ... The social laws, that sought to mitigate the problems of women in their family life, have remained unknown to a large mass of women in this country, who are as ignorant of their legal rights today as they were before Independence.[38]

Beyond the clear failure of the law in practice to safeguard certain basic equalities for women in India, there are a range of general markers which show how complex was the broader problem Nehru faced of making women equal citizens of India. Demographic statistics show how 'second class' women still are in basic matters of life and health. In 1971 there were 930 women to every 1000 men in the population, a percentage differential which had increased markedly from 1901 when there were 971 women for every 1000 men. In the decade 1961–71 life expectancy was 45.6 years for women and 47.1 for men, and the gap was actually widening. This evidence of female mortality, particularly in infancy and childbearing years, indicates the low valuation put on women's lives when it comes to family investment in health care. Female infanticide was still not unknown, given the pressures of dowry in some parts of

India, although it had been made illegal under the British. Further evidence shows that women lacked access to just those resources which might enable them to help themselves. Women's literacy in 1971 stood at 18.4 per cent compared with 39.5 per cent for men; and rural women were particularly ill educated, with a literacy rate of only 13.2 per cent. By the time the National Committee on the Status of Women had reported there was still not free and compulsory education for all children up to the age of 14, despite a constitutional directive; fewer girls than boys were being enrolled in school, and girls had a higher drop out rate than boys. An educational survey of 1965 had shown that in rural secondary schools only 17 per cent of pupils were girls. Women's lack of access to material resources in their own right was also clear from the failure of attempts to grant them inheritance rights, and from the declining role of women as paid workers in the economy. Despite the high profile of some very well-educated, professional women, the overall percentage of women workers in the labour force was declining – from nearly 34 per cent in 1911 to just under 12 per cent in 1971. In the decade 1961–71, while male and female populations both increased, the number of men workers increased by over 15 per cent while the number of women workers declined by over 41 per cent. By comparison, studies have shown the enormous amount of unpaid but vital work women put into the family economy and family reproduction and 'maintenance' broadly defined.

.   .   .

These three particular issues, so central to Nehru's vision of a new India, provide evidence of the constraints on Nehru as he sought to implement change and the weakness of the instruments at his disposal. Law was in each case a feeble tool in the context of deep cultural conservatism which was often enshrined in and reinforced by resilient socio-economic structures. The use of law in fact played into the hands of the more conservative who had a powerful and legitimate role in law-making and law-enforcement through the country's federal structure and the power vested in the state governments on specified issues. In many instances there was, moreover, simply not the administrative structure in place which could have monitored and enforced the law and the provisions of the constitution, for little had been done to transform an imperial administration geared to revenue collection and the maintenance of a stable society in order to make it capable of taking a leading role in the fostering of social and economic change. Moreover, the state itself had meagre financial resources with which to pursue the enforcement of reforming laws, or to invest in the provision of skills and resources which might have enabled the disadvantaged to help themselves.

Two weaknesses were profoundly significant. One was the lack of a vibrant and productive economy which might have generated a 'trickle-down' effect to help those at the base of society. The other was the failure of Nehru's government to give top priority in planning and investment to education. As the case studies showed, lack of knowledge and skill was a major factor in the continuing deprivation of the landless, the former untouchables and a majority of Indian women, and their inability to use the laws which were meant to help them.

Nehru was not unaware of the vital role of education in social and economic improvement for individuals and for groups. He had seen how access to modern education had transformed his own family's fortunes in the nineteenth century and how it had been central to his own development. He had seen what sort of strong and independently minded women his own sisters had become, not least because of their privileged education, and he had ensured the best education available for his daughter. Early on in his prime-ministership he was expressing disquiet about the educational system India had inherited from the raj – an elitist system with most investment in secondary and higher education, and provision for primary education which was totally inadequate for a mass educational system such as the constitution envisaged. In 1952 he wrote to a close colleague: 'I am thoroughly dissatisfied with the present system of education and I have almost come to the conclusion that it is doing more harm than good. But the fact remains that all our future progress depends upon our educational apparatus and something radical has to be done to it.'[39]

However, the major difficulties were a lack of resources for the huge investment required to educate a vast and growing population, and the fact that education was a state rather than a central responsibility and therefore subject to all the pressures and inertias of state politics and government, rather in the same way that agriculture was. Towards the end of the decade a sense of growing frustration was evident in the prime minister, as he saw how little had been done, given the magnitude of the task. At the end of 1958 he wrote to his chief ministers:

> the greatest and most revolutionary factor in bringing about political, economic and social change is education. I am not sure in my mind if everyone realizes this, but I have come to this definite conclusion. That education must be based on primary and basic education, but it has to include in its scope higher education. We cannot go far in industrialization or better agriculture or indeed better anything except on the base of such widespread education ... without education, there is no real development.[40]

By 1961 India had not fulfilled the directives of the constitution in providing mass primary education. Despite very considerable advances during the decade by 1961 just over 62 per cent of 6–11 year-olds were attending school, but the figure for 11–14 year-olds was only 22.5 per cent.

This failure to provide crucial and life-enhancing skills to those at the base of society, like the failure of broad economic development, raises basic questions about the state-centred strategy for change which Nehru adopted. The lack of change in practice, particularly in the countryside and in the lives of the poorest and the weakest, suggests the significance of change generated at the grass-roots level rather than from above, whether by parties or movements committed to local-level activism, by community-based structures of administration, or in Gandhian fashion through local determination and self-help. A mixture of such strategies was probably needed to tackle what Nehru saw as one of the greatest revolutionary experiments of the century – radical change in a democratic context. By the end of his life it was clear that the Indian state could not alone achieve the breadth and depth of change he had hoped for.

.   .   .

EPILOGUE

The final months of Nehru's life and prime-ministership were marked by the disaster of 1962, and the effects the failure of his foreign and defence policies had on India's broader development plans and on his own authority in the political system as a whole and even in his own party. The Congress party (and by extension the prestige of the prime minister) was challenged by three defeats in parliamentary by-elections in what had been thought to be 'safe seats'; and the Congress's own post-mortem on this underlined the decay in the party organisation and the way it was split by faction: 'The dissensions and mutual vilification create on the one hand a revulsion of feeling against the Congress among the people and lead to a paralysis of Congress activity on the other.'[41] Not only did Nehru suffer the pain of seeing his party's image becoming tarnished, its nationalist credentials undermined, and its efficacy as an instrument of change seriously weakened. He also faced a challenge to his personal authority as prime minister with a no-confidence motion in the Lok Sabha on his economic policy. Moreover, even within his own party his authority was slipping. A significant number of his own party members did not support him in the Lok Sabha when a constitutional amendment came before parliament directed at the legitimation of ceiling legislation. Even his own finance minister, Morarji Desai, privately opposed the prime minister's socialist approach to economic development, though he was correctly supportive in public. The food and agriculture minister refused to follow Nehru and the planning commission in their proposed strategy to deal with the food crisis by price control and state procurement of food grains. Faced by overt conservative opposition to his development strategies inside and outside the party Nehru consented to the tactic of the Kamaraj plan in order to reassert his authority and begin the overhaul of the Congress party which now seemed necessary.

However, Nehru did not have the time to carry the project through. He was no longer the robust man who had endured years in jail, who throve on the demands of electioneering and drove younger men into the ground by the amount of work he could do in a day. A kidney problem early in 1962 had visibly weakened him, even though he had spent nearly a month in bed and consented to a less rigorous round of daily work. Now at the start of 1964 he was well into his seventies. In January at the Congress session he suffered a mild stroke, and it became evident that sooner rather than later India would have in earnest to face the much-asked question, 'After Nehru, who?' But Nehru did not resign from office, and after a brief rest insisted on attempting to carry on as before. Moreover, he declined to hint whom he would prefer as his successor, and was insistent that in a democracy the leader should be chosen by properly democratic methods rather than by an act of patronage. None the less, significant members of the Congress were already beginning to manoeuvre in readiness for his death and the need to choose a successor rapidly and with little break in the continuity of government.

Nehru's final hours were spent, like the greater part of his life, in the service of his country. He cleared his desk as usual late on 26 May and went to bed. He woke the next morning, in pain and obviously very ill, having suffered major internal bleeding. He soon lapsed into unconsciousness and died within a few hours, at home in his New Delhi house with his daughter beside him. Next day he was cremated near the spot where he had witnessed the last rites of his friend and mentor, Mahatma Gandhi, amid an outpouring of grief which had not been seen since that earlier day of national mourning in January 1948. Nehru had always said that he remembered Gandhi as a pilgrim figure, striding out in the search for truth, as an individual and for his countrymen. Nehru, too, was a visionary, sustained by a sense of personal vocation to lead his country to a profound transformation which would make freedom a reality for those without place and privilege. It was symbolic of his life, and also of the constraints on his ability to achieve his vision of a new India, that he kept on his table a quotation from the poet Robert Frost:

> The woods are lovely, dark and deep,
> But I have promises to keep.
> And miles to go before I sleep.

.   .   .

NOTES AND REFERENCES

1. Nehru to chief ministers, 1 August and 25 October 1957, *LCM*, vol. 4, pp. 518, 585.
2. Nehru to chief ministers, 10 July 1961, *LCM*, vol. 5, p. 473.
3. Nehru to chief ministers, 23/24 January 1958, 18 February 1963, ibid., pp. 11–12, 579–80.
4. Nehru to chief ministers, 28 May 1959, ibid., p. 259.
5. Details for the three elections are in R.L. Hardgrave, *India. Government and Politics in a Developing Nation* 3rd edn (New York: Harcourt Brace Jovanovich, 1980), pp. 204, 206.
6. Chs 14 and 15 of S.A. Kochanek, *The Congress Party of India. The Dynamics of One-Party Democracy* (Princeton: Princeton University

Press, 1968) on the composition of the mass organisation and the parliamentary wing of the party.

7. It is noteworthy that two decades later it was a cadre-based party, the CPM, which did manage to achieve change on the ground in West Bengal. See ch. 3 of A. Kohli, *The State and Poverty in India. The Politics of Reform* (Cambridge: Cambridge University Press, 1987).

8. Nehru to chief ministers, 2 July 1959, 3 September 1962, *LCM*, vol. 5, pp. 266, 517–18.

9. Nehru to chief ministers, 1 January 1960, *LCM*, vol. 5, pp. 351–2.

10. For example, in the case of M.O. Mathai, a long-standing special assistant, who resigned in 1959 after charges of corruption had been virtually proven against him; or Krishna Menon, diplomat and minister, who was erratic and unstable and ultimately resigned after the Chinese invasion in 1962, when he was minister of defence.

11. Quoted on p. 29 of a classic work on this development, H. Maddick, *Panchayati Raj. A Study of Rural Local Government in India* (Harlow: Longman, 1970).

12. Mehta report cited in ibid., p. 54.

13. Cited in Hardgrave, *India*, p. 108.

14. Statistics on the Indian economy can be found in B.R. Tomlinson, *The Economy of Modern India 1860–1970* (Cambridge: Cambridge University Press, 1993), ch. 4; and A. Vaidyanathan, 'The Indian Economy since Independence (1947–70)', ch. xiii of D. Kumar and M. Desai (eds), *The Cambridge Economic History of India. Volume 2: c. 1757–c. 1970* (Cambridge: Cambridge University Press, 1983).

15. F.R. Frankel, *India's Political Economy 1947–1977. The Gradual Revolution* (Delhi: Oxford University Press, 1978), p. 144.

16. Cited in Frankel, *India's Political Economy*, p. 162.

17. Nehru to chief ministers, 1 August and 24 November 1957, *LCM*, vol. 4, pp. 525 ff., 606 ff.

18. Nehru to chief ministers, 12 and 27 August 1956, 20 and 24 November 1957, *LCM*, vol. 4, pp. 390 ff., 425 ff., 599–610.

19. Nehru to chief ministers, 23/24 January and 30 July 1958, *LCM*, vol. 5, pp. 17, 106–10.

20. Nehru to chief ministers, 2 July 1959, *LCM*, vol. 5, pp. 263–4.

21. Nehru to V. Pandit, 15 December 1955, cited in S. Gopal, *Jawaharlal Nehru*, 3 vols (London: Jonathan Cape, 1973–84), vol. 2, p. 255.

22. Nehru to chief ministers, 8 December 1956, *LCM*, vol. 4, pp. 463–7.

23. *Economist*, 4 April 1959.

24. Nehru to chief ministers, 1, 16, 26 October 1959, *LCM*, vol. 5, pp. 285, 297, 311.

25. Nehru to chief ministers, 4 November 1959, *LCM*, vol. 5, p. 325.

26. Nehru to chief ministers, 12 October 1962, *LCM*, vol. 5, pp. 530–2.
27. Nehru to chief ministers, 21 October 1962, *LCM*, vol. 5, p. 537.
28. J.S. Mehta, 'Nehru's Failure with China: Intellectual Naïveté or the Wages of a Prophetic Vision?', in M. Israel (ed.), *Nehru and the Twentieth Century* (Toronto: University of Toronto Press, 1991), p. 206.
29. Nehru to chief ministers, 22 December 1962, 2 February 1963, *LCM*, vol. 5, pp. 547 ff., 567–8.
30. Nehru to chief ministers, 1 August 1957, *LCM*, vol. 4, p. 523.
31. Cited in P. Reeves, 'The Congress and the Abolition of Zamindari in Uttar Pradesh', in J. Massclos (cd.), *Struggling and Ruling. The Indian National Congress 1885–1985* (London: Oriental University Press 1987), p. 163.
32. Case studies can be found in F.T. Jannuzi, *Agrarian Crisis in India. The Case of Bihar* (Austin and London: University of Texas Press, 1974); P. Reeves, *Landlords and Governments in Uttar Pradesh. A study of their relations until zamindari abolition* (Delhi: Oxford University Press, 1991); T.R. Metcalf, 'Landlords Without Land: The U.P. Zamindars Today', *Pacific Affairs*, XL (1 and 2) (1967), pp. 5–18; R.S. Newell, 'Ideology and Realities: Land Redistribution in Uttar Pradesh', *Pacific Affairs*, 45 (2) (1972), pp. 220–39.
33. Januzzi, *Agrarian Crisis*, p. 45.
34. Quoted in ibid., p. 201.
35. Quoted in M. Galantar, 'The Abolition of Disabilities – Untouchability and the Law', in J.M. Mahar (ed.), *The Untouchables in Contemporary India* (Tucson: The University of Arizona Press, 1972), p. 266.
36. Quoted by Galantar in Mahar (ed.), *Untouchables*, p. 262.
37. B. Agarwal, 'Widows versus Daughters or Widows as Daughters? Property, Land and Economic Security in Rural India', *Modern Asian Studies*, 32 (1) (1998), pp. 1–48.
38. Quoted in G. Forbes, *Women in Modern India* (Cambridge: Cambridge University Press, 1996), p. 227.
39. Nehru to G. Nanda, 8 September 1952, *SWJN(2)*, vol. 19, p. 102.
40. Nehru to chief ministers, 31 December 1958, *LCM*, vol. 5, pp. 186–7.
41. Quoted in Frankel, *India's Political Economy*, p. 222.

CONCLUSION

This 'profile in power' has followed the career of one of Asia's most notable and articulate political leaders of the generation which saw the development of anti-colonial nationalist movements, the destruction of European empires in Asia and Africa, and the making of new nation states in their place. Drawing on the remarkably rich evidence of his political career, as well as his own more leisured and reflective writing, it has been possible to see how the privileged young man of late Victorian India, who was a less than assiduous student and a big-spending man-about-town, became a radical firebrand in the nationalist movement, as it was given new direction by Gandhi. We have seen how a high-caste Hindu man became deeply concerned about the most disadvantaged in his country, regardless of community or gender, under the influence both of Gandhi and of western radical thinking; and finally as prime minister of independent India became an international figure intent on creating a new India both to give genuine new freedoms to its people and also to contribute to a new and idealistic world order.

A biographical focus in a political study can distort the lens if the later observer is tempted to ignore the wider forces at work moulding the environment in which the subject of study lived and functioned as a political figure. However, the life of a particular and influential individual can also be a window through which to see more clearly the play and strength of those forces, as well as a way of seeing how creative individuals interact with such forces to play a significant role in the history of their time. In Nehru's case it permits us to see the wider world of India's changing political system as the British raj weakened and crumbled and was replaced by a democratic

180

system on a vast scale, and the way these changes gave him a particular pathway to prominence and eventually to national leadership. But the frustration of so much of his vision in later life also indicates the range of serious constraints on his ability to exercise power in pursuit of the goals he most cherished. Focusing on his life also faces the important question of why he welcomed a public life which involved him in deprivation of the comforts and relationships private people take for granted, long years in prison, and eventually right into old age a punishing schedule of work which allowed him little rest and no eventual retirement. We are privileged to see the evolution of the inner man and his dreams and visions, his compulsion to work, his loneliness and periodic plunges into despair and near paralysis of mind and emotion, and his eventual sadness at the frustration of so much of his vision of the future.

Nehru was remarkably perceptive and at times articulate about himself and his life, and it is fruitful to consider how he might have written a conclusion to an account of his life. He would surely have seen his life in terms of a vocation to serve his country, both in helping to achieve its political independence and later in high office endeavouring to make independence a reality in the changed lives of ordinary people. He would also have noted, as he once did in an anonymous article on himself, how he recognised the importance of wielding power in the public sphere and indeed revelled at times in his influence and public repute. Yet he was also an intellectual by temperament, sensitive and deeply reflective. These were qualities which could isolate him, as Gandhi perceptively noticed when commenting how lonely a young man Jawaharlal was. Indeed, after the deaths of Motilal and then of Gandhi there were few people who came really close to him. Krishna Menon, who shared so many of his intellectual enthusiasms, was increasingly a political liability rather than a trustworthy and constructive confidant. Women friends and relatives gave some social normality to his work-driven life but seldom appear to have influenced his attitudes. The qualities which made Nehru the thinker could also on occasion make him hesitant in the harsh world of political decision-making because he could see so many aspects of a question. Apart from his recognition of the importance of political power, and particularly power that flowed from legitimate state structures, he was also motivated by a deep moral concern about the relationship of means and ends, and more generally about standards in the public life of India. This concern originated partly in his upbringing in the Nehru household, where a patrician sense of duty and responsibility was entrenched by his father, Motilal; and partly by his exposure to Gandhi and the Mahatma's insistence on the primacy of moral means. In later life he often sounded irritable and even 'colonial' in his criticism of his compatriots for what he saw as their declining standards in public life, their smallness of vision, and their pursuit of the personal, particular and local at the expense of a broad and inclusive national vision. However, this underpinned his commitment to democratic government and an insistence that free India's government must guard and foster the resources of the nation as a whole for the good of the whole, and become in a new way 'the people's government' compared to the imperial regime under which he had grown to maturity.

Nehru's life and public work was ultimately rooted, not in a religious vision of man's search for truth as was Gandhi's, but in a passionate secular vision of a new India which would be free, having its governance transformed, its economy set on the road to vibrant modernisation, and its society working to rid itself of gross manifestations of hierarchy and unequal access to resources. Such an India would, he thought, then be able to play a major role in international affairs, not only establishing itself as an independent force to be reckoned with, but also helping to create a more peaceful post-colonial world. However, by the later 1950s the great hope with which he had embarked on the novel democratic experiment of freedom and change had given place to a growing awareness of the limited extent to which he could hope to make this vision a reality. India was indeed free of colonial raj and had a democratically elected government; but the other goals which he cherished were still very far from attainment, and indeed seemed to be receding in the middle of a mounting economic crisis at the end of his life, worsened by the effects of the humiliating Chinese invasion. The constraints on his ability to use power – arising from the political system of India, the nature of his own party, the persistence of social and cultural conservatism, and India's multiple economic problems – had encompassed and trapped him, just as his own physical energy and psychological resilience were ebbing away. It was little wonder that he valued the way Robert Frost articulated a sense of having 'promises to keep' and 'miles to go before I sleep'.

This much was evident to the perceptive observer at the time. The historian has the perspective of a longer time-scale and the evidence with which to see deeper issues, some of which have yet to be resolved over three decades after Nehru's death and fifty years after Indian independence. Some problems Nehru appears not to have seen or judged significant, or to have seen but failed to tackle. Within India it became clear that the growth in population which had begun to escalate from the 1950s was to become staggering in proportions, and was to make India the second most populous country in the world by the end of the century. It was a growth which was to endanger all Nehru's hopes for increasing national prosperity, the alleviation of extreme poverty and the growth of greater equality and fraternity. The failure of Nehru's economic strategy of rapid industrialisation behind protective walls of tariffs, licences and controls, was to become the subject of severe criticism, particularly when decades later it seemed to have paralysed India's economic potential. But for his generation there was no other model of rapid economic growth which could have guaranteed international strength and attempted to address poverty of dimensions scarcely conceived of in the western world. Even more significant were the failures in education policy and provision which increased the divisions between those who could take advantage of new opportunities and those who could not, often reinforcing older ritual and status divisions in society and hardening them into class. In terms of India as a whole it created a society which was low in skill but placed great value on a literary rather than practical education available only to an elite. It therefore rendered many of its people unable to adapt to new economic opportunities and work environments, in contrast to many other Asian societies.

Nehru saw intellectually the need to transform the administrative structures and culture of India, if the country was to shake off attitudes towards government confirmed by the long years of colonial rule and develop an administrative structure geared to change and sensitive to the needs of ordinary people and local communities. But he made no significant impact here and indeed seems to have given up the attempt to struggle against the social and political forces which gained from or had come to accommodating terms with the nature of Indian administration. Nor did he concern himself adequately with the Congress party itself, and ask how a nationalist alliance could be turned into a political party which could engage in the disciplined pursuit of specific and ideologically motivated goals. This failure stemmed from his temperamental distaste for party politics and perhaps also from his yearning for a continuation of what he thought of as the old high-minded Congress of the Gandhian struggle, regardless of the vested interests entrenched within it, and the rifts and factions which had plagued it even in those years. To have turned the party into an effective force for change would have required skills he did not have, and also would have meant the end of the party as a national rallying symbol and a home for a wide range of attitudes and groups.

Beyond the purely domestic, Nehru was also incapable of resolving the multiple issues related to Kashmir and the politics of its people, partly because of a lack of political expertise in the international arena at the outset of his prime-ministership, and partly because of his vision of a secular India where Muslims, including Kashmiri Muslims, would not only be safe and equal citizens, but would be the symbol of India's inclusive identity. His failure with Kashmir not only necessitated increased expenditure on defence but weakened his own position on the international stage and made India vulnerable to Pakistan's alliances with other international players such as the United States and China. Ultimately his greatest misjudgement was with China, where he failed to see that an Asian 'brother' and socialist state could generate a resurgent nationalism as aggressive and destabilising of peaceful relations as had his old enemy, world-wide imperialism.

Nehru's experience of the highest political office in the country and his nevertheless limited ability to wield power and to achieve his stated goals also raises longer-term questions about national political leadership on the subcontinent. He was, as an English-educated Brahmin, symbolic of the earliest generations of modern-style political leaders on the subcontinent – an Indian gentleman created out of the interaction of Indian patterns of hierarchy and new opportunities afforded by the presence of the British raj. His critical contemporaries sometimes jibed at him that he was too gentlemanly for politics, and worse, he was an English gentleman. He himself once said he was the last Englishman to rule in India. This sense of being the last viceroy contained more than a little truth. In his socio-economic background and his education he was much like the last British rulers of India. He shared many of their values, including a belief in secular nationalism, the validity of the nation state, and the increasingly vital role of the state in managing a nation's economic and social as well as political life. Moreover, his political style was like theirs. He was a patrician, despite his commitment to democracy. This manifested itself in personal rectitude in the conduct of public affairs, an immense dedication to hard work for the public good, and a sense that he and his elite advisers at the pinnacle of national government knew what was best for the people at large. It also showed itself in irritation, even disdain, for what he saw as Indian weaknesses. Colonial discourse on the difference between the British and their Indian subjects had been replete with stereotypes about Indians as weak, idle, corrupt and lacking in a national and civic sense of identity and responsibility. Moreover, it categorised Indians as swayed by primitive forces of religious and social identity. Such images were to be found in Nehru's discourse, too; as he inveighed against low standards in public life, laziness and lack of public commitment, narrow loyalties, and above all at what he saw as the corrosive effects of communalism – the privileging of religious identity in politics above loyalty to an inclusive and secular nation. It was because he was so like his viceregal predecessors that he was able to inherit the raj with comparative ease, transform himself from nationalist opponent of government into India's first prime minister, and operate within a political system which owed so much to precedents established under the British raj, in style and convention, as well as in the formalities of the constitution. It was also this continuity of attitudes and style which enabled Nehru to become a significant international figure and to see the advantages for India in continuing membership of the Commonwealth, with all that was to mean for the evolution of the Commonwealth into a new kind of international association. He was thus in many senses and in several different political environments a bridge figure between an older colonial world and a new order emerging out of the destruction of the old European empires.

Although this bridging type of political leadership helped to avoid major disjunctures and upheavals for India, and gave her crucial time to achieve a new national stability, it raised major questions for the future. What sort of a leadership would be needed which could achieve both national stability and unity and genuine change in a society where rising expectations from a growing population had to be met and managed in a political environment of growing complexity and sophistication? Constitutional reform from the start of the twentieth century, combined with the evolution of the Congress party and the nationalist movement it led, had begun this process of politicisation. Nehru's rhetoric of national transformation reinforcing the experience of democratic politics only quickened this trend. However, he did not have the political skills to operate in this fast-changing environment, and this became increasingly clear towards the end of his life when he was frustrated by the challenges to his authority and the constraints on his power. What was needed was a new type of leadership, almost certainly from a less privileged backgound, which recognised the validity of the new political environment and was sensitive and skilled in its management. The skills and standards of the Brahmin and the patrician were increasingly dysfunctional in the management of India's developing political system. Nehru not only did not possess the attributes needed for the changed environment: he did not nurture those who did, but tended to rely on established and increasingly elderly Congress colleagues, with whom he shared a political culture rooted in the experience of the nationalist movement, or on technocrats and planners who were concerned with goals rather than hard political questions about the pathway to those goals.

Nehru's unique position as Gandhi's heir and embodiment of the nation's new identity in 1947, combined with the continuity ensured by leadership as prime minister, also raised but postponed answers to questions about the nature and role of a 'national', all-India leadership in the future. So much power over decision-making and resources lay with the states within the Indian Union that a continental leader did not have a free hand over policy-making and implementation, even if he had the backing of the Delhi parliament. Moreover, the nature of society and persistence of conservative cultural attitudes also imposed limitations on what a 'moderniser' could hope to achieve. In such a situation what sort of individual or combination of individuals could provide a national leadership which could channel the strengths and interests of India's diverse regions and interest groups rather than fighting against them? Linked to this was the continuing issue of Indian identity, and particularly the prevalence of a vision of India rooted in Hindu culture as opposed to the secular and inclusive vision which Nehru believed fundamental to the new India. How was a national leadership to relate to these tendencies within society and the political system: by criticism and control or by acceptance and management?

These questions remained unresolved at Nehru's death. The unexpectedly sudden death of his successor, Lal Bahadur Sastri, led to the choice of Nehru's daughter, Indira, as prime minister, as a result of political calculations among significant Congress leaders. This began to perpetuate the notion that India had a ruling 'dynasty' essential to national leadership and integration, though there is no evidence that anything like this was in Nehru's mind in his closing years. As it turned out Indira's style and self-image were even more viceregal and authoritarian than her father's had been. This only perpetuated and indeed deepened the crucial problems relating to viable and effective all-India political leadership in a changing and increasingly complex environment. The crumbling of Congress as a genuinely national party as Indira strove to assert her personal authority removed one of the few democratic institutions within which a new form of truly national yet democratic leadership could have been nurtured and which could have provided it with a secure base. By the end of the twentieth century no other party had replaced it, and central government had come to a state of periodic near-paralysis as a result. Furthermore, an ideological vacuum had opened up which gave room for gross and at times criminal self-seeking in the practice of politics, or – partly in revulsion at this – a vision of Indian renewal and purification which was far narrower and rooted in Hindu culture.

Despite the questions Nehru's style and role as prime minister left unanswered, from the perspective of the closing years of the century, after his daughter and grandson both died violent deaths as prime minister or contesting for that office, and after other prime ministers have often had but fleeting moments in office, it is apparent what a significant and creative function Nehru's transitional leadership performed for his country. He was a vital element in a continuity critical for India's survival as a new nation state and as a functioning democracy, and as a regional power in Asia and a player on the world international stage. Moreover, by putting his country first, before family, region or community, he set before India a vision of herself and a standard for public life which were contemporary and attainable, in contrast to the idiosyncratic life and vision of his great mentor, Gandhi. The later criticisms levelled at him which have arisen from a context of confusion and disquiet about India's identity and the quality of her public life are a measure of his influence and also an unintended tribute to the way he attempted to use his unique position of power.

BIBLIOGRAPHICAL ESSAY

. . .

PRIMARY SOURCES

Jawaharlal Nehru's life is very well documented for the historian. The major holdings of primary sources relating to him are his own and his father's papers, and the records of the Indian National Congress in the Nehru Memorial Museum and Library, New Delhi; and government records held in the National Archives of India, New Delhi, and the India Office Library and Records, London. A considerable amount of this primary material is also available in several major documentary collections, including: S. Gopal (ed.), *Selected Works of Jawaharlal Nehru* 1st series (New Delhi: Orient Longman), 2nd series (New Delhi: Jawaharlal Nehru Memorial Fund) (in process of publication – has not yet gone beyond 1952; volumes contain letters, speeches and articles); G. Parthasarathi (ed.), *Jawaharlal Nehru. Letters to Chief Ministers 1947–1964* 5 vols (Delhi: Oxford University Press, 1985–9); *A Bunch of Old Letters. Written mostly to Jawaharlal Nehru and some written by him* (Bombay: Asia Publishing House, 1958); S. Gandhi (ed.), *Freedom's Daughter. Letters between Indira Gandhi and Jawaharlal Nehru 1922–39* (London: Hodder and Stoughton, 1989) and *Two Alone, Two Together. Letters between Indira Gandhi and Jawaharlal Nehru 1940–1964* (London: Hodder and Stoughton, 1992); *The Collected Works of Mahatma Gandhi* 90 vols (Delhi: Government of India, 1958–84); N. Mansergh and E.W.R. Lumby (eds, Vols I–IV), N. Mansergh and P. Moon (eds, Vols V–XII), *Constitutional Relations Between Britain and India. The Transfer of Power 1942–47*

12 vols (London: HMSO, 1970–83). Nehru also wrote two major books, which give a vital insight into his mind: *An Autobiography* (London: Bodley Head, 1936); and *The Discovery of India* ([1946] rev. edn Bombay: Asia Publishing House, 1947).

.   .   .

BIOGRAPHIES

There have been many biographical studies of Nehru. The best is the authoritative three-volume biography by S. Gopal, *Jawaharlal Nehru* (London: Jonathan Cape, 1973–84), based on unrivalled access to Nehru's papers, but probably too detailed for the general reader. More popular is M.J. Akbar, *Nehru. The Making of India* (New York: Viking, 1988). The latter is less substantial on Nehru as prime minister, as is S. Wolpert, *Nehru. A Tryst with Destiny* (Oxford: Oxford University Press, 1996), a recent book which is racy narrative rather than academic analysis and makes unsubstantiated assumptions about Nehru's sexual orientation. An older but still valuable biographical study is B.R. Nanda, *The Nehrus. Motilal and Jawaharlal* (London: George Allen and Unwin, 1962), which covers 1861–1931.

.   .   .

BACKGROUND WORKS

For readers unfamiliar with Indian history there are a number of useful background books which set Nehru's life and career in historical context. Among these are B.S. Cohn, *India: The Social Anthropology of a Civilization* (New York: Prentice-Hall, 1971) and two broad and interpretive studies of twentieth-century India, R.W. Stern, *Changing India. Bourgeois revolution on the subcontinent* (Cambridge: Cambridge University Press, 1993) and S. Khilnani, *The Idea of India* (London: Hamish Hamilton, 1997). More political in orientation are Judith M. Brown, *Modern India. The Origins of an Asian Democracy* 2nd edn (Oxford: Oxford University Press, 1994) and *Gandhi. Prisoner of Hope* (New Haven and London: Yale University Press, 1989). A more detailed account of the development of Indian politics in the twentieth century is R.L. Hardgrave, *India. Government and Politics in a Developing Nation* 3rd edn (New York: Harcourt Brace Jovanovich, 1980).

. . .

COLLECTIONS

Some of the most interesting insights into Nehru's life, work and policies come from collections of essays about him. Notable among these is B.R. Nanda, *Jawaharlal Nehru. Rebel and Statesman* (Delhi: Oxford University Press, 1995), which includes chapters on Nehru and various leading contemporaries, Nehru's attitude to religion and socialism, his economic planning and policy of non-alignment, and aspects of his writing. M. Israel (ed.), *Nehru and the Twentieth Century* (Toronto: University of Toronto Press, 1991) includes essays on various aspects of Nehru's policies and his place in the century, one on his relations with Gandhi, one piece of 'personal nostalgia' by a former member of India's foreign service, and a significant contribution on Nehru's failure with China. A very significant comparative collection on Nehru and various elements in the Indian political system is J. Manor (ed.), *Nehru to the Nineties. The Changing Office of Prime Minister in India* (London: Hurst, 1994). A major interpretive essay is B. Parekh, 'Jawaharlal Nehru and the Crisis of Modernisation', in U. Baxi and B. Parekh (eds), *Crisis and Change in Contemporary India* (New Delhi, Newbury Park (Calif.) and London: Sage, 1995).

. . .

SPECIFIC STUDIES

Many of the studies of particular issues which relate to Nehru's life are referred to in the notes and references in this book. There is also treatment of many of these issues in Gopal's three-volume biography. Noted here are some major studies on some of the most significant aspects of Nehru's career, particularly as prime minister. On politics a major analysis which extends into the 1980s is P.R. Brass, *The Politics of India since Independence* (Cambridge: Cambridge University Press, 1990). Particular aspects of politics are dealt with in S.A. Kochanek, *The Congress Party of India. The Dynamics of One-Party Democracy* (Princeton: Princeton University Press, 1968) (a very substantial analysis of the party from 1946 to the mid-1960s); H. Maddick, *Panchayati Raj. A Study of Rural Local Government in India* (Harlow: Longman, 1970); R.D. King, *Nehru and the Language Politics of India* (Delhi: Oxford University Press, 1997). Two works which deal with Hindu nationalism and its challenge to Nehru's secular vision of India are B.D. Graham, *Hindu Nationalism and Indian Politics. The Origins and Development of the Bharatiya Jana Sangh* (Cambridge: Cambridge University Press, 1990) and C. Jaffrelot, *The Hindu Nationalist Movement and Indian Politics 1925 to the 1990s* (London: Hurst, 1996). There is a large literature on the issue of the development of the Muslim demand for Pakistan and the eventual partition of the subcontinent. Nanda has a very detailed essay on Nehru and partition in his collection, *Jawaharlal Nehru. Rebel and Statesman* (Delhi: Oxford University Press, 1995). Important works dealing with Muslim politics prior to 1947 are D. Page, *Prelude To Partition. The Indian Muslims and the Imperial System of Control 1920–1932* (Karachi: Oxford University Press, 1987); A. Jalal, *The Sole Spokesman. Jinnah, the Muslim League and the Demand for Pakistan* (Cambridge: Cambridge University Press, 1985); and an important collection of essays edited by M. Hasan, *India's Partition. Process, Strategy and Mobilization* (Delhi: Oxford University Press, 1994). On India's economy and Nehru's role in relation to the planning of the economy the best accounts are chapter 4 of B.R. Tomlinson, *The Economy of Modern India 1860–1970* (Cambridge: Cambridge University Press, 1993), and in much greater detail F.R. Frankel, *India's Political Economy 1947–1977. The Gradual Revolution* (Delhi: Oxford University Press, 1978). Nehru's role in deciding that India as a republic should stay within the Commonwealth is covered in R.J. Moore, *Making the New Commonwealth* (Oxford: Clarendon Press, 1987). An attempt to understand his attitude to China is J.S. Mehta's essay in M. Israel (ed.), *Nehru and the Twentieth Century.* The Kashmir issue is so disputed that no work is considered impartial by Indian and Pakistani scholars; one of the most recent works by a notable scholar from outside the subcontinent who has written a number of other books on Kashmir and on the China–India border is A. Lamb, *Incomplete Partition: The genesis of the Kashmir Dispute* (Hertingfordbury, Herts: Roxford Books).

CHRONOLOGY

1889	Born, Allahabad, 14 November
1905	Enters Harrow School, England
1907	Reads Natural Sciences at Trinity College, Cambridge
1910–12	Studies law in London
1912	Returns to India
1916	Marriage to Kamala, February
1917	Birth of Indira
1919	Jallianwalla Bagh shooting Montagu-Chelmsford reforms
1920–22	Non-cooperation movement led by Gandhi
1922–23	Nehru in jail
1923–24	Chairman of Allahabad municipality
1926–27	Visits Europe (including attendance at International Congress against Colonial Oppression and Imperialism, Brussels and visit to Russia, both in 1927)
1929	Elected president of Congress Irwin's declaration of Dominion Status as goal for India
1930–31	Civil disobedience movement led by Gandhi Nehru in jail
1931	Death of Motilal Nehru Gandhi's 'truce' with Irwin and subsequent attendance at Round Table Conference in London; Nehru deeply involved with peasant movement in UP
1932–34	Civil disobedience campaign renewed

1932–34, 1935	Nehru in jail, released to be with dying wife in Europe
1935	Government of India Act
1936	Death of Kamala in Swiss sanatorium, February
	Publication of *An Autobiography*
	Elected president of Congress
1937–39	Congress holds office in provincial government following election successes; withdraws at outbreak of war
1938	Death of Nehru's mother
	Visits Europe
1939	Visits China
1940–41	Individual non-cooperation in protest against participation in the war
	Nehru in jail
1942	Sir Stafford Cripps' unsuccessful mission to India and 'offer'
	Launching of the 'Quit India' campaign
August 1942–June 1945	Nehru in jail
1944	Finishes *The Discovery of India* (published 1946)
1945	Simla conference
1946	Cabinet Mission to India and plan for transition to independence
	Nehru elected president of Congress
	Formation of interim government with Nehru as minister for external affairs and Commonwealth relations
1947	Arrival of Mountbatten as viceroy, March
	British decision to leave immediately and divide the subcontinent, with consent of Congress and the Muslim League
	Independence for India and Pakistan, 15 August; Nehru becomes prime minister of India
	Severe communal rioting in northern India
	War in Kashmir
1948	Assassination of Gandhi, 30 January
	Police action in Hyderabad
1949	Ceasefire in Kashmir
	Visits USA
1950	India becomes republic but stays within Commonwealth

	National Planning Commission created (April) with Nehru as chairman
1951	Nehru exerts dominance in Congress
1951–52	General elections
1952–56	First Five-Year Plan
1952	Community Development programme
1954	Treaty with China recognising Chinese sovereignty over Tibet
	Visits China
1955	Bandung Conference, April
	Visits USSR
1956–61	Second Five-Year Plan
1956	Reorganisation of Indian states on linguistic lines
1957	General elections
1958–59	Beginning of *panchayati raj*
1959	Imposition of president's rule in Kerala
	Relations between India and China begin to deteriorate over Chinese policy towards Tibet and claims over the border with India
1961	Indian troops move into Goa (December)
1961–66	Third Five-Year Plan
1962	General elections
	Chinese invasion of India (October)
1963	Kamaraj plan to revive Congress organisation
1964	Suffers stroke (January)
	Dies, New Delhi, 27 May

GLOSSARY

ashram	Hindu religious community
Bapu	diminutive of 'Father' in Hindi; term of affection used of Gandhi
Bhoodan	'land gift': movement led by Vinoba Bhave after Gandhi's death to encourage the voluntary redistribution of land
durbar	the open audience of a ruler
durbari	pertaining to *durbar* (adj.)
Harijans	name given by Gandhi to untouchables: literally 'children of god'
khadi	hand-spun cloth
Khalifah	successor to the Prophet as world-wide leader of Muslims (the Sultan of Turkey)
Khilafat	pertaining to Khalifah (adj.); movement in India during the 1914–18 War to protect the status of the Sultan
Lok Sabha	lower house of the Indian parliament in Delhi
Mahatma	'Great Soul': honorific title used of Gandhi
Marwaris	caste of traders originating in Marwar, western India
memsahib	female of *sahib*; used to denote European women in India
Mizo	tribal group in north-eastern India
Naga	tribal group in north-eastern India
panchayat	caste council
panchayati raj	form of local government instituted in the 1950s
Panchsheel	five principles of peaceful international relations
purdah	seclusion of women
raj	rule

sati	the self-immolation of a widow on her husband's funeral pyre
satyagraha	'truth force'; name used by Gandhi to denote non-violent resistance to wrong; practised by *satyagrahis*
swaraj	'self rule': used to denote political independence in India, but used very differently by Gandhi as a moral concept
zamindar	landholder
zamindari	pertaining to *zamindar* (adj.): holding of land by *zamindar*

MAPS

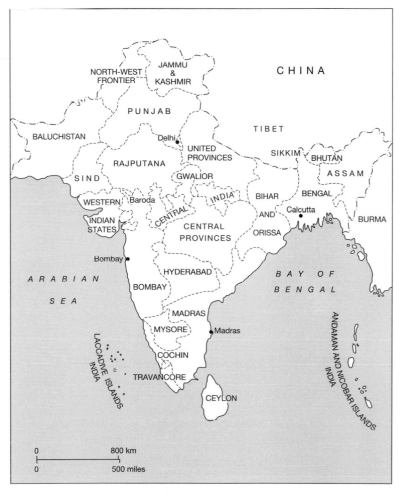

1. India under the Raj, *c.* 1930
After Judith M. Brown, *Modern India* (Oxford: Oxford University
Press, 1985, 1994)

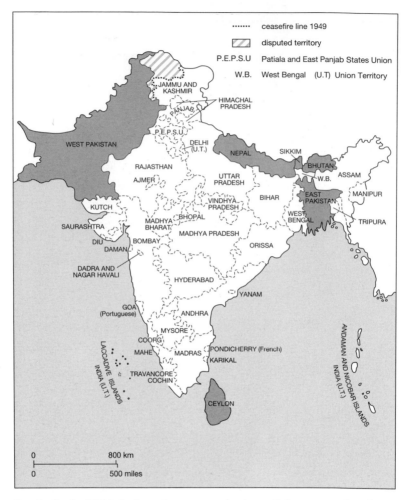

2.   India in 1954, before the reorganisation of the states, showing the area which became Pakistan

After F.C.R. Robinson (ed.), *The Cambridge Encyclopedia of India* (Cambridge: Cambridge University Press, 1989), p. 186

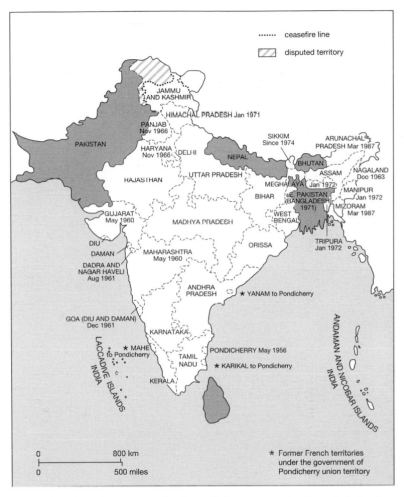

3. India after the reorganisation of the states on a linguistic basis in 1956 with later changes

After F.C.R. Robinson (ed.), *The Cambridge Encyclopedia of India* (Cambridge: Cambridge University Press, 1989), p. 187

INDEX